C000130694

PRINCESS DIANA

The Evidence

HOW MI-6 AND THE CIA
WERE INVOLVED IN THE
DEATH OF PRINCESS DIANA

by

Jon King & John Beveridge

SPECIALIST
PRESS
INTERNATIONAL

New York

PRINCESS DIANA: The Hidden Evidence Copyright © 2008 by Jon King &
John Beveridge. All rights reserved, including right of reproduction. No part of
this book may be used or reproduced in any manner without written
permission of the publisher except in the case of brief quotations embodied in
critical articles or reviews.

Specialist Press International books can be purchased for
educational, business or sales promotional use. For ordering details,
please contact:

Special Markets Department
Spcialist Press International – SPI Books
99 Spring Street • New York, NY 10012
212-431-5011 • sales@spibooks.com

For further information, contact:

New York

S.P.I. Books
99 Spring Street, 3rd Floor
New York, NY 10012
(212) 431-5011 • Fax: (212) 431-8646
E-mail: publicity@spibooks.com
www.spibooks.com

10 9 8 7 6 5 4 3 2 1

First Edition

Library of Congress cataloging-in-publication data available

ISBN (13): 978-1-56171-888-7
ISBN 1-56171-888-2

Also, by Jon King

COSMIC TOP SECRET: The Unseen Agenda
THE ASCENSION CONSPIRACY: 2013

With best wishes,

[signature]

DEDICATION

*In Memory Of Diana,
Princess Of Wales*

C O N T E N T S

Acknowledgements

In researching and compiling evidence for this book, we are indebted to all those, both named and unnamed, who were courageous enough to come forward with their information. Plus all those who kindly granted us access to their work and research, and all those who agreed to talk to us in whatever capacity. We should state that we have made every conceivable effort to contact the publishers/authors of all works quoted herein, and we are sincerely grateful for their permissions in this regard. Our sincere apologies to anyone we have been unable to track down. We would like to extend a special thanks to Mike Grey and Dave Cornish, and to several other 'silent voices'. Also to Ian Shapolsky and Specialist Press International-SPI Books for having the courage to publish this work where so many turned tail and ran.

Introduction

By Jon King

S ince the publication of this book's hardback edition in 2001, it has been a real task keeping pace with the almost daily emergence of new evidence regarding Diana's death. The case has moved forward at such a rate, with new information coming to light with every new twist, that much of the material contained in the hardback has, by necessity, been replaced in this paperback with the updated material now available, effectively resulting in a new book. Indeed, the ever evolving nature of this case has forced us to include only the most up-to-date, time-relevant evidence, and as a result, only the most pertinent chapters from the hardback are reproduced here.

That said, the thrust of our original argument has not changed. For reasons explained in the hardback, and reiterated in this edition, we firmly believe Diana was assassinated and make no bones about that. Much of the new evidence that has come to light, in fact, supports our argument even more so than the relatively meagre strips available when we wrote the first book. The new evidence has strengthened the case for murder, no doubt about that.

It should be said that much of this new evidence has emerged as a result of Mohamed Al Fayed's ongoing legal processes, which on many different counts challenge the conclusions of the French inquiry, as well as the findings of Operation Paget, the British investigation into Diana's death headed up by former Metropolitan Police Commissioner, Sir John (now Lord) Stevens. The French inquiry, of course, completed in September 1999, concluded that Diana's death was the result of a simple though tragic drink-drive accident. Chauffeur Henri Paul was drunk, Judge Herve Stephan decreed, and that was the end of it.

Not so, said the voice of the people. *We believe there was more to it and we demand a public inquiry in Britain to determine the true cause of Diana's death.* This, at least, was the general tenor of the thoughts and opinions of the thousands of people who attended our talks and book signings, tuned in to our radio talk show forums, and who also signed our online petition to force an inquiry into the incident. The general public was not satisfied with the French verdict, it seemed. Needless to say, Mohamed Al Fayed was not satisfied, either. Having publicly accused members of the Royal Family, together with MI-6, of murdering Diana and his son, citing Diana's alleged pregnancy by Dodi as the motive, in January 2004 Operation Paget was launched to investigate the deaths. Some 3 years and £4 million later, on Thursday, December 14th, 2006, the investigation was finally brought to a conclusion, and the results published in an 832-page dossier, *The Paget Report.* In large part, this new paperback is a direct response to, and cross-examination of, that report.

But it is also much more than this. For the past ten years John and I have found ourselves embroiled in an investigation we had no prior intention of involving ourselves in. We were quite happy with our lives just as they were, thank you very much. Given the circumstance resulting in our involvement, however, we feel we had little choice but to get involved; and once involved, to give it our best shot. Hence our initial three-year investigation, which resulted in the first edition of this book. And hence our ongoing investigation, which resulted in the publication of this one.

For those of you unfamiliar with the circumstance that led to our initial investigation, and those others who might be curious as to our background and how we managed to gain access to some of the sources quoted in this book, let us take a moment to explain how it all came about. Indeed, the most common questions we have been asked over the past few years are: What prompted you to investigate Diana's death in the first place? Where did you get your information? How did you manage to forge relationships with such deep-cover security and intelligence sources? The answers are as follows.

Firstly, this book was not written overnight. For reasons that will become evident, our investigation began within days of Diana's death, and over the years that followed we ploughed every ounce of our time, energy and resource into uncovering the true facts surrounding her fatal crash. My background in investigative journalism meant that I had already established a fairly broad network of sources in one area and another, and we found we were able to draw on these sources and that they in turn were able to introduce us to new sources. Quite frankly, we were surprised, not only by the number of sources willing to talk, but given the subject matter, by those willing to be named.

Secondly, as fate would have it, I happened to grow up in a fairly military environment, in Sandhurst, where we train the elite of Britain's military machine. Indeed, the elite of military machines the world over. But the Royal Military Academy Sandhurst, where Princes William and Harry recently trained to become officers in the British Army, is only one of many very sensitive military sites in the area. For a good thirty or forty-mile radius the area is literally singing with military bases and training camps, Ministry of Defence compounds, top-secret government installations etc., as well as the headquarters of other, 'less official' units. One or two of these 'less official' units form part of what we might loosely term a 'private security operation' that, in turn, forms an unofficial arm of MI-6. Staffed mainly by former SAS and other special forces and intelligence personnel, this operation has been run out of Sandhurst and the surrounding area for a good many years, and in consequence, a fair number of the young men I grew up with ended up on its payroll. In other words, they became MI-6 assets. I knew a good number of them. I was never part of the operation, but I went to school with some of those who were. I socialized with others. From high-ranking intelligence and security personnel through diplomatic bodyguards down to rank-and-file mercenaries and assassins—I knew them. For a good deal of my early life they were my peers.

True to say, then, that a fair number of the young men I grew up with ended up working in some or other area of intelligence and/or security. Thus, by the time we embarked on our investigation into Diana's death, I had a fairly broad base of military, security and intelligence sources to call on, and via which to gain access to other sources of a similar background. It was one of these sources in particular—whose identity is disguised in the book, and to whom I have always referred in my previous works as 'Stealth'—who would, one week prior to the event, forewarn me of Diana's imminent assassination.

On Saturday, August 23rd, 1997, I met up with "Stealth" at Avebury Stone Circles in Wiltshire. This US Special Forces veteran and CIA contract agent was someone I had met on several occasions previously, someone who had furnished me with good information before. On this particular occasion we met up specifically to discuss the nefarious goings on in some of the British government's top-secret deep-underground facilities—the facility that existed several hundred feet beneath a place called Aldermaston in Berkshire, for example, where for decades the Royal Dutch Shell Group, a company in which the Royal Family has invested heavily over the years, allegedly ran an undeclared nuclear reactor, and in consequence, many of the locals are now dying of cancer. But that, as they say, is another story.

Seating himself on a fallen megalith, staring thoughtfully ahead, Stealth said he had given me about as much as he could on the deep-underground programme, but that he wanted to leave me with "one last pearl" of information before we parted company. Something big was about to happen, he said, something he had known about for some time, something the higher echelons of US and British intelligence had been talking about for months. Though he did not know precisely where this event would take place, he was none the less able to confirm that it was imminent. He then proceeded to warn me of "*a plot to eliminate one of the most prominent figures on the world stage...within days from now.*"

"*I can tell you, Jon,*" he concluded, "*this one will be bigger than Kennedy.*" The full interview with Stealth is included inside.

This information was given to me on Saturday, August 23rd, 1997— precisely one week before Diana's death. Though at the time Stealth did not name Diana specifically, he nonetheless compared the intended target to JFK and Martin Luther King in terms of their massive popularity and thus their ability to sway public opinion against the status quo. He even mentioned John Lennon in this same regard. I took the information with caution, scepticism even. I knew this man to some degree; I knew his contacts, their field of activity, who they mixed with and what they were capable of. But a prime-target assassination? Who? President Clinton? Tony Blair? I dared not think it. Certainly Diana never for one moment entered my mind. I, like most people, was kind of aware of her landmines campaign, and that her face seemed to adorn the front page of every newspaper on sale. But apart from that, she never appeared on my radar. Certainly I never imagined she might have been targeted by whoever carried out political assassinations. Even so, when she died a week later, in what so many thought were highly suspicious circumstances, I knew immediately that it was Princess Diana to whom Stealth had referred, and it numbed me. Indeed, for some days thereafter I tossed unthinkable thoughts back and forth in my head, wondering who else might have known that Stealth had given me this information. How careful had he been? Who else knew about our meetings? Was I in danger? My family?

I decided to talk to the only person I knew who might be able to help, someone I knew to be very well-connected within British military intelligence. I simply cannot say any more about this contact, other than to confirm that he introduced me to a second very well-placed source who claimed to have been present at a meeting held at MI5 HQ in which Diana's assassination had been discussed. We met at a well-known landmark in London.

To my genuine surprise, between them these two sources were able to confirm everything Stealth had said, plus some. Indeed, I was told quite categorically that they had learned of the plot to assassinate Diana "*several months*" prior to the event, that in fact the plot had been tabled at least as long ago as November 1995, and moreover, that Diana's death was the result of a failed MI5 attempt to assassinate Camilla Parker Bowles. Yes, this sounds preposterous. Yes, it raises many improbable questions. But please stay with it. We have uncovered very credible evidence that these two sources were in fact correct in their assertions. Charles's and Diana's looming divorce, and the constitutional crisis foreseen as a result of Charles's intentions to marry Mrs Parker Bowles while Diana was still alive, were the primary reasons given with regard to motive. In the book we present the full body of evidence in support of this allegation, and it forms a very powerful document indeed.

And there was more information forthcoming from these same two sources. Though MI-6 and the British Establishment had their own reasons for wanting rid of Diana, they said, the princess had, in the last year or so of her life, also engendered the wrath of the CIA. Enter Stealth. It was this CIA contract agent who had informed me in the first place, I reminded myself, suggesting that the US spy agency might indeed have been more involved than anybody knew. I noted the fact. Indeed, these sources went on to tell me that the CIA had finally given its support to the already existing MI-6 plot against Diana's life because, as Stealth had affirmed, her unprecedented popularity meant that her landmines campaign had attracted massive public attention, massive media attention, and in consequence, had started to threaten not only highly lucrative US defence revenues, but the very stability of central Africa—a region glued together by CIA arms-for-oil deals in Angola and other, neighbouring countries. The fact that Diana had single-handedly persuaded then President Bill Clinton to, in effect, overturn US defence policy and support the princess's wishes for a total ban on the manufacture, sale and deployment of landmines, worldwide; and the added fact that the Angola situation highlighted by the princess's campaign threatened also to expose the illicit oil-backed loans made by Bush-Cheney to Angola's communist government, loans brokered by the CIA, served only to bolster the agency's resolve, we were told. Again, evidence to support these allegations is presented in full inside this book.

OK, before we proceed, we would like to make the following points absolutely clear.

1) Based on the evidence uncovered during our investigation, together with that uncovered by other investigators, we are convinced that Diana was assassinated. We make no bones about that. However, this conclusion does not depend at all on the information received from Stealth. On the contrary, the information received from Stealth was instrumental only in persuading us to investigate Diana's death in the first place. Our conclusion is the result of the many difficult and demanding years that followed.

2) There are many sources quoted in this book. For obvious reasons, a small percentage of these sources must remain anonymous, at least for the time being. Whether or not they ever come out is entirely up to them. But until then, we can only continue to protect their identities by remaining faithful to our initial agreements with them. In other words, by assuring their anonymity. So far as a couple of those sources are concerned, we do not know their real names anyway

> Despite this, a very high percentage of the sources quoted herein are named. The book is not based on information that cannot be corroborated or substantiated, or independently checked out. Wherever information from an unnamed source is presented, we have done our best to either substantiate or corroborate that information with supporting information from at least one named source. Any information we could not substantiate or corroborate, at least to some verifiable degree—and there was some—was in the end left out.

3) The reason we have written this book—against all the odds, it has to be said—is to present you, the jury, with the evidence, the facts as we have been able to sift and substantiate them. In this regard we have tried to piece together the entire body of existing evidence, both old and new—both that uncovered by us and that uncovered by other investigators—and present it to you as it might be presented in a court of law.

In short, this is our 'case for the prosecution'. It is our clear and unambiguous intention to convince you, from our standpoint as 'prosecuting counsels', that Diana's death was no accident, and thus that the circumstances in which she died, together with those parties involved, should be properly and judicially investigated and tried before a democratically elected, independent jury. To date they haven't been. Thus the purpose of this book is to raise public awareness and galvanize public opinion towards this end.

BOOK ONE

THE EVIDENCE

I

THE PRINCESS AND THE PLAYBOY

"**P**rince Philip has let rip several times recently about the Fayeds—at a dinner party, during a country shoot and while on a visit to close friends in Germany. He's been banging on about his contempt for Dodi and how he is undesirable as a future stepfather to William and Harry. Diana has been told in no uncertain terms about the consequences should she continue the relationship with the Fayed boy... *now the royal family may have decided it is time to settle up* [italics in original copy]."

Sunday Mirror, 31st August, 1997.

[Note: the newspaper in which the above quote appeared was already on its way to the news stands when news of Diana's death reached Britain.]

The Rats

SATURDAY, 30ᵀᴴ AUGUST, 1997:

At 1pm, local time, Diana and Dodi left Olbia Airport in Sardinia, bound for Paris. Word of their arrival would precede them. Indeed, as the Al Fayed Gulfstream-IV jet touched down at Le Bourget Airport a little over two hours later, the couple were once again greeted by the familiar hail of flash-bulbs and jostle. The usual high levels of security at France's busiest airport, it seemed, had failed. Ordinarily, the electronically-wired gates and high security fences would have been sufficient to repel the attentions of the paparazzi. But not today. Today the rats had swarmed. And Le Bourget's VIP lounge was bearing the full burden of this twentieth-century plague.

In an attempt to regain control of the situation, airport staff advised that the couple remain on the aircraft. A police escort had been requested, they were informed, but neither Dodi nor Diana wished to wait around for the escort to arrive. Time was pressing: Dodi wanted to get to the Ritz as soon as possible and with the least fuss; Diana, too. As it was, only one night of their holiday remained. They wished to spend it in Paris, quietly, privately, intimately. They wished to be alone. This was, after all, a day of celebration— the sole reason they had decided to stop off in Paris was to collect the engagement ring Dodi had ordered some three weeks earlier in Monte Carlo. It was now ready for him to collect. Indeed, much to the disdain of the British Royal Establishment, it was now ready for the princess to wear.

Instead of accepting the offer from the airport staff, then, and waiting for *Pest Control* to come and remove the rats, Dodi called on his personal staff—already waiting at the airport—to bring the cars out on to the tarmac, to the plane, so that he and Diana may be driven directly from the aircraft and out through customs, avoiding the waiting press and cameramen. In the melee that followed, Dodi's bodyguard, Trevor Rees-Jones, attempted without success to persuade the paparazzi to follow him in a decoy car. At the same time, Dodi's driver, Philippe Dourneau, drove the official car to the aeroplane steps.

At this point the couple were forced to make a dash for it. Hurriedly disembarking they crossed the short stretch of tarmac at the foot of the aeroplane's steps and made their way over to the black Mercedes which had just pulled up at the edge of the runway. Airport staff described the couple as "*courteous*" but "*anxious*" at this point; though eager to escape the promise of yet another photo call, Diana was said to have taken the time to greet the staff personally before climbing in the back of the Mercedes with Dodi. As she did so, she would have noticed a second car waiting there, parked immediately behind the Mercedes—a dark-green Range Rover deployed both as back-up vehicle and baggage hold. Behind the wheel was the Deputy Head of Security for the Ritz Hotel, Paris. His name was Henri Paul.

Conscientiously Henri Paul followed the Mercedes out of Le Bourget Airport and on to the highway that would take them back towards the centre of Paris. But they would not travel there directly. At Dodi's request they would first stop off at Windsor Villa, the former residence of the Duke and Duchess of Windsor in Rue du Champ d'Entrainment, Paris. There, Dodi would proudly show off to Diana what he hoped would soon be their new home, as husband and wife. Indeed, later that afternoon he would ask his father for the keys.

Having spent around thirty minutes viewing the property, the ill-fated couple continued their journey to the Ritz.

Unidentified Faces

I f the newspaper reports are to be believed, the journey from Le Bourget Airport that afternoon was little but a dress rehearsal for what was to happen later that evening. Indeed, the Mercedes in which the couple were travelling was badgered and hounded virtually all the way to the steps of the Ritz Hotel by the hungry rats—on their motorbikes and in their cars. At one point, prior to stopping off at the couple's proposed new home in Bois de Boulogne, a press vehicle, reported to have been a black Peugeot 205 sedan, deliberately swerved in front of the Mercedes while the latter was driving at some speed. It was an act that forced the Mercedes to brake sharply. At which point a motorbike pulled alongside and its pillion passenger, camera in hand, fired off a volley of high-powered *flashes* through the passenger-side window, temporarily blinding both driver and passengers alike. In some respects the couple were fortunate not to have been driven off the road there and then. But then, perhaps that wasn't part of the plan.

By now word had spread to just about every paparazzo in town. Plus some. Soon after 4 pm, anticipating the couple's arrival, the cameras and the flash-bulbs and the tripods plus their owners had already begun to assemble outside the exclusive Ritz Hotel in Place Vendome, Paris. Most had arrived on motorbikes and scooters, though some smaller number had arrived in cars. Each had arrived in time to stake out their place for the evening's entertainment: the arrival of a princess and her playboy lover. They did not have to wait long. According to the time signal on the Ritz security cameras it was 4.35 pm when the couple's black Mercedes finally pulled up outside the front entrance. As though the symptom of some strange and morbid custom, the paparazzi were once again there to greet them. But not only paparazzi. Security footage shows that, by this time, the waiting cameramen had been joined by several *unidentified faces*. According to eyewitness reports, together with video footage retrieved from the Ritz's own security cameras, these *unidentified faces* would remain posted in and around the Ritz for the entire evening. They would make their presence known soon after midnight.

For the next couple of hours Diana and Dodi enjoyed some private time in the hotel's most exclusive apartment—the US $10,000-a-night Imperial Suite. Complete with eighteenth-century antique furniture, oak and marble bathroom, and a private balcony overlooking the fashionable Place Vendome, the Imperial Suite was not an unfamiliar sanctuary. Diana knew it from a weekend spent there secretly with Dodi a month earlier; Dodi, of course, knew it like home. When in Paris, but not staying at his luxury apartment on the Champs Elysees, he would stay at the Ritz. And when at the family-owned Ritz he would of course occupy the Imperial Suite. Indeed, it was to this palatial apartment, at around 5 pm, that Ritz Manager, Claude Roulet, would deliver Diana's US $200,000 engagement ring, a *'Dis Moi Oui'*—'Tell Me Yes'—ring, which Dodi had selected from one of Europe's most exclusive jewellers, *Alberto Repossi*. He would present it to Diana later that evening.

But not before the couple had first returned to Dodi's apartment, where they were scheduled to spend the night. They had not intended to return to the Ritz at all that evening. Instead they were to dine at Paris's exclusive *Chez Benoit* restaurant on Rue Saint Martin, where a reservation had been made earlier by Claude Roulet. Following a romantic 'engagement dinner', the plan was to return to Dodi's ten-room apartment for the night before flying out of Paris the next day. But it was not to be. The traffic was too dense, the city too busy, and too many paparazzi were already staked out outside Dodi's front door for the couple to cross from the apartment unnoticed, unmolested. In consequence, and with some reluctance, they decided to drive back to the Ritz and dine there instead. At least there, they figured, they could dine in peace.

According to the Ritz security cameras the couple's Mercedes arrived back at the hotel at 9.53 pm. If Diana, Dodi and the entire Ritz workforce were surprised at their unscheduled return, strangely, the paparazzi were not. As the couple left the car and entered the hotel it is estimated that well over fifty rats and their cameras were milling outside—some at the front, some to the rear, all seemingly a little uneasy with the mounting tension now evident. And for some reason the tension was even more aggressive than usual. Insults flew. Scuffles broke out. Shouts went up as bodies jostled for position. The video footage of the couple entering the hotel certainly betrays a sense of tension about them, too. But then again, who could blame them for that? By anyone's standards they had suffered a gruelling day. The long haul from Sardinia to Paris, dodging paparazzi. The almost military operation necessary to escape the paparazzi on arrival at Le Bourget Airport on the outskirts of Paris. Paparazzi *en route* from Le Bourget to central Paris, in particular the incident when their car was almost driven off the highway. More paparazzi on arrival at the Ritz. More on their departure. Yet more paparazzi on arrival at Dodi's apartment, forcing the couple to make last minute changes to their preferred schedule and drive back across town to the Ritz for dinner. Even more paparazzi waiting for them there. Indeed, one might be forgiven for wondering who in truth was organizing this almost military-precise press operation: *for wondering who was tipping these guys off.* Someone with an ulterior motive for wishing to exhaust the couple's inner reserves, perhaps— cause them tension, fear, anxiety? Could these tactics have been part of the operation that would, later that same evening, claim their lives? As a result of this action, for example, would Dodi be tempted to encourage Henri Paul to drive just that little bit faster, take just a little less care than perhaps he normally would? The possibility cannot be ruled out. After all, the couple were anxious. They were hungry. They were tired. All they wanted was to find somewhere quiet to eat. And sleep. In military terms, they were, quite simply, sitting targets.

Finally, at around 10 pm, the couple entered the Ritz for dinner. And even then they were forced to retire to the Imperial Suite in order to avoid the scrutiny of other diners in the Ritz's own *L'Espadon* restaurant. Perhaps if they had simply given in to their own exhaustion at this point, and decided to remain at the hotel until morning, they would have survived to tell their own story of this fraught, frenetic day. They did not, of course. They did not stay and they did not survive. Indeed, according to the evidence now available, they were not meant to do either, as we shall see.

The Operation

By the time the couple were ready to leave for Dodi's apartment once more it was 12.15 am. They had been at the hotel for a little under two-and-a-half hours. As Henri Paul prepared to make his getaway from the rear of the building, down Rue Cambon via Place de la Concorde and along the Champs Elysees, two Ritz decoy cars screeched away from the front of the hotel in a bid to lure paparazzi off the chase. They circled the square at the front of the hotel, once, and straight away returned to the hotel's front entrance. To some extent the ploy worked. But not entirely. Perhaps on a hunch, perhaps on a tip-off, it is now known that a small number of *unidentified faces*—posing as paparazzi—were already waiting at the rear of the building. There they watched from the shadows as Diana and Dodi left by the back door and climbed in a spare car—a black Mercedes S280 VIP limousine. They then sped off in pursuit of that spare car, those *unidentified faces*. It was now 12.20 am.

Precisely what happened during the four minutes following Henri Paul's departure from the rear of the Ritz cannot be so clearly defined; for some bizarre and still-unexplained reason, the ten CCTV cameras lining the route, plus those situated in the Place de l'Alma itself, failed to capture any images of either the chase from the Ritz to the crash tunnel, or of the crash itself. This, at least, remains the official line.

At 12.21 am Diana's car was forced to stop at traffic lights in Place de la Concorde. It is reported to have jumped those traffic lights in order to escape the close attentions of paparazzi and other, as yet *unidentified pursuers*. At 12.22 am, still being pursued by paparazzi—but also by a second Mercedes and a high-powered motorbike complete with driver and pillion rider—the car was forced to take an unscheduled detour. Instead of taking the more direct route—turning right off Place de la Concorde and heading up the Champs Elysees—Henri Paul was forced to take an alternative route along the right bank of the River Seine and through an underpass, which he negotiated safely. But there was another underpass ahead.

At 12.24 am Diana's Mercedes entered the Place de l'Alma underpass, later to be identified as Diana's 'crash tunnel'. It was at this point that the operation truly kicked in. As the Mercedes approached the tunnel's entrance, Henri Paul endeavoured to take the slip-road off the riverside highway in order to head back towards Dodi's apartment, but the slip-road was blocked by a motorbike parked broadside across the exit. Henri Paul was forced to drive on into the tunnel. A split-second later a second motorbike— the high-powered motorbike that had followed them along the riverside highway—was seen to suddenly pull alongside, and then sweep ahead. As it sped past Diana's Mercedes, Henri Paul inexplicably lost control of the vehicle and it started to spin out of control, first one way, then the other, then back again into the thirteenth concrete pillar lining the tunnel's central reservation. At some point the Mercedes also clipped the back of a white Fiat Uno, grazing its rear wing and smashing its rear driver-side brake light (traces of white paint belonging to a Fiat Uno, fragments of a rear light-casing and a Fiat Uno wing mirror were later found by investigators at the scene of the crash). On impact, the Mercedes was hurled round a violent 180 degrees, plus a little more. When it finally came to rest its mangled front end faced back towards the Ritz.

Meanwhile, the motorbike screeched to a halt some way further into the tunnel. Here a second operation vehicle—perhaps the Mercedes seen speeding away from the scene moments later, perhaps the white Fiat Uno described in some detail by a number of eyewitnesses—was already waiting to ferry operatives from the scene in the event of injury. So far as we know, none of the operatives were injured in the operation. The vehicle was ready and waiting just the same. Just in case. But that was not the end of it. According to Britain's foremost crash expert, Professor Murray MacKay of Birmingham University (whom we interviewed), and contrary to initial reports, Diana's Mercedes was travelling no faster than 60/63 mph at the moment of impact. And what is more, Diana herself was seated directly behind the passenger-side front seat—which, according to Professor MacKay, should have been the safest seat in the car. The "most survivable" seat. Even so there was only one survivor, and it was *not* Princess Diana. Operatives at the scene were on hand to make sure of that. But they had only seconds in which to complete the operation.

Having satisfied themselves that Diana's condition was fatal—having *ensured* that Diana's condition *would be* fatal—they evacuated the scene at high speed, as reported by a number of eyewitnesses. Mission accomplished. It should be added that, even though involved in a major road traffic accident in the centre of one of Europe's largest and busiest cities—and moreover, an accident involving the death of a British Royal—none of the persons involved, nor their vehicles, have ever been traced by the French authorities. Curious, to say the least. Indeed, the assumption must now be that these vehicles will never be traced. And that, in consequence, their occupants—and those for whom they were working—will never be brought to justice. *Fait accompli.*

Though deliberately speculative in its conclusion, this version of events is otherwise based on the facts as known regarding the final few hours of Princess Diana's life. Perhaps details of the final few minutes will never be known. We cannot say. What we can say, however, is that the above conclusion is not necessarily so far-fetched that one should automatically dismiss it out of hand. For one thing it is based on information gleaned from several intelligence and security sources (as presented in the ensuing chapters), and from eyewitnesses to events immediately prior to and following the crash. As we shall see, eyewitness testimonies that do not support the 'drink-drive' theory were simply brushed aside by the French investigation team, as well as by Lord Stevens and Operation Paget. Other eyewitness testimonies—which include detailed descriptions of the high-powered motorbike, the second Mercedes and the Fiat Uno observed at the scene of the crash—have simply not been acted upon with any degree of vigour. Certainly not with any degree of success. To add to this, intelligence services are known to have employed the 'road traffic accident' in other assassination operations, both in England and other European countries, with some large degree of success. Indeed, in security circles the 'road traffic accident' is known as the most reliable form of deniable operation, as our evidence will demonstrate.

In any event, when the full body of available evidence is considered, the conclusion posited above becomes all the more plausible, certainly more so than the official, and wholly contrived, 'drink-drive' theory so vigorously promulgated by the authorities. In our opinion no one in an official capacity has yet proposed anything like a satisfactory explanation regarding Diana's death. And what concerns us even more is that, unless we force the issue, no one in an official capacity ever will. Why would they? Certainly we can expect that the forthcoming Royal Inquest will simply uphold the 'evidence' presented in Lord Stevens' Paget report, as though it tells the whole story. It does not. It is a sham, a flagrant and predetermined whitewash of the real evidence, as presented in this book. All we ask is that you read this evidence with justice rather than prejudice in mind.

—2—

THE WITNESSES

"The officer [senior French police officer, David Laurent] was driving towards the Alma tunnel when a white car overtook him and raced past. As the officer approached the tunnel he again saw the car, which he recognized as a Fiat Uno. But this time, the Uno appeared to be creeping along very, very slowly a few metres from the mouth of the tunnel. It had no reason to slow down or stop, but it had come to a virtual standstill just before the tunnel entrance... The officer drove past, leaving the Uno at the tunnel entrance... Later that night he heard about what had happened on the news... He now believes the Uno was waiting for...the Mercedes carrying Princess Diana."

Mirror, Thursday, 4th June, 1998.

A Second Mercedes and A High-Powered Motorbike

According to early reports, the Mercedes S280 VIP limousine in which the couple died was doing in excess of 100 mph at the time of the crash—an attempt on behalf of driver Henri Paul, they say, to escape the attentions of the chasing paparazzi: *click, click.* The evidence, however, as we now know, tells an altogether different story.

Somewhat conveniently, many have since commented, the crash occurred as the princess and Dodi were driven through the Place de l'Alma underpass on the right bank of the River Seine. If the reports are to be believed, Henri Paul was already worse for a cocktail of drink and drugs by the time he was summoned to drive the couple from the Ritz Hotel to Dodi's apartment. Indeed, if the reports are to be believed, Henri Paul was in no fit state to be driving *any* car at *any* speed, much less an unprotected Mercedes

S280 limo plus royal passenger at more than 100 mph. This coupled with the claim that the pack of out-of-control paparazzi was still snapping at the Mercedes' heels as it entered the underpass was the official reason given for the cause of the crash at the time. But as we discovered, eyewitness reports tended to seriously challenge this explanation.

More than one witness, for example, recalled seeing a second Mercedes on the royal tail. It is said to have pursued Diana's Mercedes as driver Henri Paul was forced to accelerate through a set of red traffic lights on exiting Place de la Concorde. Initial reports claimed that this mysterious 'second Mercedes' contained American tourists. However, the Mercedes seen speeding away from the scene of the crash moments after impact was not being driven in a manner consistent with how we might expect tourists to drive—in particular in a foreign country's capital city at half-past midnight.

Other reports speak of a high-powered motorbike swerving in front of Diana's Mercedes as it entered the underpass, only seconds before the crash. This vehicle was seen and described in some detail by several witnesses. But to no avail; it has never been traced. Confirmation that Diana's Mercedes was indeed followed by this high-powered motorbike came in an exclusive interview with Dodi's personal bodyguard, Trevor Rees-Jones (the *Mirror*, Monday, 2nd March, 1998). In the interview Mr Rees-Jones stated quite unequivocally that he recalled being followed into the tunnel by a high-powered motorbike. He also recalled being pursued by two other vehicles, one of which he described as a white hatch-back, similar to a Fiat Uno. Not one of these vehicles has ever been traced. Why?

Explosions

Another witness—London lawyer, Gary Hunter, staying at the Royal Alma Hotel on the night in question, overlooking the road leading away from the crash tunnel—claims that he heard two explosions inside the tunnel. Moments later, he says, he saw a Fiat Uno or Renault Clio together with a larger vehicle—'probably a Mercedes'—speeding away from the underpass. Mr Hunter described these two vehicles as travelling "*bumper to bumper*" at high speed. As Lord Stevens' Paget report states:

"*At 12.25am on Sunday, 31 August, 1997, Gary Hunter heard an 'almighty crash' followed immediately by the sound of skidding tyres and then immediately a further very loud crash. He took the time from the digital clock on the hotel room television. He jumped from his bed and looked out of the window. He looked to his left, in the direction of the sound and heard the constant tone of a car horn sounding. He then saw people running from the junction at the bottom of the road, across the grass area towards the direction of the noise. He watched for approximately one minute but could not see what was happening so he returned to bed. His wife was still sleeping.*

"Hunter lay on the bed for what 'felt like a minute—it may have been less'. He then heard the noise of tyres from a car screeching at the bottom of the road from the direction that he had heard the earlier sounds. Immediately returning to the window and looking to the left, Hunter saw a small dark vehicle, which had 'completed its turn' into rue Jean Goujon. This vehicle was immediately followed by a larger white vehicle, which he thought might have been a Mercedes.

"He stated that the Mercedes 'completed its turn' at speed, immediately behind the smaller darker vehicle, and the two vehicles proceeded 'in tandem' along the rue Jean Goujon, passing under his bedroom window. He described both vehicles travelling at 'inordinate speed'. He noticed that the Mercedes was not manoeuvring or signalling to pass the smaller dark car. This made him believe the Mercedes was shielding the rear of the small black car." [Operation Paget Report, Page 494]

And further, in an exclusive interview with EIR magazine, Mr Hunter said: "There was an almighty crash followed by the sound of skidding, then another crash. My initial thought was that there had been a head-on collision. I went to the window and saw people running towards the tunnel. I heard a screeching of tyres. I saw a small dark car turning the corner at the top of the road. I would say it was racing at 60 to 70 mph. My own feeling is that these were people in a hurry not to be there. I am confident that car was getting off the scene. It was obvious they were getting away from something and that they were in a hurry. It looked quite sinister. I can't recall the type of car, but it was a small dark vehicle. It could have been a Fiat Uno or a Renault. The dark smaller car was followed, on its tail, by a white Mercedes."

[Note: as explained in *EIR*, forensic experts later told *Time* magazine's Paris bureau chief, Thomas Sancton, and its Middle East correspondent, Scott McLeod, that the lighting in the tunnel and along the

Paris streets makes it virtually impossible to differentiate colours at night. The lighting, the experts affirmed, can make a white or light-coloured car appear dark-coloured to the naked eye. The fact that Mr Hunter described the Fiat Uno as "dark", then, when in fact it is now known to have been white, is not altogether surprising.]

A Fiat Uno and An Intense Flash of Light

Another witness who saw the Fiat Uno is senior French police officer, David Laurent. Back in June 1998 we were told that the French investigators had been given new evidence by Monsieur Laurent, who was off-duty on the night the Uno sped past him on approach to the tunnel. As reported in the *Mirror* (4th June, 1998):

"The officer was driving towards the Alma tunnel when a white car overtook him and raced past. As the officer approached the tunnel he again saw the car, which he recognized as a Fiat Uno. But this time, the Uno appeared to be creeping along very, very slowly a few metres from the mouth of the tunnel. It had no reason to slow down or stop, but it had come to a virtual standstill just before the tunnel entrance. At that stage there was no Mercedes in sight and no evidence that there had been an accident ahead. The officer drove past, leaving the Uno at the tunnel entrance ... Later that night he heard about what had happened on the news."

Mirror reporter Nic North, who wrote the article, went on to affirm that the police officer in question, David Laurent, was indeed a "*senior officer.*" The report concluded: "...He [Monsieur Laurent] now believes the Uno was waiting for another car, quite possibly the Mercedes carrying Princess Diana."

Another witness was American tourist, Brian Anderson, who was approaching the crash tunnel in a taxi when it was overtaken by Diana's Mercedes. Anderson says that, as they approached the tunnel, he saw an intensely bright flash of light.

"*It was at this point that from greater intensity from my left eye, I saw a flash coming from what I thought was in front of us. This flash looked like out of place light. I could not give an estimation as to the distance of the source of the flash, but it was an intense flash. I liken it to be so bright like magnesium igniting. I then heard a very loud explosion which seemed like it was coming from ahead of us."* [Operation Paget Report, Page 452]

We recall here the testimony of former MI-6 officer, Richard Tomlinson, who claims he saw an MI-6 document detailing a plot to assassinate Slobodan Milosevic by 'road traffic accident'. According to Tomlinson, the planned operation involved the use of an antipersonnel flash gun, or strobe gun, designed, he says, to blind the driver for up to three minutes. Indeed, the flash is so intensely bright, he claims, it has been known to cause irreversible retinal damage. Was this the *"intense flash"* of light seen by Brian Anderson? Though Tomlinson's claims are cleverly debunked in the Paget report, we should none the less include here the testimony of yet a further eyewitness, Francois Levistre, who claims he too saw an intense flash of light immediately prior to the crash.

"From as early as the Brazilian Embassy, I had seen the headlights of a car and of another car a little way from it, and the headlights of the accompanying motorcycles. I said to myself that I had enough time to go in front of those vehicles and so I accelerated in order to enter the tunnel. When I got to the hump just before the descent into the tunnel, one of the cars that I had seen overtook me. It was a white car. I do not know what make. It was a small car. I must have been travelling at 120 or 125 km/hr at that point, and I think he must have been doing 130."

"The white car went past. I am sure that there was no contact with that car. I continued driving through the tunnel, and when I was at the exit, just before going up the incline, I saw a motorbike accelerating. It was to the left of a large car that was behind me. The motorcycle, it was large and the two riders had full-face helmets on, cut up the large car in order to get in front of it. At that point, there was a sort of big white flash. The car zigzagged to the left, to the right and to the left again, and at that moment I came out of the tunnel. I saw all this in my rear view mirror. I stopped on the white strip at the exit to the tunnel. I remained there for 3, 4 or 5 minutes, when my wife said we should leave or I would get myself into all sorts of trouble again. As I left, the motorbike that I had seen, which had remained in the underpass while I was stationary, itself came out of the tunnel and overtook me. It was at that point that I noticed that there were two people on the bike." [Operation Paget Report, Page 455]

Francois Levistre suffered what can only be described as a full, public media crucifixion for daring to tell his story, which is serially picked to pieces in the Paget report. None the less Levistre's account was the first to describe the presence of a "white car" at the scene, and at the time Levistre gave this account on September 1st 1997, the presence of the white Fiat Uno now known to have been involved in the crash was not public knowledge. Francois Levistre's account should not be taken lightly, then.

In any event, there were other witnesses who caught snapshots of the crash in their minds. Several reported hearing a "terrific explosion" the instant Diana's car entered the tunnel. Others claimed—as did London lawyer, Gary Hunter—that they heard not one but two explosions inside the tunnel. The second 'explosion' could of course have been the sound of the Mercedes slamming into the reinforced concrete pillar with which it finally collided. But this still does not account for the first 'explosion'.

The Blockbuster Bomb

In an endeavour to shed some light on this mystery, we spoke to former SAS sergeant Dave Cornish, who informed us that the first explosion could have been due to a Special Forces device known as a Blockbuster Bomb—a small remote-controlled, non-detectable explosive concealed beneath the bonnet (hood) and designed to incapacitate, say, the steering column and/or the brakes. Employed by Britain's intelligence and security forces, it is a device capable of causing precisely the kind of 'accident' in which Diana was killed. Indeed, according to Mr Cornish, it is a device that has been employed against suspected terrorists in Northern Ireland for some years. "We used the Blockbuster so many times in Northern Ireland, we got it down to a fine art," Dave told us. It is particularly interesting to note in this regard that, as reported by the official French investigation team, Diana's Mercedes had been stolen at gunpoint prior to the crash. During its week-long absence the 'Blockbuster' could easily have been planted, Dave said.

He explained: "That's exactly how they would've done it—borrow the car for a couple of days, fix it, and send it back looking good as new." And further: "It's how they've always done this kind of job. People think: 'How did they know they would use that particular car on that particular night? How did they know Dodi and Diana would stop off in Paris that night?' But, you know, your average man on the street hasn't got a clue. These people can work bloody magic if necessary."

Also of note is that, during this same time frame, the car's EMS (Electronic Management System)—essentially a microchip that controls the steering and brakes, among other functions—had been ripped out by the thief(s) and was later replaced. This is particularly interesting for the fact that the EMS had no substantial re-sale value—it is highly unlikely, therefore, that it was stolen for financial gain. One wonders: if not for financial gain, for what reason would a VIP limousine be stolen, at gunpoint, and then conveniently 'found' minus its original EMS? Could it have been to replace the system with one that had been tampered with, we wondered?

Dave Cornish certainly thought that this could have been the case.

"The new system would have been programmed to override the steering and brakes. Like the Blockbuster, it would've been triggered [remotely] from the tail car when it got close in. There would've been absolutely nothing the driver could have done to regain manual control. Absolutely nothing."

Dave also told us that the 'accident' bore all the hallmarks of a calculated intelligence—"*probably MI-6*"—operation, though he said that the "hit" itself would have been ordered from "*beyond the normal channels*" and carried out by a "private firm"—a private security firm—"*hired by the agency*" (see The Clinic— *Chapter 3*). It should be added that this is precisely what we were told by another security source, also—that, in the event that the 'accident' had been arranged by British intelligence, it would most certainly have been executed by a private security firm hired specifically for the task. It should be noted in this regard that some of Britain's so-called 'private security firms' are far from the sleazy, backstreet operations their image might suggest. On the contrary, they are often multimillion-dollar operations set up to supply arms, mercenaries and other forms of 'assistance' to the agencies, such as MI-6, who hire them. And what's more, according to more than one mercenary we interviewed, these other forms of assistance include political assassination.

Dave Cornish concluded: "There'd been word of something like this happening for quite some time. But I never thought they'd actually do it ... From the minute the decoy car left the Ritz to the moment the tail car closed in ... it was obvious what was going down. Anyone who knows what they're talking about'll tell you the same."

And further: "It wouldn't be the first time this method has been used in a deniable op."

Evidently not, as we were to discover in *Chapter 3*.

BOSTON BRAKES

"**M**eier knew from experience that once he had taken over the control of Horsley's car, he could steer it as he pleased."

Sir Ranulph Fiennes, The Feather Men, 1991.

The Clinic

In our efforts to corroborate the claims made by former SAS Sergeant, Dave Cornish, we came upon the following account of a true-life assassination operation carried out by a 'private security firm' similar to the one described to us by the former SAS man in Chapter 2. The incident involved a former Special Forces officer, Major Michael Marman of the Sultan of Oman's Armed Forces, and a former Equerry to the Queen, Air Marshall Sir Peter Horsley. Only one of the two men survived to tell its tale.

In his autobiography, *Sounds From Another Room*, Air Marshall Sir Peter Horsley describes in chilling detail what happened to him on Tuesday, 11th November, 1986, while driving from his home in Wiltshire to a business meeting, due to take place in Plymouth. Sir Peter recounts that, on the day in question, he was driving his BMW along the westbound carriageway of the A303, at approximately 60 mph, when he was involved in a very serious 'accident'. As he approached the megalithic monument of Stonehenge, he says, he saw a grey Volvo closing on him "*at high speed*" in his rear-view mirror. He then saw the Volvo take up position "*immediately behind*" him.

But what is most intriguing so far as we are concerned is that, just as Sir Peter was about to wave the Volvo past, quite suddenly and inexplicably, he says, he lost control of his BMW.

"...With alarming suddenness," he explains in his book, "my BMW spun sharply to the left, and then, with tyres now screeching, equally sharply to the right and then back again." (Precisely what happened to Diana's Mercedes moments before it crashed.) Sir Peter's BMW then careered across the central reservation and ploughed broadside into an oncoming Citroen 2CV—driven by one Major Michael Marman.

Sir Peter wrote: "Out of the corner of my eye, I saw the grey Volvo accelerating past me at high speed. My car had now developed a mind of its own as it swung broadside and skidded down the road. With a lurch it hit the central reservation, mounted the grass verge separating the two lanes of the highway and crossed over into the opposite carriageway. I just had time to see a small car approaching from the opposite direction. I hit it sideways on with tremendous force. In a split second the driver's horror-stricken face was visible and I clearly heard his hoarse scream above the tearing metal of the two cars momentarily locked together; then came silence as the small car [the 2CV] disappeared, catapulted off the road by the sheer force of the impact."

Though Sir Peter survived the 'accident', the driver of the 2CV, Major Michael Marman, was killed instantly. The question is, of course, was Major Marman the victim of a tragic though innocent 'road traffic accident'? Or was there something more to it?

According to world famous explorer, personal friend of Prince Charles and former SAS officer, Sir Ranulph Fiennes, Major Marman's death was in fact the handiwork of a European 'private security firm'—a firm of professional assassins known as The Clinic. In his book, *The Feather Men*, Fiennes reveals that, due to his tour of duty with the Sultan of Oman's Armed Forces, Major Marman had for some time been the target of a Yemeni assassination plot. He further reveals that The Clinic had been hired to carry out that plot; indeed, that The Clinic's speciality is carrying out assassinations which to all intents and purposes look like accidents. The road traffic accident in particular, he says, was first used in Boston, and for this reason it had become known as the 'Boston brakes'. By employing the 'Boston brakes' method, Fiennes says, Major Marman's death was made to appear like an accident—much like Diana's—when in reality it was the result of a pre-planned and well-rehearsed assassination operation.

Fiennes writes: "On the night of Monday, 10 November [the night before the 'accident'], five members of the gang assembled outside Sir Peter's secluded Victorian house ... Three remained on watch while Jake and Meier began the work of fixing the apparatus to the BMW's braking system ... Meier knew from experience that once he had taken over the control of Horsley's car, he could steer it as he pleased."

In other words, due to the Special Forces device planted on Sir Peter's car the night before the incident, at precisely the intended moment, Clinic member Meier was able to take remote control of Sir Peter's BMW and "*steer it as he pleased*'—which in this instance was into the oncoming Citroen 2CV driven by assassination target, Major Michael Marman. The former SAS officer never stood a chance.

Similarly, then, might the driver of the Fiat Uno, or indeed, the motorbike's pillion rider, have 'taken over the control' of Diana's Mercedes as it entered the tunnel? And having done so, might he then have been able to "*steer it as he pleased*," as described by Sir Ranulph Fiennes? Once inside the tunnel, Diana's Mercedes certainly acted in a very similar manner to Sir Peter Horsley's BMW, in that it too lurched "*sharply to the left, and then ... equally sharply to the right and then back again.*" And then into the thirteenth concrete pillar lining the tunnel's central reservation.

As Fiennes explains: "[From inside the chasing Volvo] Meier took over Horsley's car and... he steered the BMW across the centre of the reservation into the path of Marman's approaching car ..."

And further, in order to cover their tracks: "That night two members of The Clinic broke into the garage and quickly removed all the apparatus from Horsley's car."

In other words, they removed all evidence of the device which had enabled them to remotely control Sir Peter's car. Fiennes concluded: "The police arrived the following morning and... did not have the slightest suspicion that they had been duped."

One wonders who might have been the first to 'examine' the wreckage of Diana's crashed Mercedes, then. The highly organized assassination team who caused the crash in the first place, perhaps? The agency for whom they were working? One thing we know for certain is that it was not the fully qualified Daimler-Benz engineers, the very engineers who perhaps should have been called upon to analyze the wreckage. In fact the Daimler-Benz engineers—who indeed offered their expert assistance to the French authorities—were refused permission to go anywhere near the wreckage. Very strange.

Or perhaps not. After all, who knows what they might have found? The remains of a Blockbuster device, perhaps? Or some other device—a remote-control receiver/transmitter? As outrageous as it may sound, the possibility should not be dismissed out of hand—certainly not according to Prince Charles's personal friend and former SAS officer, Sir Ranulph Fiennes, at any rate.

And there is further evidence to be considered. According to independent eyewitness, Aubrey Allen, who was driving some short distance behind Sir Peter's BMW when it crashed, what appears to have been a small explosion occurred moments before Sir Peter lost control of his BMW. As Mr Allen testified to the inquest into Major Marman's death: "The BMW was travelling normally down the centre of the road in front of me when a large puff of smoke came out of the left rear side of the car." As a result, Mr Allen concluded, Sir Peter's BMW spun out of control.

The question, then, must surely be asked: what caused the "*large puff of smoke*" seen by Mr Allen to emerge from Sir Peter Horsley's car moments before he lost control? A blown tyre? No. No evidence of a blown tyre was found. A blown engine, then, a piston ring, a gasket?

No.

Might, then, the smoke have been the result of a small explosion, perhaps the result of a 'Blockbuster Bomb' triggered from the passing Volvo? The Volvo, remember, was the vehicle in which the assassins—The Clinic—were travelling.

The fact is that this question has never been answered, much like the many other questions which frankly still remain with regard to the crash that killed Diana. Indeed, the patent similarities in the deaths of Major Marman and the princess simply cannot be ignored.

And other than the 'Blockbuster' and 'Boston rakes' methods described by our SAS source and Sir Ranulph Fiennes, neither can they be explained.

— 4 —

DRUNK AT THE WHEEL

“**I** don't think there's evidence from the video that can suggest
he looks drunk. You wouldn't look at that... and say
'goodness me, that's a drunk person we're looking at'...
There's nothing in his demeanour, from these videos, to suggest
that there were any problems with his competence.”

Behavioural psychologist, Dr. Martin Skinner, 1998.

A Spurious Blood Test

According to the results of the official French inquiry, published in September
1999, Diana's death was entirely the result of a drink-drive accident.
Chauffeur Henri Paul was three times over the permitted alcohol limit, Judge
Herve Stephan concluded. Case closed. Having ruled out foul play for lack of
smoking-gun evidence, the results of Henri Paul's forensic blood test comprised
the sole basis for this verdict.

*The results of Henri Paul's forensic blood tests comprised the sole basis for
this verdict.*

Maybe, then, we should take a closer look at these forensic blood
tests—how they were performed, under what conditions, by whom. Certainly
the tests claiming Paul was three times over the legal limit seem spurious
enough. Indeed, highly contestable. For one thing, apart from the alleged
alcohol content, Paul's blood was found to contain 20.7% carbon monoxide
poisoning. According to medical experts, including carbon monoxide expert,
Dr. Alastair Hay, this is an inexplicably high level sufficient to cause nausea,
dizziness, unconsciousness, even death, in particular when combined with
alcohol and drugs. And yet security footage of Paul's behaviour at the Ritz for
the two hours prior to the ill-fated journey suggests that he was not even

drunk, much less that he was suffering from 20.7% carbon monoxide poisoning (about the level you might expect to find in the blood of someone who has committed suicide by locking themselves in their car and inhaling exhaust fumes). As behavioural psychologist, Dr. Martin Skinner, told ITN's investigative documentary, *Diana: Secrets of the Crash:* "I don't think there's evidence from the video that can suggest he looks drunk. You wouldn't look at that not knowing what has happened, and say 'goodness me, that's a drunk person we're looking at'. The pictures of him walking up and down the corridor are straight and smooth—he's standing very still. There's nothing in his demeanour, from these videos, to suggest that there were any problems with his competence."

In the same programme, carbon monoxide expert Dr. Alastair Hay was even more forthcoming: "It doesn't strike me when you look at the [video] pictures of Henri Paul [that] the man is really suffering. It doesn't look as if he's got a headache; he's not massaging his temples to try and reduce the pain in any way. He seems to be someone who is quite relaxed in his environment, in control—he's talking to people, giving orders; he's affable with the people he comes into contact with, smiles at what I assume were guests and so on."

And in conclusion: "I find it difficult to rationalize everything. I certainly think with a blood/carbon monoxide level of 21 per cent ... and a blood/alcohol level of about 180 milligrams per hundred mil, that this would be someone who would have a much slower reaction time. [It] would certainly be someone who would be slowed up in the way they did things. It would probably also be somebody who was in some pain. But none of those [things] seem to be evident from the pictures that we see of him. So it is a bit of an enigma."

Indeed it is. In particular when you consider that neither Diana nor Dodi—nor indeed Trevor Rees-Jones—suffered any carbon monoxide poisoning whatever. Which of course means that Paul could not have been poisoned by, say, exhaust fumes that might have leaked into the car. Nor by inhaled smoke from cigarettes or cigars. In fact Henri Paul did smoke the occasional cigarillo, but medical experts say that around 8% carbon monoxide trace is high even for the heaviest of smokers. Any higher than this and the symptoms as described above start to kick in, and with some vengeance. And in any event, Paul was not a heavy smoker; according to friends he smoked only a few cigarillos a day. So where, why, when and how was he poisoned? Just how did this amount of carbon monoxide find its way into Henri Paul's blood? It simply could not have been during the two hours prior to the crash because carbon monoxide trace decreases by roughly half every four to five hours. This means that, if the carbon monoxide level in Paul's blood was around 21% soon after the crash, then two hours prior to the crash it would have been somewhere in the region of 30%, or even 35%. According to the experts, these kinds of levels can be lethal. And yet the Ritz security footage shows Paul calm, congenial and coherent throughout the two hours prior to the crash. Very curious indeed.

As is the claim that Paul's blood contained very high levels of alcohol, and yet he was able to act and function as though completely sober. Contrary to many press reports, of course, Henri Paul was not a heavy drinker. True, were he an alcoholic—or even someone who drank alcohol more than most— then his alcohol tolerance might have been higher than that of the normal person. Thus he might perhaps have been able to disguise his alleged inebriated condition. But Paul's autopsy showed clearly enough that his liver was in good condition; there was no sign whatever that Paul was a heavy drinker. This being the case, then, what are we to make of a blood test that claims a very high alcohol level mixed with a concoction of prescription drugs and a level of carbon monoxide poisoning sufficient to incapacitate a mountain gorilla? He should have been on his back, reeling in pain. Yet he clearly was not. It simply does not add up.

And there are other anomalies. For one, it seems beyond all reason to even consider the possibility that trained VIP bodyguards such as Trevor Rees-Jones and Alexander 'Kes' Wingfield, both of whom spent two hours with Henri Paul immediately prior to the fateful journey, would have allowed him anywhere near the wheel of a car—even more so *that* car—if they thought for one minute that he had consumed the equivalent of one-and-a-half bottles of wine, the amount he is alleged to have consumed. Indeed, Trevor Rees-Jones said as much himself. In his much-publicized interview with *Mirror* editor Piers Morgan (the *Mirror*, Monday, 2nd March, 1998) the former Al Fayed bodyguard stated quite categorically that, in his professional opinion (and his opinion is indeed a professional one) Henri Paul was not drunk. It should be remembered that Trevor Rees-Jones has run operations with the British Army's elite Parachute Regiment and is a fully trained VIP bodyguard. He is a professional observer, trained to react to irregular situations and behaviours. He saw nothing irregular in Henri Paul's behaviour that night.

The same can be said of his colleague, Alexander 'Kes' Wingfield, who said that he was within feet of Henri Paul on several occasions during the two hours prior to the departure from the Ritz. Not once did he suspect that Henri Paul might have been drinking heavily. Not once did he doubt Henri Paul's ability to drive the Mercedes, even though it contained the Princess of Wales and Dodi Fayed. Indeed, in the professional opinion of both these highly trained men, Henri Paul was not drunk. If we are expected to accept the experts' opinion when it supports the drink-drive theory, then equally we should consider it when it does not.

Indeed, it is our contention that the drink-drive theory holds about as much water as a sieve might hold. Which is not very much at all.

— 5 —

THE FIAT UNO AND THE MISSING TYRE MARKS

"The Fiat Uno would have been weighed down low to the ground, probably with bags of cement or concrete blocks, so that it held the road when it collided with the bigger vehicle... so that it didn't roll on impact. That's basic ABC."

Dave Cornish, former SAS Sergeant, 1998.

Speed Of Impact and an Unseen Hand

Despite initial efforts to convince us that Henri Paul was travelling at 121 mph at the time of the crash, we now know that in fact he was travelling at no more than 63 mph—around 60 mph slower than claimed. In fact, Mercedes' chief engineer said all along that the speedometer was not stuck at 121 mph following the crash, as reported by the tabloid press. In the event of an accident, he affirmed, it is designed always to revert to zero. Which it did. This statement, however, was overridden by the '121 mph' story—which, incidentally, was first concocted and published by one of the British establishment's major propaganda outlets, *The Daily Telegraph*, before being blasted across the world as part of the establishment's drive to discredit Henri Paul. The fabricated story was also supported by the French police. Indeed, as we have seen, Mercedes' offer to send a team of highly qualified engineers to Paris in order to help in the analysis of the crashed Mercedes was rejected by the French authorities. The car manufacturer was forbidden to make any statement regarding the crash and/or the subsequent investigation.

In any event, it has since been confirmed by the French investigation team that the speedometer did indeed revert to zero immediately following the crash. This leaves the true speed of the car at the moment of impact to be determined by crash experts.

Enter Professor Murray MacKay of Birmingham University—Britain's foremost Road Traffic Accident expert. Professor MacKay, who employed state-of-the-art computer-simulated reconstructions of the crash to enhance the accuracy of his findings, has been studying the causes and effects of car crashes for more than thirty years. When we interviewed him, he made it clear that he did not wish to add to the speculation surrounding the crash. Given his position, of course, this was understandable. He was nonetheless very affable, indeed forthcoming, in particular with regard to the two most crucial factors concerning the crash itself—the speed of the Mercedes and the part played by the officially still-missing white Fiat Uno.

According to Professor MacKay, who has visited the Place de l'Alma underpass on several occasions, Diana's Mercedes was travelling at approximately 60 mph when it collided with the concrete pillar. This figure was calculated, he said, "without having to rely on any eyewitnesses".

He explained: "The speed on impact was about 60-63 miles an hour. That's based on the whole reconstruction process ... From the photographs you can compare the state of the car with that of an undamaged car, the amount of frontal crush, where it actually is ... so you get a pretty good idea as to the extent of the damage and the shape of the impact zone. From that there are crash reconstruction techniques. You can compare the crash with experimental crashes around the speed mentioned. You can use comparative techniques. When you crash any car it starts off relatively soft in terms of the structure, but then when you begin to hit the engine and destroy the engine mountings you get these heavy structures. The resistance builds up and then when you get even further into destroying the structure it starts to deform the transverse bulkhead and the actual body-shell of the passenger compartment. Then you get into some really stiff structure. I am saying this because you have to make assumptions about how the structure is deformed...

"...So there's some estimating to be done. That gives you what's called the 'Delta D', which is the 'change in velocity'. The change in velocity is something in the order of 50-54 miles an hour, based on the analysis. We know where the vehicle finished up in relationship to the point of impact—that's pretty well-defined from the police reports, and from the videos and photographs taken at the scene ... so the final position would be well-fixed. On impact [the Mercedes] span out around 180-210 degrees ... anyway it spun round, and its distance from the pillar was something around 10 or 12 feet. We then do calculations in terms of the exit velocity of the car's impact with the pillar, which was around 5-8 miles an hour ... and that tells us that the over-the-road speed into the pillar was something in the order of 60-63 miles an hour."

Professor MacKay went on to say that, according to the reconstruction techniques employed by his team, Diana's Mercedes would have been travelling at around "*80 mph*" when it entered the tunnel. It must then have collided with a "*second vehicle inside the tunnel*", he concluded, and in consequence would have spun out of control. When we questioned him on the somewhat suspicious presence of this "*second vehicle*", he commented: "It does make you wonder. But whether it [the Uno driver] was an innocent bystander who just wanted to maintain a low profile, [who] had his own reasons not to want to have contact with the police, well, you know. It may mean nothing more than that. The rest is speculation."

Indeed it is, to a certain extent. But the question has to be tabled: if the driver of the still-missing Fiat Uno was purely an innocent bystander, then is it not reasonable to assume that this person was/is a regular French citizen? And if this person was/is a regular French citizen then where is he now? Why has he not been traced? And moreover, given the fact that motor vehicles, their owners and their licence numbers are these days registered and logged on highly sophisticated central computing systems, how is it that the car has not been traced, either? True, it may have belonged to a foreign visitor who just happened to be driving around the centre of Paris at midnight. It may even have been an imported car that had escaped the notice of the French authorities. Perhaps an *illegally* imported car. But in reality, of course, this explanation seems no more substantive than all the other anomalous assumptions made with regard to this case. Less so. Indeed, is it not more likely that the Uno and its driver might have been part of an organized intelligence operation? Certainly if this were the case then one would not expect to trace either the vehicle or its driver. And that is precisely the situation as it stands—officially, at least. It should also be remembered that, despite several detailed eyewitness descriptions of a high-powered motorbike also involved in the incident, and of a second motorbike seen to block Henri Paul's exit off the riverside highway, forcing him to drive straight on through the crash tunnel, these vehicles and their drivers remain unaccounted for, too. As does the Mercedes seen speeding away from the scene plus its crew. Remarkable. No less than five vehicles involved in a major incident in the centre of Paris. Three of these vehicles—the motorbikes and the Uno—seen and described in some detail to the authorities by at least seven eyewitnesses. And yet none have been traced. Not one. Which only serves to demonstrate what a complete and utter hash the French investigators made of their inquiry.

Either that, or their efforts have perhaps been thwarted by an unseen hand at play. This latter possibility, of course, throws into question the entire investigation. In particular when you consider, too, the fact that at least 10 CCTV cameras line the route from the Ritz to the crash tunnel. Yet according to the French authorities, no CCTV footage exists, either of the chase from the Ritz to the crash tunnel, of the crash itself, or of any of the other vehicles leaving the scene of the crash. We can only surmise from this that all of these highly sophisticated pieces of technology were somewhat conveniently 'facing the other way' on the night in question—which to us seems an absurd notion, even though this is precisely what the French authorities claim, as we shall see. Indeed, if these cameras truly were blind on the night in question, then either somebody turned them all inwards at the appropriate moment. Or somebody has watched a re-run of the entire tragic event and is refusing to share their information.

And either scenario implies a cover-up.

"Abnormal Driving"

There is another factor to consider. Professor MacKay confirmed to us that "*tyre marks*", as distinct from 'skidmarks', had been found at the crash scene. It was estimated by the French investigators, as well as by Professor MacKay, that these tyre marks belonged to Diana's Mercedes—that they had been made as Henri Paul had swerved in order to try and avoid contact with the white Fiat Uno. However, what is interesting in this regard is that no tyre marks were made by the Fiat Uno. No skidmarks, no tyre marks. In other words, having been struck by a meaty Mercedes travelling at 80 mph; and further, having then witnessed that Mercedes slamming into a concrete pillar less than 2 seconds later and only a few metres in front of him, the Uno driver did not slow dramatically, did not stop, but smoothly drove on, skilfully missing the crumpled wreckage of Diana's car as it bounced around in front of him in the middle of the road. And thus—and only thus—there were no tyre marks made by the Fiat Uno. A most unlikely scenario, to be sure. After all, if you had been driving a smaller, flimsier car that was hit by a hefty Mercedes travelling at 80 mph, would you not have instinctively performed a correction manoeuvre that might have left tyre marks on the road? And further, if that Mercedes had then proceeded to slam into a concrete pillar just a few metres in front of you, would you have had the presence of mind to brake very gently in order to avoid leaving tyre marks on the road; casually change down a gear; change lanes in order to avoid colliding with the Mercedes' wreckage, and simply drive past as if nothing had happened—all in the space of less than 2 seconds?

We put the question to Professor MacKay, who was understandably reluctant to commit himself. None the less he did agree that it seemed strange the Uno driver had not braked rather more sharply—either on contact with the speeding Mercedes, or when the Mercedes had slammed into the concrete pillar less than 2 seconds later, right in front of the Uno. Or indeed, that the Uno driver had not performed some other manoeuvre in order to rectify the jolt of being clouted by four tons of speeding metal. After all, a Fiat Uno is not the sturdiest of cars; the slightest graze at a speed of around 80 mph (estimated speed of Mercedes as it entered the tunnel) would surely have had its effect on the smaller, lighter vehicle. And if this smaller, lighter vehicle (the Uno) was being driven by, say, a regular French citizen going about his business in a routine manner, then surely they would, at the very least, have been forced into a reflex correction manoeuvre on contact with the considerably heavier, considerably faster Mercedes. Yet the evidence suggests otherwise—no skidmarks; no tyre marks, either on the road or against the kerb where it might have scraped its tyres or wheel rims on collision with the Mercedes. Apart from the smashed rear-light casing belonging to a Fiat Uno; the broken wing mirror belonging to a Fiat Uno; the traces of white paint belonging to a Fiat Uno (all found at the scene)—and, of course, the numerous eyewitness statements describing the Uno in some detail—it is as if the Uno was not there at all. But of course it was there. And the fact that it was suggests that it was being driven by a very skilful driver indeed. Even Professor MacKay agreed that, in his opinion, some rather "*abnormal driving*" had occurred with regard to the Fiat Uno. His status and reputation, of course, prevented further speculation on his part. We would none the less like to thank Professor MacKay for being as frank and honest as he was.

Next we put this same scenario to our SAS source, Dave Cornish, from whom we were able to glean a somewhat different picture. Without hesitation he told us that the Uno driver would indeed have been highly skilled. And further, that in his experience the Uno would have been "*custom-weighted... fitted up*" for the job.

"It would have been weighed down low to the ground," Dave explained, "probably with bags of cement or concrete blocks, so that it held the road when it collided with the bigger vehicle ... So that it didn't roll on impact. That's basic ABC."

And further: "It would have had a very skilled driver who would've clipped the Mercedes just enough ... he would've dipped in front of the target vehicle at just the right moment so that the other driver was forced to swerve ... just enough to nudge it [Diana's Mercedes] off the road. When you're doing that kind of speed—60-70 miles an hour—a nudge is usually enough."

So in his opinion was this scenario consistent with an intelligence operation?

"Oh, yeah. Look, I've already told you, but I'll tell you again. I've still got good contacts in the right places. Some are old mates. I keep my head low these days but I still keep an eye on what's going on, you know. I'm telling you straight, this was a hit. Everything about it—it just stinks of it. When you've done the things I've done and seen the things I've seen done in the name of queen and country—I'm telling you this was a hit. You'll never ever prove it because that's the way it works. But it was a classic deniable op. I've seen it and done it. If you can find anyone else like me they'll tell you the same."

One final question. If you were still in the SAS, would you have agreed to take part in such an operation, knowing the identity of the target?

"These boys weren't SAS, I'll tell you that now. There may've been one or two old boys, but the [SAS] wouldn't be used for something like this. Too f**king risky ... But yeah, there was a time I would've done. There's plenty of old boys around who would, that's for sure. You know, it's the ultimate, isn't it, Princess Di ... It's like a drug. It's the ultimate high. You're paid by the government so you know you probably won't get caught. You *can't* get caught, because if you do it leads right back to the government. You're a professional working for other professionals who know how to cover their tracks. At the end of the day, whether it's a princess or some African dictator, if you get your hands dirty then the government's in the shit. And if the government's in the shit then you're in even bigger shit ... When I say the government I don't mean the MPs or those idiots at MI5. I'm talking the real professionals, probably MI-6, but they never say they are ... But that's who would've done it, one of MI-6's D-op [deniable operations] units. It would've been organized by them but the actual hit would've been ordered from ... well let's just say from beyond the normal channels. The hit itself would've been down to some private firm, mercenaries hired by the agency. There's always plenty of them looking for a few quid. And they don't mind how they earn it, either."

Evidently not.

— 6 —

THE RESCUE OPERATION

"Diana could still be alive, had it not been for the incompetence of the doctors. They simply let her bleed to death."

Dr. Wolf Ullrich, Head of the European Commission on Crime, 1998.

Many Questions

One further point to be considered is of course the rescue operation—the fact that the emergency services took so long to reach the scene of the crash, and then took even longer to ferry Diana to what turned out to be the furthest hospital from the crash scene. Many questions arise in this respect.

Why, for instance, did Dr Frederic Mailliez, the first doctor to examine Diana at the scene, initially describe her condition as "*not catastrophic*"? What prompted him to conclude that she "*did not seem desperate*", when some small time later she was dead? Why did paramedics take almost a quarter of an hour to reach the scene of the crash? According to official reports there was no traffic congestion in Paris that night.

And further: why was Diana treated by doctors and paramedics for more than 90 minutes, both at the crash scene and in the back of the ambulance *en route* to hospital? Why was she taken to Pitie Salpetriere hospital—the furthest from the scene—at a snail's pace, when at least two other, closer hospitals could have dealt equally well with the emergency? Surely if her condition was so delicate that the ambulance was forced to travel at a suspiciously slow pace then prudence would dictate she be taken to the nearest possible hospital for the swiftest possible medical attention. In this regard, one of Paris's most noted and, indeed, best-equipped hospitals, Hotel Dieu, is less than two miles from the scene of the crash. The ambulance drove straight past this hospital on its way to Pitie Salpetriere, which is a further mile away from Place de l'Alma. When travelling at an average speed of less than 10 miles an hour, as the ambulance was, a mile can make the difference between survival and death. Indeed, it seems it did.

And there is a further question to be asked of the French emergency team. Having for no apparent reason chosen the hospital furthest from the scene, why did the ambulance then stop for a further 10 minutes outside Paris's Natural History Museum, when Pitie Salpetriere's casualty department—and thereby the expert attention necessary to save Diana's life—was literally only seconds away? Less than half a mile separates the hospital from the museum. An ambulance travelling at, say, 60 mph, would thus have taken around 30 seconds to reach the hospital from the museum. And yet Diana's ambulance, having already taken almost two hours to get her that far, stopped for a further 10 minutes before completing the final 30-second leg of the journey. Why?

Not for the first time in the course of this investigation, it seems, something here simply does not add up. One might surely be forgiven for suspecting that the so-called 'paramedics' who attended the crash were working for someone other than the French health authorities. Either that, or they were hijacked by someone who was. Indeed, in an article run by the German newspaper Bild Zeitung, intriguingly titled: *Diana Died Because She Was So Famous* (14th January, 1998), criminologist, lawyer and Head of the European Commission on Crime, Dr. Wolf Ullrich, charged that in his professional opinion: "*Diana could still be alive, had it not been for the incompetence of the doctors. They simply let her bleed to death.*"

Sadly, all the evidence suggests Dr. Ullrich could be right.

Note: In the hardback edition of this book, we carried an interview with noted US investigative journalist, Jeff Steinberg, as well as Paramedic Supervisor, Andy Palmer, who both agreed that, in the case of such a trauma, the first assumption must always be that the victim might have suffered internal bleeding. While we do not wish to question the integrity of the French doctors and paramedics at the scene of Diana's car crash, we must question why it took such a suspiciously long time to get her to hospital, in particular as we now know that Diana's blood pressure dropped so dramatically at the scene of the crash that she suffered a heart attack and had to be revived. Such a dramatic fall in blood pressure is *the* tell-tale sign that the victim is bleeding internally, and that, therefore, they need to get to a hospital, *soon as possible*. True, the French emergency teams do things differently to their British and US counterparts, claiming that their SAMU ambulances are effectively operating theatres on wheels. But it has to be said that this argument is, in practice, phoney. Even they can do little, at the scene of the crash, to save the life of someone who is bleeding internally, which is why in Britain and the US the golden rule is to get the victim to hospital within an hour. It took the French team precisely one hour and forty-three minutes to transport Diana 3.25 miles to hospital, an anomaly we will explore in more depth later in the book (see *The Paget Report*).

7

THE AVEBURY MEETINGS

by Jon King

" . . . [T]his information] came into my possession some short while ago, and it concerns a plot to eliminate one of the most prominent figures on the world stage... I do not know precisely where or when the hit will take place. I do not know the precise schedule. But so far as I have been made aware it has been planned for a good many months and it will take place within days from now... very soon... I can tell you, Jon, this one will be bigger than Kennedy."

'Stealth', US Special Forces veteran and CIA contract agent,
23rd August, 1997—one week prior to Diana's death.

The Contact

In the *Introduction* I explained that our investigation into Diana's death was the result of information received one week prior to the crash in Paris. I should stress that, while our investigation does not at all depend on this information, it was none the less the catalyst that initiated our interest. For this reason we have elected to include this chapter here.

What follows is a minimally edited account of how this information was received, plus a detailed rendering—so far as I am permitted—of precisely the information involved. On its own it bears little credibility; we are acutely aware of this. But given that we are assuming the position of 'prosecuting counsels' in this case, we feel bound to present you, the jury, with *all* the evidence—certainly to call our main sources to the witness stand so you can hear first-hand what they have to say. Of course, we could easily have omitted this chapter; it would have weakened our case not at all, perhaps even strengthened it. The fact that some unseen, anonymous source elected to supply us with information, in secret—and the added fact that this information has been corroborated only by two other anonymous sources—simply would not stand up in a court of law, we know. But the fact remains that it was this information that first prompted us to investigate this case. Thus, in our endeavour to be as open and frank as we possibly can—to tell you the whole story, as it unfolded—we have elected to present this information here, in its raw state: *as it came to us.* In so doing we hope its relevance and credibility will in the end become evident enough.

"Mr. King?" It was copy deadline week, and accordingly I was to be found staring blankly at my computer screen, endeavouring with little enthusiasm to polish the final draft of a story which had been dumped on my desk a few moments earlier. But then, I guess that has always been the problem with copy deadline week: leave aside any current investigations, no matter how pressing, and attend to the mundane bread-and-butter task of editing—preparing this month's copy for public consumption. In this respect the call I had just taken was a welcome distraction.

"Speaking." Hitting the button on my tape recorder I leaned back in my seat and checked my wristwatch, a habit. It was 11:45 am. "I've just read your article on the US government's covert activities underground," the American accent calmly informed me. "Project Noah's Ark. Very interesting."

"Thank you."

"Sure."

"So how can I help you?"

"The article prompted me to call. I have some information."

"Go on."

A short pause, then: "It would be best if you left your office," I was told in a more critical tone. "We'll talk on another line. Go to a public call box and call this number, soon as you can."

A mobile (cell) telephone number was given; I took it down. "Can you tell me your name?" I said, probing, still jotting down the contact number, suspicious the man I was talking to would turn out to be yet another time-waster, one of a good many who had called in the past bearing similar promises, but who in the end had proved to be either hoaxers or people of unstable mind. At the same time, of course, I was hopeful he would turn out to be one of the very few who in the end prove genuine. "Who should I ask for?" I ventured. "Can you... Hello?" But the line was already dead; the caller had hung up.

Duly intrigued I reset the telephone in its cradle, turned off the tape recorder (which was wired to my telephone), waited a further minute or so, then got up from my desk and left the office, discreetly. So far as any of my colleagues knew I was off to purchase a sandwich for lunch.

As the caller remarked, I had recently been investigating government activities underground. Claims made by a number of independent witnesses, for a number of different reasons, pointed to the fact that a series of highly covert and extremely controversial military-industrial test programmes were in process, both in Britain and the United States. Or more precisely, several hundred feet *beneath* Britain and the United States. In short, many witness claims suggested that, deep inside some of the British and US governments' most top-secret deep-underground installations, some pretty nefarious activities were taking place. In the main these activities were said to involve secret-technology and biotechnological programmes, many of which were being illegally run and fuelled by underground nuclear reactors. It was my report concerning the US programmes in particular that had prompted the mystery caller to contact me. My hope now was that he would be able to pass some relevant information my way regarding Britain's endeavours in this same regard. I was not to be disappointed.

"...It's Jon King returning your call." A gusty November wind was whipping through the call box in which I now stood. I guessed it was probably a group of local kids with nothing much better to do who had smashed the glass panels on the call box door, both at face-height and again three panels further down. Indeed, I wondered if it was this same purposeless gang who had partially unhinged the door into the bargain—a gap tall enough for an ambitious limbo dancer to slither under now existed between the foot of the door and the concrete on which I stood. To make matters worse, the line was bad, the stranger's voice faint and breaking up. I pressed a thumb to my ear in an attempt to silence the drone of passing traffic.

"We should meet," I managed to decipher through the fizz of the mobile's poor-quality signal. "It would be easier that way."

"Well, with respect I'm a busy man," I said, fencing. "I really need to know…"

"It'll be worth your time," the voice calmly assured. "But the information I have for you is … best not divulged over the telephone."

I paused for a brief moment at this point, quickly trying to measure the man—his tone, his character, his quiet, almost serene authority. Such cursory assessments are not always successful, of course. But more often than not they are. And in any case, in situations such as these there is scarcely the time to compile a casebook. He seemed sound enough. And until I could shake him by the hand and look him in the eye, that was all I had to go by.

"Do you have anywhere particular in mind?" I said.

"Avebury," came the reply. "Avebury Stone Circles in Wiltshire. You know the place?"

"I do, yes." In fact I knew it very well. "When?"

"This Saturday, midday, in the car park opposite the Post Office."

I made a note. My pad was recording the conversation as we spoke it. "OK," I said, finally. "How will I recognize you?"

"You won't," the voice affirmed. "I'll recognize you. Saturday. Midday. Avebury. Opposite the Post Office. Are we agreed?"

"I'll be there."

That said, the line clicked dead. Not for the first time that day the stranger hung up on me. Whereupon the call box ate my change. I headed for the baker's shop. At least next time there would be no windy call boxes involved, I thought to myself as I braved the chill, autumnal weather and made my way back across the street towards the smell of bread and cakes. At least next time we would talk face to face.

Stealth

Avebury was even colder than the call box had been. But at least it was good, clean country air, and aesthetically a good deal more pleasing than the high street in which the call box had stood. I consoled myself with these thoughts as I wrapped up against the bleak November day.

I had arrived at the Avebury car park about fifteen minutes earlier than our arranged meeting time. As usual it was more or less full, but from what I could make out my contact had not yet arrived. Having parked my car and gathered my attaché case I wandered over to the car park entrance and sat myself down on the vacant wall, watching for the arrival of a single middle-aged male, which was the mental picture I had formulated on speaking to the mystery caller on the telephone. I did not have to wait long for his arrival. Moreover, as he drove into the car park I noted that the mental picture I had formulated was about right. In fact he looked how you might imagine a mildly successful, late middle-aged businessman to look—around six feet, slightly overweight, thinning to grey on top and driving a silver Vauxhall Carlton. His handshake was firm.

Following a brief introduction we wandered out through the car park's rear entrance—a wooden field-gate that led into a grazing meadow famed for its sheep and megalithic standing stones. Despite the chill weather there were a good many other people strolling around the field, but none seemed too interested in anyone else. On the contrary, all seemed preoccupied with their own private business—taking photos of the stones, the sheep, generally being tourists. In this respect it was a good place to talk about matters secret and classified.

My contact gave no name. For purposes of identification I have always referred to him (in my previous works) as 'Stealth'. On this particular occasion Stealth told me a little about his background and his reasons for wishing to pass information my way. He described these reasons as "personal", though this was said with some bitterness, as though by betraying his employers he was able to gain some amount of personal satisfaction. Possibly even revenge. I should stress, however, that this is my own interpretation.

He did imply, though, that he and a small faction within "the Agency" were keen to ensure that "certain information" made its way out into the public domain. On more than one occasion he voiced—in no uncertain terms—his disapproval of the high levels of political power wielded by the "corporate-funded intelligence community". He believed in democracy, he said. And he did not like what he had discovered with regard to the manipulation of democratically elected governments by extremely powerful cabals within the military-industrial complex. In particular, he said, he was unhappy with the way the intelligence community had, in effect, become the instrument by which much of this political manipulation was achieved. Indeed, in many respects, it had become little more than a "*corporate watchdog*", he said.

With regard to himself, Stealth told me that he was a US Special Forces veteran of several campaigns, that he had been involved in numerous covert operations run by the CIA, and that lately he had been assigned to a highly covert CIA/SIS cell stationed in Britain (SIS: Britain's *Secret Intelligence Service,* broadly known as MI-6). He did not tell me exactly what this cell had been set up to achieve, though he did say that it operated at the bidding of a very powerful cabal within the British and US-based military-industrial complex.

"SIS and CIA do the bidding of these people," he told me with some disdain. "We always do the bidding of these people."

According to Stealth, the higher echelons of British and US intelligence work hand-in-glove. Certainly he affirmed that this was the case with regard to the most covert levels of MI-6 and the CIA. In this regard, the joint British/US intelligence cell to which he had been assigned was so furtive, he said, its operations so secret, that its orders seldom, if ever, issued from the appropriate departments, from the offices of our elected representatives in Government. Rather they issued from some unseen and democratically unaccountable cabal made up of what Stealth referred to as "*financial, industrial and political godfathers ... [who] operate quite independently of the law*".

Some very high-level military and intelligence chiefs also comprise part of this cabal, he said. He also said that many of the operations carried out at the behest of these people are veiled behind the smokescreen of National Security. He emphasized this point. The National Security screen was formulated to protect military secrets, he wanted me to understand—to ensure that top-secret military operations, experiments and programmes could be conducted behind closed doors, away from the prying eyes of Cold War Soviet spies and/or terrorists. But these days, he said, these same laws were being enforced illegally. The most dangerous secrets were no longer military, he explained; they were corporate. The most dangerous secrets were no longer being kept from Soviet spies, but from the public at large. The Cold War, he was keen to remind me, ended almost a decade ago.

"It's the kind of behaviour that flies in the face of democracy and the democratic freedoms on which our world is allegedly run," he said with some fervour. "And it is wholly unacceptable. These people are getting away with murder, sometimes literally."

He went on: "If I were to tell you all I know about the military-industrial complex, Jon—about the quasi-security and intelligence agencies and their underhand operations; about the modus operandi of some of the complex's most powerful chiefs—you would quickly become as old and embittered as I am." He let a half-smile lighten his face at this point.

A heartbeat later he banished it. "Not very far from here there are secret-technology programmes and experiments being carried out that would shock and astound you. But you cannot see them. You cannot see them because they're being conducted underground. And what is more they're being conducted in secret, concealed by what you have in this country—the Official Secrets Act. That is illegal. It is illegal because of the nature of the programmes involved. They are using the laws of National Security to further their own secret political ends. It riles me. It is fundamentally wrong."

Over the course of the following months Stealth was to underline precisely what those 'fundamental wrongs' were.

It was for these reasons that Stealth had decided to seek me out and talk to me, then. He had read my reports concerning my own investigations into these matters, he said, and he had decided to pass what relevant information he could my way, in particular with regard to the secret technological and biochemical programmes being carried out by the British and US-based military-industrial complex, underground. And more specifically—so far as I was concerned at the time—those being carried out by the super-secret aerospace industry, both in Britain and the US, also underground. Much of that information forms the basis for my previous works.

But it's the information that is not contained in any of my previous works that is of paramount importance here. Indeed, it is this very information that, in effect, led to the publication of this book.

And once again, it came my way during a meeting with Stealth at Avebury.

One Last Pearl

I met up with Stealth twice during the summer of 1997, and on both occasions he voiced his concerns about how long our meetings could and should continue. As it turned out, the second meeting that summer proved to be our last.

But before parting company he told me that he wished to leave me with *"one last pearl"* of information, designed, for the most part, to substantiate his credential. He would tell me something that had not yet come to pass, he said. When it did come to pass, I would at least be assured that he was party to information unavailable in the public domain, and therefore could feel more confident about the information he had given me in the past. In essence, he said, this was the motive behind his decision to pass the following information my way.

Seating himself on a fallen 'standing stone', staring thoughtfully ahead, Stealth left me with the following, astonishing monologue—during which, I feel I should offer fair warning, *he did not mince his words.* I should add that the transcript has been minimally edited for publication.

"Remember I told you how certain people were taken out, people whose message was a threat because of their popularity, and because of their ability to mobilize public opinion—Kennedy, Martin Luther King, John Lennon, and others...?"

I do, yes.

"Well, Jon, I have in my possession some information. It might make an angle on which to build your story. It might not. But, well ... whatever you choose to do with it is fine by me...

"...[This information] came into my possession some short while ago, and it concerns a plot to eliminate one of the most prominent figures on the world stage, someone like Martin Luther King and John Lennon, someone with the ability to undermine the social and political control mechanisms currently in place...

"...I do not know precisely where or when the hit will take place. I do not know the precise schedule. But so far as I have been made aware it has been planned for a good many months and it will take place within days from now ... very soon ... I can tell you, Jon, this one will be bigger than Kennedy

... even my own sources are extremely nervous about this one. Provision for public reaction has already been considered. They have good experience of how to deal with public reaction... It's being taken care of as we speak. The media is being primed, as we speak."

He went on: "I'm telling you this so that you can believe more readily what I have told you already, so that at least you'll know the information I have given you is genuine ... so you can be assured that my sources are genuine. I really can't say what use this information will be to you other than that ...

"...You must understand that I do not expect you to put your neck on the line with this. This is not evidence; you will never find the hard evidence necessary to prove a thing with this. I'm aware that you're unlikely to believe what I'm saying anyway, and I can't blame you for that." He turned and caught my eye at this point: "At least until it happens," he added. "At least until what I'm telling you actually happens. Then you'll believe it."

Just then a small party of tourists ambled by, some in conversation, others seemingly prone to a world that existed only in their own thoughts. Momentarily Stealth fell silent. As the last of the tourists passed us by, I couldn't help but wonder how people might react should Stealth's information prove correct: should someone of global renown—"*within days from now*"—truly meet an untimely end, the result of political assassination. The prospect was chilling. So much so that, in a perverse kind of way, I was glad when Stealth resumed. It snapped me away from the growing sense of trepidation which was by now everywhere in me.

"...I was told that this person has to go for a good many reasons," he went on. "Not the least because they have become 'carcinogenic to the system. That's a quote, which basically means they have become a threat to the stability of corporate government, just like John Lennon and the others before him, the others I've told you about. To the bastards who run things this person has become a cancer in the system; this is what I was told, verbatim. Listen carefully to what I'm saying here, Jon. This person has become a 'loose cannon on a world stage'. That's another quote. This person has upset an awful lot of very influential, very powerful people ... people of the calibre I have already told you about."

Can you tell me who this person is?

"I'll tell you what I know, Jon—you must read between the lines this time ... Someone big is going to get hit. That is all I can say for now." He added a few moments later: "So far as I have been made aware ... well, you'll know soon enough who it is. And then you'll know that what I'm telling you is live intelligence. It's hot. So keep your lips sealed and your ear to the ground. Watch the news networks ... I can promise you one thing: it'll be bigger than Kennedy."

This information was imparted to me on Saturday, 23rd August, 1997, one week prior to Diana's death. Though Stealth never mentioned either Princess Diana or Dodi Fayed by name, it soon became evident who he'd been talking about. Indeed, it has been said I should have been more acute: that I should have recognized Stealth was talking about Diana from the hints he dropped into our conversation, particularly when he referred to her as a "*loose cannon on a world stage*". But this was 1997, remember; I'd frankly never heard that term applied to Princess Diana. As stated in the *Introduction*, she was quite simply not on my radar. I took little if any notice of her or her life, other than being vaguely aware that she was campaigning to have landmines banned. The Royals were not my 'thing', and so far as I was concerned back then, Diana was a Royal, even though by that time she had apparently had her 'HRH' title taken off her, like a naughty child might have a favourite toy confiscated. Pathetic really.

In any event, a week later, when news of her death became the day's sole headline, I realized clearly enough that Diana was almost certainly who Stealth had been referring to. I still cannot be certain that Stealth's information and Diana's death are linked, of course. On the other hand, I will never be convinced they are not.

8

THE SQUIDGYGATE AFFAIR

"They [MI5] do it regularly. They have literally hundreds
of hours of transcripts... Even as I speak, Diana is being
bugged. They think she is unstable and could go off
and do something. They want to know exactly what is in her mind."

James Whitaker, Royal Correspondent for the Mirror,
(quote from the People, May 16th, 1993).

Intimate Conversations, Dark Threats

In 1993, investigations revealed that MI5 had been illegally listening in on
intimate telephone conversations held by both Prince Charles and Princess Diana.
This much-publicized revelation, and the investigation that followed, became
known as the 'Squidgygate Affair'.

Initially, it was claimed that radio hams—one in particular, retired
bank manager, Cyril Reenan—had inadvertently tuned in to a private
telephone conversation involving Princess Diana and a 'male friend', James
Gilbey. It was reported that Mr. Reenan had subsequently sold the tapes on
to the tabloid newspapers. While this is ostensibly true, later investigations
revealed that the conversation recorded by Mr. Reenan had actually taken
place four days prior to the day on which he recorded it. In consequence, it
soon became apparent that MI5 officers at GCHQ (35 miles from Mr.
Reenan's home) had themselves recorded the *"high-quality"* tape, and had
then rebroadcast it on a frequency known to be used by radio hams in order
to ensure the leak. Mr. Reenan himself is certainly convinced that he was
used by the Security Service in this way. Though he refused to say whether
or not he had been personally approached by MI5, he confessed that the
attitude shown him by police officers investigating the case was unusually
"lenient". In fact he said the police had treated him *"almost like a film star"*.

The added fact that Mr. Reenan was parked in a lay-by when he made the recording, and yet there is no sound of passing traffic on the tape; and further, that he was able to listen to the high-quality broadcast for an unusually long time without losing the signal, makes it almost certain that the signal was being broadcast from nearby GCHQ.

And that the broadcast was in fact a rebroadcast of the conversation originally eavesdropped and recorded by MI5 four days previously.

Following Mr. Reenan's revelations, transcripts of the alleged telephone conversation between Princess Diana and James Gilbey, plus those of a further telephone conversation between Prince Charles and his years-long paramour, Camilla Parker Bowles, made front-page headlines across Britain. As did a taped conversation between Prince Charles and Princess Diana as the couple argued over Christmas arrangements regarding their children. In this instance, however, both Charles and Diana were in the same room, at the Prince of Wales's country residence, Highgrove (again, scarcely a whisper from GCHQ). It soon became evident, then, that the taped conversation was the result of a highly sophisticated remote bugging device, and not a telephone tap. Indeed, according to the *Mirror's* royal correspondent, James Whitaker, Charles and Diana are not the only Royals to have had their conversations bugged. The Queen, too, has suffered this same indignity, he said, and on a regular basis.

"The security services don't do it from time to time," he told *The People* (May 16th, 1993), "they do it regularly. They have literally hundreds of hours of transcripts... They are bugging all the Royals from the Queen downwards."

And further: "Even as I speak, Diana is being bugged... They think she is unstable and could go off and do something—they want to know exactly what is in her mind."

Mr. Whitaker confirmed that his information had originated with a source inside GCHQ.

In one of the taped telephone conversations, Prince Charles and Camilla Parker Bowles—caught in a long-distance, bedtime tryst—are heard to declare their undying love for one another. In parts the conversation is extremely intimate, and sexually explicit. In the second of the taped telephone conversations, Princess Diana tells Mr. Gilbey of her *"torture"* in being married to Prince Charles—a fact that would later become public knowledge via the BBC's now-famous Panorama interview, during which the princess openly stated, among other things, that there had always been *"three people"* in her marriage. During the conversation between Diana and James Gilbey— in which Mr. Gilbey refers to Diana as 'Squidgy'—the name of yet another of the princess's 'male friend's' is mentioned. His name is James Hewitt.

So far as we are concerned, the love affair between Princess Diana and former Guards officer, Major James Hewitt, is particularly revealing. Major Hewitt has repeatedly claimed, for example, that he received 'warnings' from Princess Diana's personal police protection officers—warnings to the effect that he should end the affair immediately. He also revealed that a member of the inner Royal circle—indeed, a member of the Royal Family— warned him that his affair with the princess was dangerous, and that he should end it forthwith.

"Be extremely careful," Major Hewitt was advised. "Your relationship is being investigated by MI5. Be on your utmost guard."

And the warnings did not end there. Major Hewitt received no less than six similar warnings in as many weeks, to the point that he began to fear for his life. In one such warning, for example, he was told that *"it was not conducive to [his] health to continue the relationship"*. And during an interview conducted by ITN's royal correspondent, Nicholas Owen, Major Hewitt again claimed that he had received repeated warnings about the affair from Princess Diana's personal police protection officers. He further confirmed that he had received several more *"threatening"* warnings from an 'unknown source' in this same regard, plus a personal warning from a member of the Royal Family. "Your relationship is known about," he was plainly told. "It is not supported."

And further: "We cannot be responsible for your safety or security. [We] suggest that you curtail [the relationship] forthwith."

When asked if he thought there were those who would *"wish ill"* on the Princess of Wales herself, sufficient that they might *"do something really terrible to her"*, he replied: *"Yes, I do think there are people like that."* Indeed, fearing for his life, and possibly for that of the princess herself, Major Hewitt took the advice he had received and curtailed the relationship *"forthwith"*. He is reported to have told a close friend that, had he ignored the warnings, he feared that he might have ended up having an 'accident'. He already knew, of course, what had happened to a former confidant of the princess, Sgt. Barry Mannakee—who, for a period during the 1980s, was Princess Diana's personal bodyguard. According to our main MI5 source, Sgt. Mannakee had not only become 'too well-acquainted' with the princess; he had also informed her that MI5 was actively monitoring her movements, that her private apartments were bugged, and that her telephones were tapped. In consequence, the princess started to show signs of concern, even mild paranoia. At which point her much-publicized eating disorders and emotional instabilities came to the fore, and they did so publicly. In short, being told that MI5 was actively monitoring her every move took its toll. From that day forth the princess repeatedly voiced her anxieties about 'dying in an accident'.

Indeed, as this book was going to press we were fortunate enough to talk to one of Sgt. Mannakee's professional peers, Royal Personal Protection Officer, Mike Grey, who was able to confirm Sgt Mannakee's claims that Diana had indeed been wiretapped by MI5. Mike told us:

"Clandestine surveillance by the Security Services on the most intimate of situations was to culminate later in the assassination of Diana, Princess of Wales, of this I have no doubt."

And further: "I have no doubts whatsoever, given my twenty years experience within various sections of the security industry, that Diana, Princess of Wales, was assassinated. The Security Service hallmarks are plain to see..."

And again, speaking of the crash in Paris: "[The operation bore all the] classic hallmarks of a security service assassination—twenty years experience in the industry give me absolutely no doubt."

Interestingly, we recall in this same regard the words of former SAS Sgt Dave Cornish, quoted in *Chapter 3*. Dave told us:

"From the minute the decoy car left the Ritz to the moment the tail car closed in... it was obvious what was going down. Anyone who knows what they're talking about'll tell you the same."

Mr. Grey, of course, does indeed know what he is talking about; he has worked as personal protection officer to some of the most important VIPs in the world, including royalty. And because he has, his observations—like those of our SAS source, Dave Cornish—should be considered in the highest regard.

In any event, what is known for certain with regard to the princess and Sgt. Barry Mannakee is this. In September 1986, father-of-two Sgt. Mannakee was relieved of his post as the princess's personal bodyguard, and was transferred to the Diplomatic Protection Corps. Evidently, members of the 'inner circle' had stated their concern that the princess and the bodyguard had become 'too familiar'. But what is most chilling of all about this particular case is that, eight months after leaving his post as Diana's personal bodyguard, Sgt. Mannakee was killed in a 'road traffic accident'. Diana and Sgt. Mannakee, it seems, had continued their relationship despite the bodyguard's transfer, and several sources close to the princess, as well as Diana herself, have since voiced their concerns that Sgt. Mannakee's death was in fact the result of an MI5 operation.

Indeed, these suspicions were confirmed to us by our own sources, who told us quite unequivocally that Sgt. Mannakee had been *"taken out"* because he had been *"too willing"* to impart information to the princess regarding MI5's surveillance of her.

But whatever the truth, it is clear that from this point on Diana became increasingly concerned for her own safety. And for the safety of others who might also be deemed to have 'overstepped the mark'—to have become 'too close' to her. *"Any gentleman that's been past my door... all hell's broken loose,"* she would later tell BBC's *Panorama.* And as her own tragic fate would later attest, of course, her concerns were not unfounded. And neither, it seems, were those of the man Diana openly confessed to have been in love with, Major James Hewitt. On the contrary, it is little wonder that Major Hewitt took so seriously the warnings he received from his royal contact. To put it bluntly, it would appear that 'road traffic accidents' are flavour of the month with regard to official assassinations, as affirmed by the death of Major Michael Marman (see *Chapter 3*).

Indeed, this would seem particularly evident when yet another, similar incident is entered into the equation: the attempted assassination of Prince Charles's mistress, Camilla Parker Bowles.

9

CAMILLA AND THE CONSTITUTIONAL CRISIS

"**S**he thought it was an MI5 job—that MI5 was trying to kill her. She was right, of course, but it all went stupidly wrong ... The reports had to make it look like an innocent accident."

Intelligence Source, February, 1998.

A Bungled Operation

According to our source, who we first spoke to in February 1998, Camilla Parker Bowles had been the subject of a concerted MI5 surveillance operation for some years. Indeed, this information has since been confirmed by another source who until recently held a senior rank within a British Military Intelligence department. This source—who has now 'retired'; indeed, who has suffered in no small measure for the fact that he was party to the assassination scenario from its inception—informed us that a "*loose plan*" to assassinate Diana had "*for some considerable time*" been debated by both British and US intelligence agencies. And perhaps more surprisingly, that a parallel plot to assassinate Camilla Parker Bowles had also been tabled by MI5 chiefs. Indeed, it had been attempted and bungled.

According to this source, an attempt on Mrs Parker Bowles's life had been made—and bungled—by MI5. And what is more, the assassination attempt had once again taken the form of a 'road traffic accident', as we shall see.

The decision to assassinate Mrs Parker Bowles had been taken, we were told, to *"clean up the constitutional mess"* caused by Prince Charles's intention to marry his long-term mistress while his former wife was still alive. Indeed, we were told that the reason top executives within MI5 finally gave their support to the already existing MI-6 plot to assassinate Diana was precisely because their attempt on Mrs Parker Bowles's life had failed. To add to this, at the time of the 'Camilla Incident', the existing MI-6 plot had recently won the support of its American bed partner, the CIA. Evidently the CIA had finally given its blessing in this regard due to the unprecedented success of Diana's landmines campaign. In effect, Diana's ability not only to mobilize public opinion in her favour, but also to persuade the world's most powerful man, President Clinton, to support a worldwide ban on landmines, had caused no small concern within the higher echelons of the US-based military-industrial complex. It emerged that arms-trade godfathers, who were still making a handsome buck out of arms sold to warring factions in Angola and other African states, as well as to Western-backed forces in Bosnia and the Balkans—arms which of course included antipersonnel landmines—were furious that the President had acceded to the princess's wishes. This point will be more fully elucidated later on in the book. But let us begin by presenting a summary of the sequence of events that, according to our sources, led to Diana's assassination finally being given the green light.

Following Diana's much-publicized *Panorama* interview (BBC, November 1995), during which she publicly attacked the Royal Family, and indeed expressed her opinion that Prince Charles was not fit to be King, furious oligarchs within the British Royal Establishment initiated moves which eventuated in a plot to assassinate the princess. As British author, AN Wilson, commented in *The New York Times* (25th November, 1995) in response to the *Panorama* interview:

> *"...When it comes to fighting a war, the Establishment can get very nasty indeed ... for all her undoubted popularity, if she continues to rock the boat in this way, the Establishment will simply get rid of her."*

Indeed, in the end, it seems, this is precisely what the Establishment did.

But at this early stage, and according to our sources, there were still those who opposed the proposed plot to assassinate the princess. Though MI5 had for some years prior to the interview conducted a massive and intrusive surveillance operation on Diana, even so it had always been considered by MI5 chiefs *"too risky for the Princess of Wales to die in mysterious circumstances... on home soil"*. And in any case, according our sources, MI5 chiefs were reluctant *"from the beginning"* that the princess should be the one to be assassinated. It was argued that a parallel plot to assassinate Mrs Parker Bowles should instead be initiated, and this for several reasons.

One: the death of Mrs Parker Bowles would serve equally well to clean up the *"constitutional mess"* resulting from Prince Charles's marital and extramarital predicament;

Two: the consequences of Mrs Parker Bowles's death *"on home soil"* would be *"far easier to deal with"*; indeed, the sudden and mysterious death of Mrs Parker Bowles would be extremely unlikely to engender the same massive public protest feared by the authorities in the event of a similar misadventure befalling Diana, *"no matter where in the world she died"*;

Three: the sudden and mysterious death of Mrs Parker Bowles would serve as a chilling reminder to the princess; in effect it would frighten her into submission and thus act as a *"deterrent"*, a means to rein her in, force her to *"toe the line"*.

In short, MI5 argued that the sudden and mysterious death of Mrs Parker Bowles would not only resolve the *"constitutional mess"* facing the Establishment. It would also be *"far easier to deal with"* and at the same time would terrify Diana into submission. Thus, at this stage, MI5 argued against the proposed plot to assassinate the princess. And instead to concentrate their efforts in this same regard on Mrs Parker Bowles.

However, the immediate problem—*"the constitutional mess"*—was to be further compounded when in the summer of 1996 Diana's divorce from Prince Charles became absolute. In consequence, speculation regarding the future King's intentions to marry Mrs Parker Bowles, herself a divorcee, began to assume a new and more evident significance. In the event that Charles were to marry Camilla, of course, on his accession to the Throne she would become Queen Consort. However, in the summer of 1996 Diana was still alive. And that was the problem. As everyone in Britain is—presumably— aware, while it would seem constitutionally acceptable for a king (or queen, for that matter) to enjoy extramarital relations, it is wholly unacceptable for him to divorce and remarry. When a British monarch accedes to the Throne, by constitutional design they also assume the office of Supreme Governor of the Church of England. And herein lies the problem. The Church of England forbids the remarriage of divorcees in church, and as the Church's Supreme Governor, Charles would be expected to either uphold this Jurassic edict or abdicate his responsibilities in a manner similar to his great uncle, King Edward VIII, who chose to marry American divorcee Wallis Simpson rather than remain King. But even Edward's situation was less complicated than the situation facing the Establishment in 1996. Indeed, the situation in 1996 was even further exacerbated by the fact that Camilla could not, constitutionally speaking, become Queen while Diana remained alive, a fact acknowledged by the Lord Chancellor's office (now the Department for Constitutional Affairs), when on 18th July 1997, just six weeks before Diana's death, the Parliamentary aide to the Lord Chancellor, Tony Wright, stated in no uncertain terms that a constitutional crisis regarding the marriage of Prince Charles and Mrs Parker Bowles would result in the "*disestablishment*" of the Church, an unprecedented move that would have amounted to the single biggest constitutional reform since the days of Henry VIII. Simply put, the United Kingdom of Great Britain would have become a secular state for the first time in its history, and all because of the "*constitutional mess*" caused, in the first instance, by the Prince of Wales's philandering.

In any event, it was for these reasons that MI5 came under increased pressure at this time to remove the cause of that "*mess*", and thus free up Prince Charles to marry whomsoever he chose. MI-6 and the British Royal Establishment, of course, saw *Diana* as the cause of that mess. MI5, on the other hand, saw *Camilla* as the cause of that mess. The result: stalemate.

It should also be said that, at this time (July/August 1996), the problem remained more or less a British one. Pressure brought on MI5 to sort out the 'mess' came solely from British Establishment oligarchs—the very same oligarchs who had for some time desired that Diana should be removed. Though the divorce gave added impetus to their appeals, nevertheless MI5 chiefs remained reluctant to act on that impetus and give their support to the proposed plot to assassinate Diana, preferring still their alternative solution—to assassinate Mrs Parker Bowles. According to our sources, it was at this point (circa January/February 1997) that a new factor entered the equation. It was at this point that Establishment oligarchs were joined in their appeals by "*American parties with vested interests*". As stated above, American support for Diana's removal was the result of her meetings with Bill and Hillary Clinton, and the former President's subsequent pledge to support a worldwide ban on landmines. Or as our sources put it:

"Certain parties became very disenchanted with Clinton when they found out that he was prepared to—effectively—overturn US defence policy on the strength of what they considered the whim of a meddling British Royal. Especially as she was no longer officially royal... The fact that she was an attractive young woman didn't help matters, of course. Apparently Clinton's partiality for attractive young women had been noted."

According to our sources, then, it was at this point that the CIA threw its weight behind the already existing MI-6 plot to assassinate Diana. *The word from then on was that, if MI5 wouldn't do it, then the CIA and MI-6 would*", we were told. The reason for CIA involvement was of course to repair relations between Clinton and the arms trade; once Diana was out of the way Clinton would be free to renege on his pledge and opt out of the proposed worldwide ban on landmines. Which, less then three weeks after the princess's mysterious death, is precisely what he did. America was the only Western power to U-turn in this regard and refuse to sign the Landmines Treaty, as we shall see.

With these new developments, the plot to assassinate Princess Diana—which until now had not substantially progressed beyond the fact that it had been tabled—began to assume new momentum. So much so, in fact, that MI5 stepped up its operation with regard, not to Diana, but to Mrs Parker Bowles. MI5 chiefs still held that the death of Mrs Parker Bowles would be less likely to engender public suspicion and backlash, would adequately resolve the constitutional problem and at the same time would terrify Diana into submission. However, at about this same time yet another factor entered the equation: one Dodi Fayed. Though American interest was scarcely affected by this development, the British Establishment was outraged. As Andrew Golden commented in the *Sunday Mirror* (31st August, 1997) in an article written only hours before the fatal crash in Paris:

"Diana has been told in no uncertain terms about the consequences should she continue the relationship with the Fayed boy... *now the royal family may have decided it is time to settle up.*" [Italics in original copy.]

To add to this, Dodi—referred to by Prince Philip as an "*oily bed-hopper*"—was the son of a major financial player, Mohamed Al Fayed, a high-profile Muslim with an ambiguous business past, whose petitions for British citizenship had for some years been thwarted by a well-publicized series of Establishment chicaneries. Indeed, by the time Diana and Dodi started their relationship, Mohamed Al Fayed had already been ostracized by the British Establishment. For the past decade and more he had endeavoured without success to muscle his way in to the royal circus and become part of that Establishment, but to no avail. Establishment oligarchs thus interpreted Dodi's relationship with Diana as a political manoeuvre on the part of Mohamed Al Fayed—an attempt to manoeuvre his way not only in to the Establishment, but in to the heart of the Monarchy itself. In consequence, the excessive levels of pressure already brought on MI-5 intensified even further. So much so that MI5 chiefs soon realized that failure to take action with regard to Mrs Parker Bowles would mean that MI-6, together with the CIA, would implement their own plan—a plan which, all along, MI-6 and Establishment oligarchs had endeavoured to foist on MI-5: the removal of Princess Diana.

According to our sources, then, at some point in or around May/June 1997 the situation reached fever pitch. Something had to give. MI5 was finally forced to act on its plan regarding Mrs Parker Bowles or face the reality that MI-6 would hit Diana, on home soil, thereby leaving MI5 (Britain's domestic intelligence service) to take the rap and deal with the aftermath. At least this is the scenario according to our sources, and indeed, when the following account is considered, there is every reason to conclude that our sources might just have been right .

On the night of 11th June 1997, just two months prior to Diana's fatal 'road traffic accident' in Paris, Mrs Parker Bowles was herself involved in a similar, though non-fatal 'accident'. The incident occurred as Mrs Parker Bowles was travelling to meet Prince Charles at his country residence, Highgrove—on a stretch of country road between the villages of Norton and Easton Grey in Wiltshire, about 8 miles from the prince's estate. According to police reports, Mrs Parker Bowles was travelling at some speed when her car, a green Ford Mondeo belonging to Buckingham Palace, seemed to lose control and plough head-on into an oncoming vehicle—a Volvo estate driven by one Carolyn Melville-Smith of Easton Grey. As a result of the collision, Ms Melville-Smith's car overturned in a ditch at the side of the road. She suffered chest injuries. Mrs Parker Bowles, on the other hand, was relatively unhurt; indeed, she immediately climbed out of her car and fled the scene in a self-confessed state of "*sheer terror*", leaving Ms Melville-Smith trapped and in pain in her overturned car.

For some days and weeks thereafter the incident became the focus of intense media interest, the details of the crash seeming to alter slightly with each passing day. Initial reports claimed that Mrs Parker Bowles had fled the scene of the crash in fear that she was being kidnapped by terrorists and/or that she was the intended victim of assassination. Certainly it is known that she fled the scene in fear for her life.

"I panicked out of sheer terror", she told reporters. "I have constantly been warned that one day I might be attacked and I thought this is what might have happened."

The question is, of course, attacked by whom: terrorists? Or MI5?

Precise details of the crash are difficult to establish; there were no witnesses to the incident. But what is known for certain is that, following the incident, Prince Charles ordered that Mrs Parker Bowles's personal security be considerably stepped up—a curious response to an innocent 'road traffic accident', it has to be said. What is also known is that Mrs Parker Bowles did indeed leave the scene of the crash in something of a hurry; she did not attempt to discover to what extent the other driver (Ms Melville-Smith) might have been injured, and neither did she wait around to exchange names and addresses. A police investigation was thus launched into the incident, but no charges were brought against Mrs Parker Bowles, even though it is an offence in Britain (under the Road Traffic Act 1988) to evacuate the scene of a crash without first exchanging names and addresses with all parties involved.

Failing to report an accident is also illegal. As Ms Melville-Smith commented in *The Independent* (14th June, 1997): "You should never leave the scene of an accident. If I had done it, I would be in a lot of trouble right now."

No doubt about that.

The official explanation came in a statement from royal sources some days after the event, and contained few surprises. It was claimed that Mrs Parker Bowles had not evacuated the scene of the crash without good reason. She had climbed out of her car, the sources said, had checked to see that Ms Melville-Smith was alive and well (a claim refuted by Ms Melville-Smith) and had then returned to her car in order to salvage her mobile phone. She had then run away from the scene in order to call the emergency services from the brow of a nearby hill, from where she was able to obtain a clearer signal. Having alerted the emergency services she had then called Prince Charles, who immediately dispatched his own police protection officer together with two royal valets and two other staff members to the scene of the crash.

It was also claimed that Mrs Parker Bowles had left the scene so abruptly due to security reasons; evidently she had been under instruction to leave the scene of such an incident due to the risk of terrorist attack. Which in itself seems plausible enough. However, it has to be said that, if Charles and his personal security operation had been so concerned about the possibility of such an attack, then it seems curious to say the least that Mrs Parker Bowles should have been permitted to drive alone, at night, along deserted country roads, thus leaving herself entirely vulnerable to such an attack—to kidnap, or indeed, assassination.

In any event, our sources had a different story to tell.

"She knew she was under some degree of surveillance, and that her position as Prince Charles's mistress was a precarious one," we were informed.

And even more explicit: "She thought it was an MI5 job—that MI5 was trying to kill her. She was right, of course, but it all went stupidly wrong. The reports had to make it look like an innocent accident."

Can you tell us if MI5 operatives were present at the scene of the crash?

A moment's pause, then: "If they were it was too late by then to effect the necessary outcome. The operation had already failed."

Yes but can you tell us if MI5 operatives were present at the scene of the crash?

A further pause, then: "Let us just say it was a bad day at the office for MI5."

It should be stated here that, in citing this incident as a bungled MI5 operation, we are in no way intending to implicate Ms Melville-Smith as an MI5 agent or accomplice. Indeed, Ms Melville-Smith would seem to have been entirely the innocent party. As we have seen with regard to the Diana crash (or indeed, the crash in which Major Michael Marman was killed—see *Chapter 3*) it is perfectly feasible that Mrs Parker Bowles's car, in particular as it belonged to Buckingham Palace, could have been tampered with at some stage prior to the incident. And that this could have caused her to lose control of the vehicle moments before it ploughed head-on into Ms Melville-Smith's Volvo estate. This is of course a speculative scenario. But similar thoughts would certainly seem to have troubled the mind of Prince Charles—who, remember, ordered that his lover's personal security be considerably tightened following the incident, even though the only other party involved was, allegedly, Ms Melville-Smith. To add to this, Mrs Parker Bowles herself believed that her life was in danger. Even though the official spin-story maintains that she saw Ms Melville-Smith alone and trapped in her overturned car (and thus would have realized that she was not the victim of a terrorist attack), she nevertheless felt sufficiently threatened that she fled the scene in terror—in fear for her life. Curious, it has to be said.

But whatever the truth in all of this, the fact remains that two months prior to the crash that killed Diana, Camilla Parker Bowles was involved in a similar 'road traffic accident', one that could just as easily have killed or seriously maimed her. Indeed, according to our sources, this was precisely the intention. Perhaps Mrs Parker Bowles should be thankful it was an MI5 operation, then. Had it been the handiwork of MI-6 and the CIA (or indeed, The Clinic—see *Chapter 3*) it is far more likely she would have lost her life.

And that, ironically, Diana would almost certainly be alive today.

10

A DRESS REHEARSAL
FOR MURDER?

"This is BBC Television from London. A few moments ago, Buckingham Palace announced that Diana, Princess of Wales, has died in a car crash. Normal programmes have been suspended."

Extract from BBC News dress rehearsal conducted before Diana's death.

How To Announce The Death Of A British Royal

Our sources also highlighted other events in the sequence which led to Diana's death. Perhaps most significant was that a top BBC executive confided to one of our sources that, ten days prior to Diana's death, a "*dress rehearsal*" had been conducted by the BBC with regard to "*how to announce the death of a British Royal*". Despite our own efforts to corroborate this claim—which involved several telephone conversations and a meeting with a somewhat anxious spokesperson—the BBC flatly denied that such a dress rehearsal had taken place. Indeed, the officials we spoke to denied that any such dress rehearsal had ever taken place. Which, to us, seemed odd. After all, the British Broadcasting Corporation is effectively the Establishment's public voice. In effect it is Britain's state-owned television company, in any event the only one for which the British public is forced by law to pay an annual licence fee, and which is traditionally a mouthpiece for the Establishment. The very idea that the BBC would not maintain a well-oiled contingency in this regard seemed to us preposterous. The announcement of, say, the Queen's death—or that of any other high-ranking royal—would by necessity require the utmost sensitive and strategic planning. Surely we were not expected to believe that the BBC would simply cast pearls to fortune and fumble its way through such an announcement without prior rehearsals. This, at least, remained the niggling suspicion at the forefront of our minds as we struggled to corroborate our source's information. And it did prove a struggle. In the end we were unable to confirm that a dress rehearsal had been conducted ten days prior to Diana's death.

But we did discover that such a dress rehearsal had been conducted some few weeks earlier, on Saturday, 5th July, 1997. And that the information contained in a BBC script for such a rehearsal revealed clearly enough that, contrary to BBC denials, the Corporation does maintain such a contingency. This same well-oiled contingency, moreover, included a startling and strangely prognostic announcement to the effect that Princess Diana had been killed in road traffic accident.

As journalist Chris Blackhurst reported in *The Independent on Sunday* (13th July 1997): "At 1.15 P.M. last Saturday ... transmission was interrupted by this announcement: 'This is BBC Television from London. A few moments ago, Buckingham Palace announced that Her Majesty Queen Elizabeth, the Queen Mother, has died. Normal programmes have been suspended.' Announcers on BBC 1 and BBC 2 had reached for their black ties, which they are required to keep close at hand, and the ritual began. It was a dress rehearsal, of course, but it says a lot about the relationship between the monarchy and the BBC."

Indeed it does. But what is even more revealing is that Chris Blackhurst's article, penned six weeks before Diana's death, also included the following, astonishing revelation:

"Previous rehearsals have been much more dramatic than the Queen Mother's last weekend. A BBC executive reveals that in the past the Corporation 'killed off' Diana in a car crash."

Perhaps we should repeat that.

"A BBC executive reveals that in the past the Corporation 'killed off' Diana in a car crash."

A stunningly accurate prognosis, to say the least. One wonders why the BBC should have elected to rehearse the announcement of Diana's death in this way.

In any event, several salient factors emerge from this disclosure:

One: that the BBC does maintain a contingency policy with regard to the announcements of royal deaths;

Two: that eight weeks prior to Diana's death the BBC did effect a dress rehearsal with regard to announcing the death of the Queen Mother;

Three: that in the past the BBC had conducted a similar dress rehearsal with regard to announcing the death of Princess Diana;

Four: that on this occasion the BBC announced that Diana had been killed in a 'road traffic accident';

Five: that, according to our sources, a top BBC executive revealed that a similar dress rehearsal had been conducted on Thursday, August 21, 1997, ten days prior to Diana's death. It should be reiterated here that point *Five* has been flatly denied by BBC officials. But then, as we discovered, such a denial is nothing short of what we should expect. When, for example, we spoke to an ITV spokesperson we were told:

"These arrangements are of necessity strictly confidential. I am surprised and saddened that Mr Blackhurst was able to obtain the script ... the secrecy is out of respect for the feelings of the Royal Family."

In any event, it was not long before the BBC was able to implement its script for real. On 31st August, 1997, the black ties and the practised words informed us that Diana, Princess of Wales, had indeed died in a 'road traffic accident'. And as the rest of us mourned, the British Royal Establishment was heard to utter an enormous sigh of relief.

"The Media Is Being Primed, As We Speak."

Is it possible, we wondered, that the BBC had been manoeuvred by its Establishment overlords to prepare for the death of Princess Diana—even though BBC staff in general would of course have remained unaware that they were being manoeuvred in this way? Is it possible that a *"dress rehearsal"* for the announcement of Diana's death by 'road traffic accident' could have been part of an MI-6 preparation schedule, and thus surreptitiously introduced into the BBC itinerary? It was our original source, Stealth, remember, who told us one week prior to the princess's death:

"Provision for public reaction has already been considered. They have good experience of how to deal with public reaction ... It's being taken care of as we speak. The media is being primed, as we speak."

If the BBC was being covertly primed in this way, we figured, our source's assertions that a dress rehearsal regarding the announcement of Diana's death—that it had been conducted ten days before she died—might thus prove correct. But in any event, the question remains: might the BBC have been manoeuvred by the Establishment to prepare the British public for news of Diana's death? It is a question which should be considered in context with the sequence of events detailed thus far, and reiterated here for clarity:

One: Diana's close relationship with her personal police protection officer, Sgt. Barry Mannakee—who, having informed Diana that she was a target for MI5 surveillance, was removed from his post, transferred, and eight months later killed in a 'road traffic accident'.

Two: Diana's subsequent relationship with James Hewitt—who, we recall, was warned by a member of the Royal Family that his relationship with Diana was *"not supported"*, and that, in consequence, he too had been placed under MI5 surveillance. We also recall that Major Hewitt was further warned by the Royal Family that *"we can not be responsible for your safety or security"* should you continue your relationship with the princess. In consequence, Mr. Hewitt ended the relationship *"forthwith"*, and at the same time confided in a close friend that, had he ignored the warnings, he feared he might have ended up having an 'accident'.

Three: MI5's intensified surveillance of Princess Diana, the so-called 'Squidgygate Affair' being a primary case in point. Indeed, *"Clandestine surveillance by the Security Services on the most intimate of situations was to culminate later in the assassination of Diana, Princess of Wales,"* we were told by Royal Personal Protection Officer, Mike Grey, a man who for twenty years has worked in a similar capacity to that of Sgt. Barry Mannakee, and who affirmed to us that Diana had indeed suffered *"clandestine surveillance by the Security Services"*.

Four: MI5's equally intensive surveillance of Camilla Parker Bowles, in particular following the divorce of Charles and Diana.

Five: MI5's directive to *"clean up the constitutional mess"* caused by Prince Charles's philandering, and further compounded by his divorce from Princess Diana.

Six: MI5's decision to focus its attention on Camilla Parker Bowles in order to clean up that *"constitutional mess"*.

Seven: The increased pressure brought on MI5 by Establishment oligarchs following Diana's infamous *Panorama* interview, for which the BBC was severely chastized by the Establishment.

Eight: The intense interest shown in Diana by MI-6 following her attack on the Monarchy and her subsequent activities in Angola and Bosnia, where, as we shall see, MI-6 and the CIA continue to carry out covert operations on behalf of the British and US governments.

Nine: The emergence on the scene of the CIA at this time due to the success of Diana's landmines campaign in oil-rich Angola, where illicit oil-backed loans and CIA-brokered arms-for-oil deals were key to a future Bush-Cheney White House. Also, the princess's meetings with Bill and Hillary Clinton and the President's subsequent decision to support a worldwide ban on the manufacture, sale and deployment of antipersonnel landmines.

Ten: The subsequent emergence of Dodi Fayed—whose surprise arrival only served to compound even further the already severe constitutional crisis brought about by Charles's and Diana's divorce. This crisis was so severe, remember, that Establishment oligarchs even considered the disestablishment of the Church in their desperate attempts to find a solution. Following Dodi's arrival, however, such a constitutional move would have proved largely ineffectual. The crisis would not only have remained; it would have proved unresolvable no matter how drastic the constitutional reform(s) implemented, in particular if Diana had in the end elected to marry Dodi— who, remember, was an Arab Muslim and son of a major international player already loathed by the Royals and the Establishment.

Eleven: The inevitable attempt on Camilla Parker Bowles's life by MI5, the bungled and mystery-laden 'road traffic accident' that Camilla survived. We should remember that, following the incident, Camilla's personal security was considerably tightened by order of Prince Charles himself.

Twelve: The mysterious *"dress rehearsal"* for the announcement of Diana's death by 'road traffic accident', said by our sources to have been conducted by the BBC ten days prior to the fatal crash in Paris, a fact disputed by BBC officials. In any event the dress rehearsal that did take place on Saturday 5th July, 1997, regarding the announcement of the death of the Queen Mother, and the fact that during a previous dress rehearsal the BBC, in a strangely prognostic announcement, did report that Diana had been killed in a 'road traffic accident'.

Thirteen: The equally mysterious and tragic 'road traffic accident' in Paris during the early hours of Sunday, 31st August, 1997—an accident that Diana did not survive, despite the fact that, medically speaking, she could have. Indeed, the sheer volume of anomalies and still-unanswered questions regarding this case only serve to highlight even further the likely involvement of British and US intelligence agencies in the princess's death. And the fact that 'road traffic accidents' are indeed employed by the intelligence services today as a well-practised and wholly deniable method of assassination.

11

MI-6 IN PARIS

"**T**he paparazzi in London and Paris are crawling with British intelligence. Some are freelancers on the MI6 payroll, others are our own deep-cover agents... Even if only to monitor the movements of Princess Diana and Mr. Fayed, the Paris paparazzi, on the night in question, would undoubtedly have accommodated a number of our intelligence agents. It would be foolish, quite naive for anyone to imagine otherwise."

Intelligence Source, 1997.

MI-6
And The Paparazzi

The very idea of MI-6 being a group of stuffy, upper-class government spies housed in an office block in London could not be further from the truth, and in itself serves as one of the Secret Intelligence Service's greatest propaganda triumphs. True, the agency sets down its roots in the shadowy world of Whitehall's most exclusive clubs and power cabals, but MI-6 cells, some embassy-based, others not, exist the world over, forming an internationally-coordinated network of foreign-city 'stations' via which foreign intelligence is gathered, collated and sent back home, and filed away on a securely encrypted intranet database at 85 Vauxhall Cross, MI-6's central headquarters in London. This, at least, is the official word on James Bond's top-secret employer.

But in reality, this 'internationally-coordinated network' is set up to achieve far more than basic intelligence gathering. Via its connections in the corporate and commercial worlds, for example, covert operations in economic subversion and industrial espionage are planned and executed, as well as other, more political and military-based operations in some of the world's more hostile territories. The media also is a hotbed for undercover operations, with local media outlets and networks crawling with undercover operatives. Indeed, when the sheer weight and efficacy of the network is viewed in all its glory, it is easy to see how complex, international operations are arranged, coordinated and executed, *in secret*. With regard to the assassination of Princess Diana, for example, intricate planning and coordination of events would have been imperative to a successful operation. As we know, following their flight from Sardinia, the couple were hounded by so-called paparazzi from the moment they touched down in Paris. Many of their movements were spontaneous and unplanned. Yet, as if by some gift of precognition, the paparazzi seemed to know in advance the couple's every move—even the fact that they would, on the spur of the moment, and as a direct consequence of being harassed by 'paparazzi' outside Dodi's apartment, choose not to dine at their prearranged restaurant, *Chez Benoit*, but instead return to the Ritz. Indeed, it was reported that more than fifty paparazzi were their to greet the couple on their unscheduled return at around 10 pm. The question is, of course, how did they know the couple would return to the Ritz when the word on the street was that they had already booked a table elsewhere? Who leaked this information? And moreover, who acted upon it?

What is known for certain is that an unusually high number of MI-6 agents were stationed in Paris during the days that led up to the princess's death. A British Embassy leak reported that, on the night itself, there were at least six MI-6 agents in Paris—more than comprise the entire (official) number of MI-6 agents in Moscow. To add to this, former MI-6 Officer Richard Tomlinson has told us that, not only was there an unusually high number of MI-6 personnel in Paris on the night in question, but that those personnel included MI-6 Chief David Spedding's personal secretary. And what is more—in a statement released on 12th May 1999—Tomlinson revealed that, on the night Diana died, two senior MI-6 Officers were in Paris on an "*undeclared*" basis, and that their directive was to liaise with MI-6 informant, Henri Paul.

Mr Tomlinson stated: "In Paris at the time of M. Paul's death, there were two relatively experienced but undeclared MI-6 officers. The first was Mr. Nicholas John Andrew LANGMAN, born 1960. The second was Mr. Richard David SPEARMAN, again born 1960. I firmly believe that either one or both of these officers will be well acquainted with M. Paul, and most probably also met M. Paul shortly before his death. I believe that either or both of these officers will have knowledge that will be of crucial importance in establishing the sequence of events leading up to the deaths of M. Paul,

Dodi Al Fayed and the Princess of Wales."

Further: "Mr Spearman in particular was an extremely well connected and influential officer because he had been, prior to his appointment in Paris, the personal secretary to the Chief of MI-6, Mr. David SPEDDING. As such, he would have been privy to even the most confidential of MI-6 operations. I believe that there may well be significance in the fact that Mr. Spearman was posted to Paris in the month immediately before the deaths."

Needless to say, neither Mr. Spearman nor Mr. Langman were questioned by the French inquiry with regard to their activities on the night in question, and this despite the fact that Jean-Pierre Chevenement, French Minister of the Interior at the time of the crash, had the power to do just that. At the very least he should have been informed that these two senior MI-6 officers were stationed at the British Embassy in Paris on the night in question, and should have acted on that information and found out precisely what they were doing there.

As Henri Paul's family lawyer, Francois Meyer, told Britain's *Sunday Express* (September 7, 2003): "We know there were two agents at the British Embassy in Paris on August 31, 1997 [the night Diana died]. If there had been any action planned by any secret service agent from Britain on French territory, Mr. Chevenement should have known about it."

And further: "If the secret agents had been in Paris in order to protect Diana, then why did they not do so? There is something not right here."

Indeed there is. For one thing, if Spearman and Langman were in Paris on royal surveillance duty, then why did the British Embassy deny this? Why did the British Embassy inform Judge Stephan, and later Lord Stevens, that it had no knowledge of Diana's presence in Paris? After all, half the world and its sister knew about the couple's arrival at the Ritz Hotel that afternoon; it was all over the news networks like a cheap suit. If, on the other hand, as Lord Stevens claims in his Paget report, Spearman and Langman were not in Paris to protect Diana, or spy on her, then it follows that they must have been there on other business—possibly even *undeclared* business. Of course, the British Embassy now claims the two officers were in Paris in an official capacity, Spearman as the 'First Secretary (Political)', and Langman the 'First Secretary (Economic)', this after having first denied that either had been there at all. But in any event, evidence of MI-6 involvement in Diana's death does not depend at all on whether Tomlinson is right about Spearman and Langman. The two may well have been stationed at the Embassy on legitimate business, and the job of monitoring Diana assigned to more covert operatives. Certainly the Embassy would have been perfect cover for any undeclared officers on royal surveillance duty. True, the Embassy claimed that, as Diana was no longer officially 'Royal', and that she had herself requested that her personal protection be withdrawn, neither the Embassy nor any MI-6 staff stationed at the Embassy were aware of the princess's visit to Paris, and thus no official surveillance was carried out. Which is very difficult to swallow. It is true that Diana had requested her personal protection be withdrawn, but she was referring to the Personal Protection Officers who would normally have travelled with her, some of whom were actually part of Prince Charles's protection staff and thus the princess no longer wanted them following her around. But the fact is, MI-6 does not, never has and never will desist from spying on a target simply by virtue of the target's request. This is a ludicrous argument.

Dear MI-6, please would you stop spying on me now that I am no longer with Prince Charles. Yours sincerely, Diana.

Of course, darling, absolutely no problem at all. Have a wonderful life.

Lest we forget, Princess Diana was still the mother of the future King of Great Britain. It is inconceivable that Great Britain's Royal Intelligence Service would not have been monitoring her movements, in particular now she was gallivanting around the Mediterranean with the nephew of the world's most notorious arms dealer, Adnan Kashoggi (more later). Back home she was royal enemy number one. In the US she was the floozy who had persuaded Clinton to ban landmines. In the eyes of the public she was more popular and more loved than The Beatles and Elvis combined. And yet we are expected to believe that while every paparazzo in France had turned out in anticipation of the princess's arrival, the British Embassy *"had no knowledge"* that Diana was in Paris until after the car crash. Nonsense.

And speaking of the paparazzi. It is of course known that both MI5 and MI-6 agents regularly pose as freelance journalists and paparazzi. It is common policy for intelligence operatives worldwide to gain employment with major newspapers and journals, if only to write stories designed to promote some or other agenda, to disseminate 'appropriate information' and, in many cases, disinformation. In 1977, for example, renowned *Washington Post* journalist, Carl Bernstein, famous for exposing the Watergate scandal that forced President Nixon's premature resignation, revealed that more than 400 journalists in the US alone were either deep-cover CIA agents, or they were on the CIA payroll. There is no reason to believe that this situation is any different today. On the contrary, there is every reason to suspect that it still prevails. As much as anything else it provides the intelligence agency concerned with a public voice, as well as providing the agent concerned with an effective cover. And as we were told by our own intelligence source soon after the crash:

"The paparazzi in London and Paris are crawling with British Intelligence. Some are freelancers on the MI-6 payroll, others are our own deep-cover agents ... Even if only to monitor the movements of Princess Diana and Mr. Fayed, the Paris paparazzi on the night in question would undoubtedly have accommodated a number of our intelligence agents. It would be foolish, quite naive for anyone to imagine otherwise."

That the paparazzi in Paris on the night in question included MI-6 agents, then, as well as one or two CIA agents, is not out of the question. Indeed, given that Diana and Dodi were in Paris it is nothing more than should be expected. Certainly when the meticulously organized, military-precise operation that seemed to orchestrate the paparazzi's every move is considered, one can only surmise that intelligence information was being gathered on the couple's movements on a minute-by-minute basis. Moreover, once gathered, this information was then—*somehow*—being successfully disseminated throughout the paparazzi network (again, minute by minute), affording the paparazzi up-to-the-minute knowledge of where the couple were. And where they were headed. This would suggest, of course, that an informant, perhaps on the MI-6 payroll, was working on the inside, close to either Diana or Dodi, or both, and was thus able to glean relevant information and transmit it back to the agents in charge of the operation. But if this is the case, who could that informant have been? There is powerful evidence, of course, that suspected MI-6 informant and photojournalist James Andanson, 'godfather' of the paparazzi, was in Paris that night. More on him later. But what about Henri Paul? His position as Assistant Director of Security at the Ritz Hotel certainly meant he would have been ideally placed for such a role. But what evidence is there in support of this allegation?

Henri Paul, Secret Agent

Well to begin, Henri Paul was himself a secret agent, of sorts. It is known that he was on the payroll of France's domestic intelligence service, DST, because two DST contact numbers were discovered in his address book after his death, prompting the DST to confirm that Paul indeed worked for them, and was *"specifically tasked with enquiries in hotel circles"* (again, more on this later). But what about Paul's connections to MI-6? Certainly it would be reasonable to assume that the Deputy Head of Security at one of Europe's most prestigious hotels would have been targeted by foreign intelligence services, and that he would have been handsomely rewarded for the highly sensitive information he would have been able to gather on their behalf. Indeed, at the time of his death, US $350,000 was sitting in more than a dozen bank accounts and a safe deposit box, most of them in Paris, all in Henri Paul's name. And this despite the fact that he earned only US $40,000 a year. According to close friends, he spent at least that much on an annual basis. He spent large sums of money on personal pursuits, for example. Among those pursuits was his love of flying. Paul was an accomplished pilot. He flew regularly. And each time he took to the cockpit it cost him around US $600, best part of his week's wages. To add to this, it is also known that a large percentage of the money paid into his various bank accounts had been deposited in cash deposits of $8,000. Indeed, he was found with the equivalent of about $2,500 in cash on the night he died—an amount, according to Richard Tomlinson, consistent with that paid to part-time agents on a 'cash-for-services' basis. And during the eight months immediately prior to his death he is known to have deposited around $8000 on five separate occasions—a total of $40,000, an amount that would normally have taken him a year to earn. Once again these deposits were made in cash. But where did the money come from?

As we will see a little later, Lord Stevens postulates the ludicrous theory in his Paget report that Henri Paul might have accumulated this fortune by way of receiving cash tips from wealthy Ritz clients. But according to his best friend, Claude Garrec, Henri Paul had worked for both British and French Intelligence for at least eleven years—the length of time he had worked at the Ritz. As stated, given his position as Assistant Director of Security at the Ritz Hotel, Paris, where international businessmen, politicians and power-brokers alike often meet to discuss their secret affairs, the fact that he might have been recruited by intelligence agencies is far more likely than not. Indeed, a senior French intelligence officer openly admitted as much to ITN's royal correspondent, Nicholas Owen, during the making of the programme, *Diana: Secrets Of The Crash*, screened in Britain to mark the first anniversary of Diana's death and presented by Owen himself. And there is further evidence to this same end. Former MI-6 officer Richard Tomlinson testified to the French magistrate in charge of the official investigation, Judge Herve Stephan, that Paul was indeed on the MI-6 payroll. According to Tomlinson, he once saw an MI-6 document naming Paul as a French informant, codenamed 'P', who worked at the Ritz Hotel. Tomlinson also revealed to Judge Stephan, remember, that the blueprint for an MI-6 plot to assassinate the Serbian president, Slobodan Milosevic, mirrored the operation that killed Princess Diana. In the Paget report, Tomlinson strangely backtracks on these assertions, which formed part of his original affidavit, thus:

"In 1992, I was working in the Eastern European Controllerate of MI-6 and I was peripherally involved in a large and complicated operation to smuggle advanced Soviet weaponry out of the then disintegrating and disorganized remnants of the Soviet Union. During 1992, I spent several days reading the substantial files on this operation. These files contain a wide miscellany of contact notes, telegrams, intelligence reports, photographs, etc., from which it was possible to build up a detailed understanding of the operation. The operation involved a large cast of officers and agents of MI-6.

"On more than one occasion, meetings between various figures in the operation took place at the Ritz Hotel, Place de Vendome, Paris. There were in the file several intelligence reports on these meetings, which had been written by one of the MI-6 officers based in Paris at the time (identified in the file only by a coded designation). The source of the information was an informant in the Ritz Hotel, who again was identified in the files only by a code number. The MI-6 officer paid the informant in cash for his information."

Tomlinson went on: "I became curious to learn more about the identity of this particular informant, because his number cropped up several times and he seemed to have extremely good access to the goings on in the Ritz Hotel. I therefore ordered this informant's personal file from MI-6's central file registry. When I read this new file, I was not at all surprised to learn that the informant was a security officer of the Ritz Hotel. Intelligence services always target the security officers of important hotels because they have such good access to intelligence. I remember, however, being mildly surprised that the nationality of this informant was French, and this stuck in my memory because it is rare that MI-6 succeeds in recruiting a French informer.

"I cannot claim that I remember from this reading of the file that the name of this person was Henri Paul, but I have no doubt with the benefit of hindsight that this was he. Although I did not subsequently come across Henri Paul again during my time in MI-6, I am confident that the relationship between him and MI-6 would have continued until his death, because MI-6 would never willingly relinquish control over such a well-placed informant."

He concluded: "I am sure that the personal file of Henri Paul will therefore contain notes of meetings between him and his MI-6 controlling officer, right up until the point of his death. I firmly believe that these files will contain evidence of crucial importance to the circumstances and causes of the incident that killed M. Paul together with the Princess of Wales and Dodi Al Fayed."

In relation to these claims made by Richard Tomlinson, we should note an incident that occurred in July 2006. In the Paget report, Lord Stevens systematically picks Tomlinson's testimony to pieces, reducing the former MI-6 spy to a mush of confusion; indeed, to the point even where he 'confesses' his claims might have been made as a result of feeling embittered towards his former employer. As we will see a little later, the report carries with it a strangely sinister, almost scary edge—almost as if Lord Stevens has the power to say and do whatever he pleases in order to whitewash the evidence and thus arrive at his predetermined conclusion: it was an accident. So many established facts regarding the case are simply brushed aside, while others are boldly refuted without rhyme or reason, the result being a statement effectively made by Lord Stevens that has now become the definitive truth: *The Paget Report*. In one instance the former police chief informs us that MI-6 afforded him and his team "*full access*" to its "*entire database*" dating back to 1990, and cites this unlikely event as evidence that MI-6 had no record of its alleged involvement in Diana's death and thus was innocent of all charges. He also claims that no files identified by Tomlinson to the French inquiry regarding Henri Paul could be found. In effect he brands Tomlinson a liar.

But in his testimony, as presented in his 1999 affidavit, a sworn and testified statement made to the French inquiry, Tomlinson does not come across as someone who is making his story up. Neither does he make vague, general claims. Rather his assertions are explicit and detailed, even to the point where he identifies specific MI-6 files he says should still exist and challenges the inquiry to subpoena those files and check them out. This is scarcely eighteen months after the event, remember, not ten years later, when Lord Stevens and his team were finally granted "*full access*" to MI-6's "*entire database*", by which time the top-secret spy agency had had all the time in the world to revise that database, or indeed, manufacture a new one. And in any event, it has to be said that the tenor and detail of Tomlinson's original statement does not appear to reflect the character of a man who would later, in effect, retract his statement and 'confess' that he might have been mistaken. In other words, something doesn't add up. Perhaps the following incident might give us an insight.

On July 3rd, 2006, the *Daily Express* carried the following front-page headline:

'DIANA: ARREST DRAMA—Ex-MI-6 Spy's Home Is Raided'.

The accompanying story proceeded to claim that the raid was "*linked to the Princess Diana inquiry*", and revealed that the former MI-6 spy in question was none other than Richard Tomlinson. Evidently, the story revealed, agents from the French security service (DST), at the request of MI-6, ransacked Tomlinson's home in southern France and confiscated telephone and computer equipment, together with his personal organiser, personal papers and files (including his bank account details), and perhaps more to the point, both his passports, as well (Tomlinson bears duel British and New Zealand nationality). This action was taken, we were told, because MI-6 feared Tomlinson might be called to testify at the Royal Inquest in London, and as a result, information would be revealed implicating MI-6 in Diana's death. Without a passport, of course, Tomlinson would be unable to travel to London, and thus unable to attend the Inquest should he be called to testify.

However, as revealed in the Paget report, detectives from Operation Paget had already 'interviewed' Tomlinson, twice in fact, and they had confiscated computer disks they later claimed contained original manuscripts for his book, *The Big Breach*. These manuscripts, they further claimed, differed from Tomlinson's later assertions regarding not only Henri Paul, but the so-called 'Milosevic Plot', as well, proving that his testimony was false, or at least mistaken. In fact everything Tomlinson had ever told us, the Paget team asserted, was untrue. And for whatever reason, instead of attempting to defend his statements, Tomlinson rolled over like a chastized dog and capitulated, tail firmly between his legs. Curious, then, that anyone should have needed to raid Tomlinson's property. After all, why would MI-6 fear what Tomlinson might say at the inquest when Operation Paget had already nailed him? They had already 'proved' his story was false, so there was no need to revisit the man and confiscate everything he owned all over again. Indeed, it has to be said that the manner of Tomlinson's submission suggests a different reason for this visit entirely.

For the record, the article, quoting an unnamed source, concluded:

"Tomlinson has not committed any offence under French law, and this shows that MI-6 and the French security services are joined at the hip— just as they were on the night of Diana's death."

And further: *"His testimony could be crucial. This is one of the reasons that the authorities picked him up. There is a feeling that, if Tomlinson agreed to give evidence, there would be all kinds of trouble … It is certainly true that the authorities in France and Britain will stop at nothing to prevent Tomlinson from giving evidence."*

No need. They 'helped' him change his mind instead.

Henri Paul, Patsy

Much of the evidence we presented regarding Henri Paul in the hardback edition of this book has by necessity been omitted here. This is partly due to lack of space, but mostly to the comprehensive coverage given to Henri Paul a little later, in the chapters dealing with the Paget Report, where the evidence has been very much updated. None the less we did wish to retain these few words here, if for no other reason than to present our opinion, based on the evidence we have gathered, on the role played by Henri Paul in Princess Diana's death.

One of the anomalies surrounding Henri Paul has always been the seemingly conspicuous dearth of information regarding his movements on the night in question. At best this information is sketchy. Having met the couple at Le Bourget airport earlier in the day, and having escorted them back to the Ritz, Henri Paul is said to have finished work at around 7 pm and retired for the night. Later that same evening, Paul returned to his place of work, and as we now know, was elected to drive the ill-fated Mercedes in which he was killed.

But where was Henri Paul during his three-hour absence from the Ritz earlier that evening? Liaising with British intelligence operatives, perhaps? Collecting yet another pay packet from his MI-6 handlers, money in advance of the operation that would, ironically, cost him his life? US journalist Gerald Posner, strangely quoted in the Paget report, claims that NSA sources told him that Henri Paul met with agents, not of MI-6, but of French intelligence (DGSE) during this period, but that the meeting had nothing to do with Diana and Dodi's presence in Paris. We have to say we find this very difficult to believe. Though France's foreign intelligence service, DGSE, denied having a relationship with Paul, they would none the less have wanted live information on the couple, and who better to talk to in this regard than their 'man at the Ritz Hotel', Henri Paul? Phone contact numbers found in Henri Paul's address book prove that he did work, on a part-time basis, for France's domestic intelligence service, DST, but according to our sources, it was his MI-6 handler that Henri Paul met up with during the three hours he was absent that evening. It was in any event his MI-6 handler who gave him final instruction and who paid him the 12000 francs for doing whatever it was he was asked to do. Of course, at this time he would have had no idea he was to play such a central role in the operation planned for later that night, much less that he would be placing himself at such personal risk. And even less would he have known that, like former CIA employee Lee Harvey Oswald before him, he was being set up as a patsy, a stooge whose blood tests would later tell the lie that he had been drunk at the wheel, as well as being further intoxicated with drugs and carbon monoxide. Little would he have suspected that, twenty-four hours later, his name would be blazoned across newspapers worldwide, and that beside his name would be a photograph of a short portly man looking slightly worse for wear, drink in hand, and a headline that accused him of manslaughter. On the contrary, he would have thought his part had been played in keeping his benefactors abreast of the couple's plans and movements. And possibly helping them in other ways, too—like bugging the Imperial Suite, the luxury Ritz apartment occupied by Diana and Dodi. Or furtively suggesting alternative plans of action to his boss, Dodi Fayed, cleverly manipulating events to ensure that, say, Dodi ordered *him* to drive the couple back to his apartment, and to take an unusual route in order to outwit the chasing pack of paparazzi. Still unaware of the enormity of the operation in which he was participating, perhaps even thinking that the entire operation had been devised simply to cause the couple further duress, in particular the princess, Paul would have taken to the wheel with dollar signs in his eyes, perhaps even planning to collect the remainder of his reward the following day. But, of course, there would be no following day for Henri Paul. The following day Henri Paul would be dead.

Indeed, when you think about it, what better plan than to hire the services of the man acting in charge of the princess's personal security on the night she is fated to die? And in order to cover your tracks, kill him, too.

12

LOOSE CANNON

"I 'm a particularly conservative Conservative. I like to think the future King of England at least starts off the job without a blemish. And I don't think he could have done with Dodi as the stepfather."

Sir James Hill, Conservative Constitutional Committee, 1997.

A Coporate Oracle

I n this twenty-first-century global village of ours, the media has become something of an oracle. It is to the media we turn for our daily fix of wisdom. As in classical antiquity the ancients would address the oracle for advice, prophecy, guidance, so we in the so-called modern world turn to the media to inform us, to entertain us, to guide us. While most of us are these days aware that radio and television, together with the daily newspapers, are little more than socio-political tools, ever ready to feed us the preconceptions and prejudices of their owners and sponsors, nevertheless we tend largely to be persuaded by the opinions disseminated in the media. It thus becomes a truism that opinions are formed on the less than expedient counsel of this latter-day corporate oracle. Like some acquiescent pendulum, public opinion is swayed, first this way and then that way, in accordance with oligarchic agendas, as was amply demonstrated in the build-up to Britain's 1997 general election, when corporate publishing mogul Rupert Murdoch struck a deal with Tony Blair. In consequence, Murdoch's extreme right-wing British tabloid, **The Sun**, bamboozled its readership into switching its political allegiance from far-right to centre-left—from the fiercely patriotic Tories to a Europhile New Labour. The shepherd changed his tack, and the flock followed suit.

Another, perhaps more pertinent example of how the media acts as a propaganda machine for its corporate owners is demonstrated in the way the

British press elected to represent Princess Diana. Following her separation and divorce from Prince Charles, for example, left and right-wing tabloids and broadsheets turned on the princess like a field of vipers on their prey. Indeed, during the last few years of Diana's life, the vipers' venom comprised a viciously barbed tirade of personal abuse aimed squarely at demeaning the princess's public image. And undermining her self-esteem. Of course, no one is suggesting that Diana was entirely the innocent party. By her own admission she harboured personal agendas, most of which, it would seem, born of her attempt to outshine the royal circles from which she had been excluded. And the media served these agendas well enough.

But the point is the media also harboured agendas. Seldom if ever did a story appear without clear propagandist design—clear political motive, one way or the other. While on the one hand editors clamoured after that as yet unseen photograph of Diana in order to sell their newspapers, on the other hand the stories that accompanied the photographs were more often than not laced with snide, often cruel attempts to hasten her fall from grace. So far as the general public was concerned, of course, these attempts backfired. But the vipers hissed and spat, just the same.

Then came that fateful night in Paris. The princess was dead. Overnight the media changed as the vipers retracted their fangs and became squirming, sycophantic worms. Diana was now the tragic victim of circumstance, the caring humanitarian whose life and memory should of course be immortalized as a touchstone for all things abiding, decent and good. In accord with this new directive the headlines changed as well. The 'Queen of Tarts' became the 'Queen of Hearts'; 'Demented Diana' became 'Saint Diana'. The so-called 'Meddlesome Princess' was overnight transformed into the 'People's Princess', as though all along the very media editors and press barons who had sold us the image of this unstable 'loose cannon' had of course loved and respected Diana as much as anybody else. At the same time, though, we were cunningly fed the line that the Princess of Wales had been tragically killed in a 'road traffic accident', and were thus encouraged to grieve on a scale unprecedented in order to keep our minds from thinking the worst, the unthinkable: that in fact she had been assassinated. The ploy was so barbed it left scars. Following her funeral, of course, we were further encouraged to 'let Diana's memory rest in peace ... for the sake of the children', as if the very newspapers that had, only days and weeks earlier, promoted her as unfit for royal office, really cared. They did not care, of course. They simply wanted us to think that way—in a way that turned our minds from mistrust, confusion, anger ... to all-consuming grief. And because by our nature we are sheep-minded, turn to grief we did.

While this is in no way intended as a slur on any individual's capacity to think and act for themselves, nonetheless public opinion does tend to succumb to periodic and often irrational mood swings. And those mood swings are, in the main, caused by collective reaction to opinions expressed in the media. It is not so much the printed word that sways minds, as the way in which that word is presented—its slant, its capacity to arouse public emotion over and above individual discrimination. It is an insidious mechanism, but it works. We are persuaded in our moral and political judgments by the brash tabloid headline on the one hand, by the intellectual argument of the broadsheet on the other. But both, of course, are instruments of the same corporate hand: the owner of the tabloid is the owner of the broadsheet; the owner of the left-wing radical is the owner of the right-wing reactionary. In the end we are like two bald men fighting over a comb, not knowing quite why we are fighting but knowing that we are, and, in the end, happy for someone else to come along and take away the comb. Tell us who to vote for. Tell us what to think. We make our choice, true enough. But it is a false choice based on at best partial, at worst extremely jaundiced information. It is an imposed choice based on a predisposed and politically weighted counsel. A Machiavellian counsel. Thus we are inveigled into the pseudo-democratic web, into the system which serves insidiously to mould, manipulate, characterize and ultimately control public thought and opinion. And it does so by the power of the word: no bullets required.

As revered journalist and former Chief of Staff at the *New York Times*, John Swinton, commented as long ago as 1953, when asked to give a toast before the prestigious New York Press Club:

"There is no such thing at this date of the world's history as an independent press. You know it and I know it. There is not one of you who dares to write your honest opinions, and if you did, you know beforehand that it would never appear in print. I am paid weekly for keeping my honest opinions out of the paper I am connected with. Others of you are paid similar salaries for similar things, and any of you who would be so foolish as to write honest opinions would be out on the streets looking for another job."

And further: "If I allowed my honest opinions to appear in one issue of my paper, before twenty-four hours my occupation would be gone. The business of the journalist is to destroy the truth; to lie outright; to pervert; to vilify; to fawn at the feet of mammon, and to sell the country for his daily bread. You know it and I know it, and what folly is this toasting an independent press. We are the tools and vassals of the rich men behind the scenes. We are the jumping jacks; they pull the strings and we dance. Our talents, our possibilities and our lives are all the property of other men. We are intellectual prostitutes."

Indeed. And we—the impressionable public—are the clients who keep those prostitutes in work.

A Personal Crusade

In January 1997, amid a storm of international media attention, Diana, Princess of Wales, touched down in the Angolan capital, Luanda, armed with a mission. It was a mission that would change her life forever.

Over the course of the following six months, Diana would campaign vigorously to highlight the massive and appalling cost to human life brought about by the deployment of antipersonnel landmines. Indeed, she would campaign for a total ban on the manufacture, sale and deployment of these insidious weapons worldwide. By her own admission the campaign was to become a *"personal crusade"*—a crusade in which she would invest so much of her own emotion, a crusade in which she would so passionately believe. Perhaps because of this, it was also a crusade that would win public and political support the equal of which has seldom before been witnessed on a global scale. Yet it was a crusade that would incense politicians and arms-trade barons the world over—as well as the world's major oil companies—as we shall see.

The princess already knew, of course, that Angola boasted the highest rate of landmine-related amputees anywhere in the world. This was due to the fact that untold numbers of landmines had been planted and abandoned during the country's so-called 'civil war'. Though ostensibly this war was an internal struggle between rival political factions following the collapse of Portuguese imperial rule in 1975, in truth it was a vicious and bloody conflict perpetrated on behalf of Anglo-American interests on the one hand, and Russian interests on the other. The reason? To gain control of the country's oil and raw-mineral reserves. A familiar story. While the CIA and MI-6 funded and armed Jonas Savimbi's merciless UNITA regime (and had indeed been responsible for the deployment of antipersonnel landmines in Angola since the late 1960s) the Soviets backed the rival MPLA faction, an equally ruthless though Communist regime which in the end won power. The irony is that, while the CIA and MI-6 were busy funding Jonas Savimbi's war effort against the MPLA—and donating millions of antipersonnel landmines to the cause—at the same time America and Britain were buying Angolan oil at a markedly reduced rate from the Soviet-backed MPLA. And they continued to do so throughout the eighteen-year war—which, in effect, rages on. It was a war in which more than 500,000 Angolans were killed. A further 200,000 were maimed, widowed or orphaned, while an inestimable number remain unaccounted for. Due to the fact that more than 20 million landmines remain unexploded beneath Angolan soil, these figures continue to rise, even today. But hey, at least it was a war that provided the West with cheap oil.

This was the country, the situation, into which Diana immersed herself heart and soul in January 1997, six months prior to her death. And it has to be said she did so to great effect—a fact that upset a good deal of very powerful people, on both sides of the Atlantic. Indeed, Diana's campaign spotlighted a major human rights problem which had been caused, on the one hand, by the political and corporate ambitions of the US and US-based multinationals. And on the other, by the financial ambitions of the British Royal Establishment. It was never simply the issue of landmines that prompted the Establishment to publicly brand Diana a "loose cannon". It was never simply the issue of landmines that prompted such a knee-jerk reaction from both British and US oligarchs, though this in itself was indeed sufficient to ruffle a fair few military-industrial feathers. No doubt about that.

But rather it was the fact that, by highlighting the Angolan problem, inadvertently Diana threatened to prise open a very unsavoury can of worms. British and US-built landmines were still ripping life and limb from Angolan women and children. British and US-based corporations were still pirating oil and diamonds in illegal arms trade-offs. MI-6 and CIA agents were—still are—active on Angolan soil. Indeed, since the early 1970s, MI-6, acting on behalf of the Royal Establishment and its neo-colonial cartel of Africa-based corporations and NGOs, has been secretly financing and equipping teams of mercenaries to carry out its dirty work in Angola, at least in part to ensure the Royal Family's vested financial interests there. In short, as well as upsetting some of the world's most powerful arms-trade godfathers, by taking the world's media to Angola, Diana threatened to expose some of the Royal Family's most unethical undeclared investments, as well.

Angolagate

But the Royal Family's vested interests in Angola were only part of the scandal under threat of being exposed. At the time of Diana's media-hyped landmines campaign in that country, the CIA was also busy trying to conceal what would later emerge as 'Angolagate'—effectively an arms-for-oil trade-off involving top French businessmen, the Angolan government and the Bush-Cheney oil syndicate. In short, in March 2002 the British-based human rights organization, *Global Witness*, revealed that George W. Bush, Dick Cheney and other major US oil oligarchs were involved in deals in which Jean-Christian Mitterand, son of the former French president, in partnership with French businessman Pierre Falcone and notorious Russian-born Israeli, Arkadi Gaydamak, funnelled billions of illicit dollars in arms and loans to Angola's government in return for lucrative oil contracts. In a report entitled *All The President's Men*, published by Global Witness, French oil giant Total-Fina-Elf was named as benefiting from these deals (see *The Paget Report*). But so were Texaco, Chevron, Philips Petroleum, BP-Amoco and Exxon Mobil, as well as Dick Cheney's old firm Halliburton and its subsidiary, Brown & Root, which secured a $68 million US Export-Import Bank loan for Angola in 1998 in return for future oil, part of a $1 billion loan scandal that year. At this time, of course, Dick Cheney was still CEO of Halliburton, and so would have benefited directly from these deals. As would a good number of the George W administration, many of whom worked for the afore-mentioned companies prior to joining the White House. Indeed, these companies, even today, are seen as a major power base propping up the Bush family's geopolitical ambitions. At the time of Diana's landmines campaign in Angola that syndicate was still preparing for office, true enough. But any hint of such a scandal, even then, could only have damaged those preparations. And the CIA, who also benefited massively from the scandal's proceeds, was not about to let that happen—certainly not at the hands of some meddlesome jet-set vamp like Diana. The CIA had invested decades of its time and resources in securing these deals. If all it took to keep the cash and oil flowing was to help MI-6 terminate the threat, then, hey—that's what allies are for, right?

As we know, back in the 1970s the CIA had trained and equipped Jonas Savimbi and his UNITA rebels in their struggle to gain power. Or more accurately, their struggle to gain control over Angola's oil fields and diamond mines. Dick Cheney in particular was an outspoken supporter of UNITA, as was Ronald Reagan, George Bush Sr, and other prominent right-wing oligarchs. But that was at the height of the Cold War, when America still feared Soviet oil gains more than it feared Soviet missiles. By the time of Diana's visits to Angola in the mid-1990s, things had changed; the Cold War was over and the man Ronald Reagan once referred to as the "*George Washington of Africa*" had lost favour with America—like Manuel Noriega, Saddam Hussein and Osama bin Laden, also at one time funded by the CIA, Savimbi had outlived his usefulness. He was now a threat to US oil interests; he had to go. Following the dissolution of the 1994 Lusaka Peace Agreement between former MPLA leader and now Angolan President, Jose Eduardo dos Santos, and the now problematic Jonas Savimbi, Bush, Cheney and the CIA turn-coated in favour of the massive oil revenues they were expropriating from Angola's black-gold reservoirs. Suddenly Savimbi was America's foe. At the same time dos Santos became America's ally; seemingly overnight he abandoned the Marxist principles for which he had so doggedly fought and converted to oil-based capitalism. All was now cosy; the new alliance was sealed. In consequence, the CIA and the Angolan Army, bolstered by units of US-based mercenaries, went after Jonas Savimbi in one of the most savage and bloodiest offensives in modern guerrilla warfare. Savimbi's UNITA rebels were finally crushed early in 1998, scarcely six months after Diana's death. Curiously, Savimbi himself, the man Reagan called the "*George Washington of Africa*", was killed on February 22—what would have been George Washington's birthday. The ironies of life, then.

Had Diana been alive today, of course, who knows what other facts might have emerged from this scandal? We already know that the Bush presidential campaign netted at least $200,000 via his links to Falcone; the money was donated by Falcone's wife, Sonia, through her health, beauty and sexual pleasure company, Essante Corporation, which, among other products, distributes a cream called Entisse, a Viagra substitute. Maybe this is the secret behind George Dubya's immutable smirk.

Or maybe it's just that he knows he's untouchable.

Sadly, Diana was not untouchable. Within weeks of her final visit to Angola she was dead, and in consequence, the eyes of the world closed on the plunder of Angola and the atrocities perpetrated in that country by Western governments. Indeed, the proceeds from Angolagate are still to this day serving to keep America and the West rich and powerful, while millions of Angolans are deprived even of the most basic necessities. Angola produces sufficient oil, diamonds and other natural resources ($3.5 billion in oil revenue alone in 2002) that none of its citizens should want for very much at all, yet three-quarters of the population live in abject poverty, on less than $1 a day. To add to this, every 3 minutes an Angolan child dies from preventable diseases (480 per day); 42% of Angolan children aged 5 or under are undernourished and underweight; and more than 3 million Angolans remain displaced within their own borders. The number of landmine-related deaths, amputations and other injuries remains astronomical.

In the meantime, the British Royal Establishment continues to wear Angolan diamonds in its Crown, and the US administration continues to steal Angolan oil with impunity, without any consideration for the consequences on Angola and her people. Indeed, the only person of any note who placed the Angolan people before diamonds and oil—before the money and power they breed—is no longer with us. One cannot help but note this fact.

— 13 —

THE LANDMINES TREATY

"**L**ast month I instructed a US team to join negotiations then underway in Oslo to ban all antipersonnel landmines. Our negotiators worked tirelessly to reach an agreement we could sign. Unfortunately, as it is now drafted, I cannot in good conscience add America's name to that treaty."

President Bill Clinton, September 17th, 1997.

Bosnia

As we have seen, by highlighting the landmines problem Diana inadvertently threatened to expose the international power games that accompany it. Some might say landmines play a relatively minor part in these games, and perhaps this is so. But let us not forget that there are somewhere in the region of 200 million landmines currently deployed around the world, a further 200 million stockpiled ready for use and an unknown number in circulation via the black market. In today's market that amounts to around $1.4 billion. To add to this, the worldwide ban on landmines proposed by Princess Diana was also to have included a total ban on the manufacture, sale and deployment of airborne mines—effectively cluster bombs, including depleted uranium cluster bombs, an evil weapon used liberally during the first Gulf War, in Afghanistan and during the second war in Iraq as well. Indeed, in Operation Desert Storm alone more than 10,000 cluster bombs were dropped on Iraq; at around $25,000 a piece, someone somewhere is making a tidy buck, especially when you realize that cluster bomb defence and neutralization systems run into $billions per fixed-price contract. Make no mistake, 'mines' are big business, even if they do only represent the tip of the arms-trade iceberg. But then, exposing even the merest tip of that iceberg none the less reveals the iceberg's existence, implying that, lurking deep beneath the revealed tip lies a mass of jagged, frozen ice so vast that its true immensity remains unknown, unseen. Certainly according to Stealth, it is the fact that the full extent of this iceberg was in danger of being revealed, if only by implication, that provoked such an instant and decisive reaction from those who wish to keep it concealed.

In short, then, Diana's landmines campaign in Angola threatened to become the *Titanic* of international arms trading. The 'unsinkable flagship' of corporate power was in danger of colliding with an iceberg that, until now, nobody had seen. The *Titanic* was in danger of sinking, and the ship's builders knew only too well that there were simply not enough lifeboats on board to save them all from drowning in the ice-flows of accountability. Fortunes would be lost. Heads would roll. Drastic measures were required, in particular when you consider that, as we know, Angola was not the only *Titanic* on the ocean that day. The Angolan situation was not alone in forcing this iceberg's tip to the surface. A similar situation existed in Bosnia, where for decades East and West have battled for political and economic control of the Balkan territories, and in the process, have left behind a legacy of millions of unexploded landmines. Diana, of course, would visit Bosnia some six months after her first trip to Angola. And once again she would take the world's media with her.

Indeed, in their efforts to avert yet another difficult situation, the powers-that-be did everything they could to prevent the princess's visit to Bosnia from going ahead. The problem was Diana exercised an uncanny knack of bringing out the humanity in people—of being filmed looking natural and easy in one-on-one situations with ordinary, everyday folk, no matter their nationality or their political bias. The last thing the authorities wanted was for us in the West to view the situation and the people in Bosnia—in particular Bosnian Serbs—through sympathetic or humanitarian eyes. The situation in Bosnia was too volatile: there were simply too many covert agendas being exercised via the Bosnian conflict, too many covert arms deals leading back to the British and American governments. The French government, as well, as we shall see. Indeed, the Balkans comprised little more than an economic and political laundry. And Diana was about to spotlight a mighty heap of dirty washing. No doubt about that.

But it is also the effectiveness of Diana's "*personal crusade*" that must be considered here. Suddenly the world was alerted to the sickening atrocities being perpetrated on innocent Bosnians and Angolans by Western-backed guerrilla warfare. Suddenly the fact that innocent people and children were being maimed and killed on a daily basis was headline news. The perpetrators, of course, did not appreciate the fact. And neither were they happy that public opinion was being so massively influenced in support of a proposed worldwide ban on landmines. Not even the most powerful military-industrial potentates can afford to turn their backs on public opinion (one reason why they go to such lengths to mould and manipulate that opinion via the media). The problem was, Diana was asserting a bigger influence on public opinion than their own propaganda machine was able to counter: the princess was out-manipulating the manipulators. According to our sources, this was a situation that demanded a swift and decisive solution. After all, if Diana was capable of so affecting public opinion with regard to landmines, then what next? What 'Diana campaign' would the public support next? Gulf War Syndrome? Palestine? Iraq?

For a moment at least, the entire corporate edifice was aquiver.

But not for long. Within six months of the campaign's start date, Diana would be dead. And the international concern engendered as a result of her campaign would, in large part, die with her. Though 'Angola' may remain a name etched dimly on people's minds, that innocent Angolans continue to face the threat of unexploded landmines, *daily*, has largely been forgotten. The fact is that, since the princess's death, the spotlight of public opinion has faded. Accordingly, concern in the corporate world has abated. The highly profitable trade in landmines and other, even more deadly weapons is today back on track. Whatever the truth behind the princess's premature death, the fact that she is no longer alive to spotlight these and other human rights issues means that those issues have quietly disappeared from public view, back behind the veil of corporate secrecy.

Did Diana's landmines campaign form part of the motive for her murder? We believe it did.

The Treaty

For those not yet convinced, there are, of course, other examples that highlight just how effective Diana's landmines campaign was. At the time of her visit to Angola, for example, it was estimated that for every person living in this war-torn African nation, there were at least two still-live antipersonnel landmines laying undetected—*unexploded*—beneath innocent feet. Many people living and working in Angola's open country fell victim to the mines on a daily basis (at the time of the princess's visit, more than 2,000 Angolans per month were losing their limbs as a result of stepping on an unexploded landmine—that amounts to around 70 people a day). The Red Cross was simply unable to cope with such a vast influx of casualties. For one thing, it was grossly under-funded. It needed cash to build and maintain the specialist surgeries necessary to care for these kinds of injuries. Plus, of course, it needed specialized equipment and an equally specialist team to operate it. Needless to say this costs money. And it was money the Red Cross simply did not have. Enter the Princess of Wales. During the year prior to the princess's visit, the Red Cross's landmines appeal failed to raise even £50,000—scarcely sufficient even to build the necessary surgeries, much less man them. In the year following the princess's much-publicized visits to Angola and Bosnia, on the other hand, the appeal raised a staggering £1,200,000. And contributions were still pouring in months after her death. But perhaps what made Diana's contribution even more telling is the fact that, almost single-handedly, she forced the issue of antipersonnel landmines into the forefront of the political arena. Until the princess's intervention, of course, the powers-that-be had been more than content to keep this issue locked safely away in the political closet. Following her visits to America and her private talks with Bill and Hillary Clinton, however, the issue was suddenly top of the political agenda. Indeed, as a result of her meetings with the Clintons, a plan was drawn up that would—and should—have amounted to a Landmines Treaty being signed by all the leading industrial and military powers. Clinton himself even agreed to the deal. In consequence, a conference was arranged for 18th September, 1997, to be held in Oslo, and to be attended by the leaders of the world's most powerful nations. However, in the meantime it would seem that someone whispered a quiet word in Bill Clinton's ear. According to our sources, Clinton was reminded in no uncertain terms that it was the very corporate czars he was about to betray whose complicity kept him in office. Enter the CIA and the President's 'sex-at-work' problems: should Clinton honour his pledge and sign the deal in Oslo, he was warned, then he would be facing serious problems, possibly even impeachment. In fact the wheels of what Hillary Clinton would later describe as a "*right-wing conspiracy*" against her husband were already in motion; the Paula Jones and Monica Lewinsky scandals were about to break, big time. As a distraught Monica Lewinsky commented during an interview with Channel 4's Jon Snow (screened in Britain as a *Dispatches Special*, 4th March, 1999):

"There's definitely a right-wing conspiracy to destroy the President. And I think I've been used as a pawn."

The threat had been issued. In consequence, the 42nd Presidency of the United States was in jeopardy of becoming only the second presidency in history to be brought to its knees. If Clinton wished to fulfil his term in office, we were told, then he would have to renege on his pledge to Princess Diana and refuse to sign the Landmines Treaty. And what is more, he would need to maintain his stance in this regard for the rest of his term in office.

"This was the reason the CIA got involved with MI-6 to take care of the princess," our sources said. "MI-6 had their own reasons for wanting rid of Diana. But from this point on it became a joint operation ... Diana's fate was effectively sealed then."

And further: "The CIA assured Clinton that Diana would be out of the way by the time the deal was to be signed... [by the time of] the conference in Oslo. With Diana gone, they knew that public focus on the [landmines] issue would diminish quickly—and that would leave the way clear for Clinton to opt out of the agreement without too much fuss."

Whether or not there were other factors involved in Clinton's sex-at-work scandal, we do not know. But what is clear is this. On 17th September, 1997, less than three weeks after Diana's death and the day before the Oslo Conference convened, President Clinton addressed a press conference at the White House, in the Roosevelt Room, where he told the waiting world:

"Last month I instructed a US team to join negotiations then underway in Oslo to ban all antipersonnel landmines. Our negotiators worked tirelessly to reach an agreement we could sign. Unfortunately, as it is now drafted, I cannot in good conscience add America's name to that treaty."

In good conscience? Or to save his political ass? Either way, as a result of this last-minute U-turn—as our sources rightly predicted—on February 12th, 1999, President Clinton duly survived impeachment.

14

THE MEDIA
AND THE
BACKLASH

"When it comes to fighting a war, the Establishment can get very nasty indeed... For all her undoubted popularity, if [Diana] continues to rock the boat in this way, the Establishment will simply get rid of her."

British author, *A.N. Wilson,* commenting in the *New York Times,* November 25th, 1995— in response to Diana's Panorama interview, screened by the BBC in Britain on November 24th, 1995.

Establishment Views

Back in Britain, senior politicians and civil servants, plus other outspoken Establishment pillars, bitterly disagreed with Diana's landmines campaign. And they said so in no uncertain terms.

Former Foreign Office Minister, Sir Nicholas Bonsor, for example, commented during an interview conducted for ITN's *The Trouble With Diana*:

"For the princess to put herself so overtly at the head of a political campaign to abandon all landmines, and deprive our own soldiers of the use of such landmines, was in my view wrong of her."

And further: "Princess Diana was potentially a threat to the

116

Establishment and a threat to the Royal Family."

Indeed she was.

Well-known constitutional historian, David Starkey, added his support.

"What is wrong, I suppose, is that she's called the Princess of Wales. She's quasi-royal. And we have had a Royal Family which, since the early nineteenth century, has steered very clear of politics. And a very good thing, too."

Possibly, if it were true. But it isn't. While on the face of it members of the Royal Family may appear to steer clear of politics, their political opinions and personal views are heard loud and clear within the hallowed halls of Westminster and Whitehall alike. There can be few doubts about that.

In any event, Diana, along with the vast majority of ordinary British people, did not see her campaign as overtly political. At least not in a 'party political' context. Though the politics of landmines deployment was undoubtedly spotlighted—the politics of international arms-profiteering, equally so—the idea that the campaign was Diana's way of making a stand on behalf of New Labour is quite simply absurd. At a speech given by the princess at London's Royal Geographical Society (12th June, 1997), she stated her humanitarian motives in no uncertain terms. At the same time she declared her utter refusal to let the issue drop. Aided by her friend, the former Minister of Information (1962-1964), columnist with *The Daily Telegraph* and fellow anti-landmines campaigner, Lord Deedes, she compiled a moving and powerful speech which stated in no uncertain terms her stance on the matter. She bravely attacked the arms trade for continuing to manufacture and sell these cowardly weapons. Moreover, she delivered a powerful and unambiguous broadside aimed squarely at the British Establishment, in particular at those she openly referred to as "*those ghastly Conservatives*"— who, she maintained, had wrongly interpreted her visit to Angola as a political statement in favour of Labour policy.

"It was not," she plainly told them. "I am not a political figure. And as I said at the time, and I'd like to reiterate now, my intentions are humanitarian."

And clearly they were.

Right-wing tabloids disagreed, however. Unashamedly siding with their Establishment supporters and sponsors they described the speech as "*an unusual gesture of support for the Blair [Labour] administration*". At the same time *The Daily Telegraph* accused her of having been caught "*on the wrong side of the political fence*". And Sir Nicholas Bonsor added:

"There was a great difference of opinion between the Conservative Government and the successor Government about landmines. And for the princess to take a stance in favour of one and against the other [is] not ... a proper role for a member of the Royal Family."

Frank Cook MP, representing the All-Party Landmines Committee, however, strongly disagreed. "It's a cross-party issue," he told ITN's *The Trouble With Diana*, screened in Britain over the Christmas period, 1997. "[It's] nothing to do with individual parties. And it's quite wrong to make it so ... Frankly I'm disappointed that any Member should be so short of media coverage that they've got to descend to this level."

But it wasn't only the issue of landmines that was getting Diana into trouble at this point; her private life was being severely criticized, as well. A week and a half after her famous landmines speech she decided to take her sons to the cinema. It was Prince William's birthday, and quite on impulse she took the boys to see a film called *The Devil's Own*. What she did not know, however, was that the film was violent and pro-IRA. Needless to say, the media leapt at the opportunity. Once again they publicly crucified her.

Though genuinely upset that she had failed to check the film's content beforehand, and although she publicly apologized for her actions immediately following the incident, this latest faux pas—the so-called 'movie affair'—was of course further ammunition for her critics. And perhaps more to the point, it was to prove yet another severe setback for her landmines campaign. It just so happened that during this same week she was due to attend a Commons Committee meeting. It was important she attended this meeting as it could and would have gained her much-needed political support for her campaign. Amidst all the brouhaha surrounding the 'movie affair', however, she was forced to cancel her attendance. The reason given for the cancellation was that Establishment protests over her public conduct and political interference had made her attendance at the meeting "*untenable*".

Once again, it seemed, the Establishment had won the day. But not the war. Not yet, anyhow.

In response to the cancellation of the Commons Committee meeting, Diana released a statement expressing her sadness and extreme frustration. It is reported that the cancellation caused her much personal regret. However, she would not be deterred from continuing her battle against the manufacture, sale and deployment of antipersonnel landmines. Quite the opposite. On 8th August, 1997, just three weeks before she died, Diana flew with Lord Deedes to Bosnia in order to further comfort the victims of these abominable weapons. And once again, the world's media, together with MI-6, followed her every move.

What The Media and The Establishment Thought About Dodi and Diana

"You can't help regretting that this beautiful woman has chosen someone so trivial."

Sarah Bradford,
the Queen's Biographer, 1997.

"I thought that the Fayeds were acting in a rather biased way—to try and get this young girl to become almost part of their inner circle. And I really didn't like it one little bit. And I don't think many people did."

Sir James Hill,
Conservative Constitutional Committee, 1997.

"I thought at the time that she was allowing her position to be prostituted. She was being exploited for publicity purposes by the Al Fayeds...
She seemed at her worst, at her most selfish."

Bruce Anderson,
political columnist, The Spectator, 1997.

"I'm a particularly conservative Conservative. I like to think the future King of England at least starts off the job without a blemish. And I don't think he could have done with Dodi as the Stepfather."

Sir James Hill,
Conservative Constitutional Committee, 1997.

———— • ————

"There's no doubt that those who care about the Royal Family were very worried in those last few months as to what this girl would get up to. I mean, she seemed capable of anything. She seemed reckless, almost demented."

Bruce Anderson,
Political Columnist, The Spectator, 1997.

———— • ————

"I think it was dangerous for the Royal Family to have a member of its clan, as it were, behaving in that kind of irresponsible fashion ... Princess Diana was potentially a threat to the Establishment and a threat to the Royal Family."

Sir Nicholas Bonsor,
ex-Foreign Office Minister, 1997.

———— • ————

"If Lady Diana Spencer had known the record of this family [the Windsors] ... she might have learnt that the Princess of Wales is a title written in tears."

Germaine Greer,
November, 1995.

———— • ————

*"The important thing is that [Diana] should set limits to her ambitions.
She has said she will not go quietly. She must, however, not go too far...
The people know how much change in the system they desire. If the Princess exceeds their wishes, it is she who will become the casualty, not the monarchy."*

John Keegan,
military historian and former Daily Telegraph
defence correspondent, November 1995.

———•••———

"No one can deny that this was a skilfully organized attack on the institution of the monarchy itself. Not just on Prince Charles. Not just on the Queen, whom Diana obviously hates. But on the monarchy...
The example of Wallis Simpson and Edward VIII should be enough to tell Diana that when it comes to fighting a war, the Establishment can get very nasty indeed, and that for all her undoubted popularity,
if she continues to rock the boat in this way, the Establishment will simply get rid of her."

British author, **A.N. Wilson**, commenting in the **New York Times** *(25th November, 1995) in response to Diana's Panorama interview, screened by the BBC in Britain on 24th November, 1995.*

———•••———

MI-6 Special Report on The Fayeds

The quote/article originally intended to occupy this space was written by Andrew Golden and appeared in the *Sunday Mirror*, Early Edition, 31st August, 1997—the day Diana died. However, for reasons best known to Colin Myler, editor of the *Sunday Mirror* at the time, we were refused permission to reproduce the article in its original form. Having taken legal advice on this matter—and having further discussed the matter with our publisher—we were informed that in fact we could reproduce the article in abridged or paraphrased form on the grounds that *(a)* it is in the public interest to do so, *(b)* at the time of writing the investigation into Diana's death is still deemed a 'current event" and *(c)* it is deemed 'fair usage'. On moral grounds, of course, we feel that we are fully vindicated in reproducing at least the main points of the article anyway, as they convey the general climate in respect of the Royal Family's attitude towards Diana, in particular her relationship with Dodi Fayed, at the time of, and immediately prior to, her death. They also suggest a Palace-sanctioned MI-6 action against Diana and Dodi during the time-frame in which the couple mysteriously died.

Queen 'To Strip Harrods Of Its Royal Crest'

The article concerned, entitled *Queen 'To Strip Harrods Of Its Royal Crest'*, began:

"The Royal Family may withdraw their seal of approval from Harrods... as a result of Diana's affair with owner's son Dodi Fayed."

In other words, due to Diana's relationship with Dodi Fayed, the Queen had been advised by her senior Palace spooks to withdraw the Prince of Wales' royal crest from Harrods, the exclusive Knightsbridge store owned by Dodi's father, Mohamed Al Fayed. So said Andrew Golden reporting in the *Sunday Mirror*. The article went on to reveal that the *"Royal Family are furious about the frolics of Di, 36, and Dodi, 41, which they believe have further undermined the monarchy"*. Prince Philip *"in particular"*, the article reported, was extremely unhappy about the relationship, even though Diana had for some time been ostracized from Royal circles and divorced from Prince Charles (who at the time, of course, had his own relationship problems to contend with). Indeed, the article reported that Prince Philip had *"made no secret as to how he feels about his daughter-in-law's latest man, referring to Dodi as an 'oily bed-hopper'"*.

But what is even more intriguing is that, according to this same article, *"MI-6 [had already] prepared a special report on the Egyptian-born Fayeds"*, which was to be presented to the Queen and The Way Ahead Group—effectively the Queen's personal advisory board and spin surgery. The Windsors were to *"sit down with their senior advisers and discuss policy matters"*, the article confirmed. The article also included quotes from an interview conducted with *"a friend of the royals"*, who said:

"Prince Philip has let rip several times recently about the Fayeds ... He's been banging on about his contempt for Dodi and how he is undesirable as a future stepfather to William and Harry... Diana has been told in no uncertain terms about the consequences should she continue the relationship with the Fayed boy..."

The article concluded: "...*Now the Royal Family may have decided it is time to settle up* [italics in original copy]."

It should be reiterated that this story appeared in the Early Edition of the *Sunday Mirror* on the day Diana died (31st August, 1997); it was already in print when news of Diana's death reached Britain. It was then withdrawn; it did not appear in subsequent editions. In consequence, most people in Britain (and elsewhere) did not get to read it—one reason we felt it imperative that at least its bones be included here.

If you would like to obtain a copy of the original article, as we did, then we suggest you contact Historic Newspapers, PO Box 3, Newton Stewart, DG8 6TQ, Scotland—and request a back-copy of the *Sunday Mirror*, Early Edition, 31st August, 1997. It should cost you somewhere in the region of £10 (or around US $20 including postage and packing).

15

NEW REVELATIONS AND CLOSING THOUGHTS

by Jon King

"This particular phase in my life is the most dangerous. My husband is planning an accident in my car, brake failure and serious head injury, in order to make the path clear for him to marry."

Extract from a note written by *Princess Diana* in October 1996, ten months before her death.

A Chilling Prediction

In October 2003, perhaps the most disturbing revelation thus far came to light, certainly in terms of corroborating the information revealed to me by Stealth a week prior to Diana's death. It also tended to corroborate information revealed to both John and myself regarding the 'constitutional crisis' foreseen by the Royal Establishment in the event of Prince Charles's proposed marriage to Camilla Parker Bowles (see **Chapter 10**).

But perhaps most disturbing of all, when viewed in the light of new information recently received by us, this same revelation cast a chilling shadow over the *real* motives behind Stealth's initial disclosures to me. Indeed, it tended to support the emerging possibility that we had been set up.

In his book, *A Royal Duty*, Diana's former butler Paul Burrell revealed that the princess was aware of a high-level plot to kill her as long ago as October 1996. It was then, a full ten months before she died, that Diana penned the now infamous note that predicted in alarming detail her own demise by 'road traffic accident'. She then gave the letter to Mr Burrell for safekeeping, as "*insurance*" for the future—so that, in the event that she did indeed die in a 'road traffic accident', the world would know that the likely cause of that 'accident' was not misfortune or reckless driving, but assassination. According to Mr Burrell, at least, this was the reason Diana wrote the note and gave it to him as "*insurance*".

In the note, which contained a chillingly accurate prediction of her own murder, Diana cited "*brake failure and serious head injury*" as the most likely cause of her death. She even named the person she suspected of being behind the plot. Staggeringly, and perhaps surprising to some, that person was none other than her newly estranged husband, Prince Charles. It should be said that we have uncovered no evidence that Charles was personally involved in Diana's death. But that doesn't mean he's innocent. Tracks leading back to the powerful institution he heads up are many and compelling. Certainly it is known that the shadowy spooks who band themselves around the unpopular prince have made no secret of the fact that they wanted rid of Diana, as we shall see a little later. Indeed, as the princess herself confided to Paul Burrell almost a year before her death, Charles's band of grey-suited spooks and protectors were constantly conniving ways to "*destroy her*". This plus the princess's flagrant suspicions that Charles himself was plotting her death—"*in order to make the path clear for him to marry*"— certainly gives weight to allegations of a high-level Royal conspiracy, in particular when we bring Camilla Parker Bowles back into the frame.

As we explained earlier, at about the time Diana wrote her letter, Britain's Royal Establishment was beside itself over fears that Charles would announce his intentions to marry his long-term mistress. In light of Diana's note, we may presume the princess herself shared these same fears—a fact that surely lends weight to the information we received from our own sources in this regard. We recall, for example, that the plot to murder the princess was being discussed very seriously at this time, and that from these discussions not one, but two plots were formulated—one: an MI5 plot to assassinate Camilla Parker Bowles; two: an MI-6 plot to assassinate Princess Diana: both by 'road traffic accident'. So far as we are concerned, Diana's note suggests very strongly that she had been made aware of this conspiracy, and furthermore, that she suspected Charles of being behind the MI-6 plot to assassinate her. From an Establishment perspective, of course, the major concern at this time was the 'constitutional crisis' foreseen in the event that

Charles pressed ahead in his ambition to marry Camilla. All kinds of problems were envisaged in this regard—not least that, constitutionally speaking, Camilla could not become Queen so long as Diana remained alive. This in itself must surely speak volumes.

But the biggest problem by far was that the Church of England forbids the remarriage of divorcees in church. As Supreme Governor of the Church of England, an office Charles will assume on his accession to the Throne, the divorced prince could not, under the existing rules, marry his divorced mistress, either in church, or indeed, with the Church's blessing. Result? Stalemate: the most damaging crisis the Establishment had faced in centuries.

In their efforts to rectify the problem, Establishment czars proposed several unparalleled measures. Perhaps unsurprisingly, these measures included moves to relax the rules regarding the remarriage of divorcees in church. But the measures went even further. At one point Britain's Lord Chancellor even considered disestablishing the Church altogether, an unprecedented move that would not only have seen Britain become a secular state for the first time in its history. It would also have amounted to the biggest constitutional reforms in Britain since Henry VIII set eyes on Anne Boleyn. This is how far the Establishment was prepared to go in the autumn of 1996 in its efforts to solve the 'constitutional crisis' caused by Charles's wanderlust. Like Henry before him, it seems, Charles wanted rid of one wife *"in order to make the path clear for him to marry"* another one—an opinion expressed by Diana in her note and an allegation that surely gives rise to the following question:

If, like Henry before him, Charles's influence is such that the nation's constitution can be ripped up and rewritten purely to suit his marital ambitions, then what other indulgences might he be granted? A good old-fashioned 'off with her head' scenario at the hands of the royal executioner, perhaps? No, of course not—not these days.

A 'road traffic accident', then, something altogether less conspicuous, more deniable—something executed by agencies whose prowess in such operations has been cultivated over decades, and whose close ties to the Royal Household are legendary? Certainly from the content of her note we know that Diana feared precisely this possibility—that Charles was plotting her death; and what's more, that her death would, like that of her former bodyguard, Sgt. Barry Mannakee, be the result of a well-rehearsed, premeditated 'deniable operation' in the form of a road traffic accident. Given the uncanny similarities between Diana's prediction and the manner in which she actually died, of course, this is a line of enquiry the Royal coroner must surely explore in full when the inquest eventually opens.

It is also of interest to note that Diana specifically cited "*brake failure*" as the most likely cause of any attempt on her life. Indeed, it is of particular interest when we consider that, according to the official French report—mysteriously leaked to Britain's *Daily Mail* (Saturday, January 24, 2004)—the Mercedes in which Diana died did indeed suffer brake failure immediately prior to the crash. The report concluded that the brakes failed to work as the Mercedes entered the crash tunnel, and in consequence, Henri Paul was forced to try and slow the vehicle down by ramming the automatic gear lever into neutral. This conclusion was arrived at following analysis of the crash wreckage by the Institut de Recherche Criminelle de la Gendarmerie Nationale (IRCGN), the official French police research establishment near Paris. According to the IRCGN team, witnesses heard an "*enormous engine noise*" immediately prior to impact—the result of Henri Paul's sudden gearshift, they concluded. They also concluded that Henri Paul applied this manoeuvre by mistake; the fact that he was unaccustomed to driving the vehicle, they deduced, caused him to 'mistakenly' make the gearshift. A strange conclusion, given the circumstances.

But even if this theory is correct, it would seem that a very obvious and fundamental question has been entirely overlooked. Namely: what actually caused the brakes to fail? Sure, if Henri Paul suddenly realized his brakes had mysteriously failed then it's certainly reasonable to assume he would have been forced to make an impromptu corrective manoeuvre—like ramming the automatic gear lever into neutral in an attempt to slow the vehicle down. But this still doesn't explain what caused the brakes to fail in the first place. On the contrary, it simply raises further questions that the IRCGN team inexplicably failed to address. *What was the cause of the failure? Bad fortune? Or foul play?* The plain fact is it simply must have been one or the other. We leave you to draw your own conclusions. Our conclusion is this:

Based solely on the evidence presented in this book, we contend that Henri Paul was the victim, not simply of bad fortune, but of a tried and trusted assassination operation known as the 'Boston brakes' (see *Chapter 3*).

We contend that Henri Paul's brakes failed not because of some luckless mechanical failure, but *because they had been tampered with*. They were meant to fail. Henri Paul's forced attempt to slow the vehicle down by ramming the automatic gear lever into neutral was thus an instinctive reaction, not a 'mistake'. Indeed, there was little else he could have done.

In any event, given the extraordinary findings of the IRCGN team, Diana's prediction that "*brake failure*" would be the cause of her death becomes all the more pertinent. Indeed, ominous.

There is one further point to consider.

Given the evidence presented in this book, Diana's foreknowledge of her own demise should come as little surprise to any of us. As we know, she had already voiced her belief that the death of her former bodyguard, Sgt. Barry Mannakee, by 'road traffic accident', was in fact the work of MI5. This belief was subsequently confirmed by our own sources, who plainly told us that Diana's close relationship with Sgt. Mannakee had resulted in the bodyguard's death. Indeed, according to these same sources, MI5 was also behind the bungled attempt to assassinate Camilla Parker Bowles—again by 'road traffic accident'—only a few short weeks before Diana's own fatal crash. Little wonder, then, that Diana feared she too would meet this same deniable fate. As Paul Burrell stated in his book, the princess had become increasingly concerned for her safety during the two years leading up to her death, a sentiment echoed by Diana's former Private Secretary, Patrick Jephson, who revealed to the British tabloid, *The Sun*, in October 2003:

"Early in 1996 the Princess assured me... that somebody had cut the brake pipes of her car and that her apartments at Kensington Palace had been bugged."

In other words, at least eighteen months prior to her death, Diana already suspected that someone was out to get her. Moreover, she believed she knew who that someone was. And if Diana was aware of a plot to assassinate her at least eighteen months before she died, surely it follows that, as our sources confirmed, select members of the security and/or intelligence community would also have known about it. Certainly Stealth (CIA) and at least two members of British intelligence whom we spoke to, claimed to have known about the plot "*months*" in advance of its execution. It was Stealth, of course, who first informed us a week before Diana's death.

And it was our sources within British intelligence who subsequently confirmed in some corroborative detail what Stealth had already said. Naturally Diana's disclosure falls short of proving any of this beyond doubt. But it does go a long way towards substantiating the fact that a plot indeed existed, and that, a week before the princess's death, characters like Stealth were already in place to ensure that plot's success.

Which brings me to a more recent and somewhat unsavoury development with regard to the motives behind Stealth's disclosures.

Gagged

I had always wondered why I'd been singled out as a recipient of the extraordinary information Stealth had to offer (see Chapter 7), and my concerns were further underlined by a recent conversation with one of our most trusted sources. After all, why did Stealth not approach the editors of the national press? Or perhaps better still, the TV news networks? Why did he choose a freelance journalist like myself as his herald when he could have chosen CNN?

I have battled with this question from the very beginning. Now, having discussed this point at some length with the abovementioned source, John and I believe we may have stumbled on the answer.

Immediately following Diana's death, the internet became jammed up with various theories about who killed Diana and why. It was Britain's Royal Mafia—otherwise known as MI-6—some said, because Diana had become a serious threat to the monarchy. It was the CIA and the US-based military-industrial complex said others, because Diana's landmines campaign had threatened to expose the lucrative though covert 'arms-for-oil-and-diamonds' deals that plagued Angola at the time, still do—deals largely brokered by the CIA. And there was a seemingly endless cacophony of other, often more exotic theories, as well. Diana was an angel incarnate who was killed by the 'lizards' who rule the world, was one of the more imaginative claims. She was still alive, was another; the whole affair had been staged to free Diana from the pressures of celebrity life, and she and Dodi were now secretly living on some idyllic island in the sun, far away from it all. Another theory put forward was that Dodi, and not Diana, had been the target; he was the nephew of the world's most notorious arms dealer, Adnan Kashoggi, the theory's perpetrators proclaimed, and his relationship with the world's most successful anti-landmines campaigner was simply not acceptable. Of course, for us the web of interconnected motives for Diana's death was vastly more complex than any one of these theories alone could explain. But the most compelling motive of all, we contend, is simply that Diana had become so famous, so popular, that not only was this 'loose cannon' beginning to seriously undermine the Monarchy and the Royal Establishment; not only was she in the process of establishing a sort of 'counter-monarchy', an alternative power base within the hallowed halls of the Royal Household (which she undoubtedly was); but also that her unprecedented popularity meant that she was now able to sway public opinion in her favour and against the status quo, something she was beginning to achieve to an ever more successful degree (her publicly-supported fight to make William king before his father, for example, which, on the Queen's death, would have elevated Diana to the office of Queen Mother, the most powerful office in the Royal Household after the monarch). This plus the Royal Establishment's uncompromising reaction to Diana's relationship with an Arab-Muslim in today's geopolitical climate, and the ever more plausible notion that she might have been pregnant with Dodi's child, was in the end sufficient to seal her fate. Of this we have little doubt.

But the question still remains: from where did the above mentioned plethora of exotic theories spring? True, some were more credible than others, and had been arrived at by a thorough and meticulous investigation of the facts. But others were sheer nonsense. Were these more exotic theories really the product of people's unbridled paranoia? Or were they the cleverly constructed brainchild of the very organizations involved in the assassination and the ensuing cover-up? Were these crazy theories deliberately promulgated in order to discredit the facts? Indeed, were they promulgated in order to discredit people like John and myself?

I cast my mind back to the first couple of years following Diana's death. It was true, of course. So many of the crazy theories circulating on the internet had indeed become associated with us. In turn this meant that, rather than being able to discuss the essential issues (why, for example, the British public should support a call for a public inquiry into Diana's death), I was forced instead to waste most of my time during media interviews endeavouring to justify our position—trying to explain that we were not 'conspiracy theorists', but investigative journalists; that we had uncovered, not 'conspiracy theory', but evidence. More recently, largely due to public opinion, the media has been forced to take our story a little more seriously, true. But we still have to contend with the odd snide remark and, more pertinently, certain commentators and presenters flippantly referring to us as conspiracy nuts. Not that we are offended personally; on the contrary, the words 'water' and 'duck's back' spring to mind. But these comments, together with the manner in which we are presented to the public, none the less continue to have an effect. First impressions are so often irreversible: if the first impression received by the public is that we are conspiracy theorists then conspiracy theorists we remain. Period. This, at least, would appear to have been the authorities' favoured method of gagging us.

But it wasn't the only one. When our book was first released in 2001, we received massive interest from a good many of Britain's national newspapers. We were hotly pursued for months by Britain's *Sunday Mirror*, for example, to whom we eventually agreed to give our story. It was to be the paper's cover story, we were told, the front-page headline, the story that would sell the paper and rock the world to boot. Twenty-four hours before it was due to be published, however, we were informed by a senior reporter at the paper that our book had received a DA Notice—effectively a directive from Whitehall preventing the mainstream media from publishing our story and/or promoting our book. Thus our front-page story was pulled. We'd been gagged.

And there is a further example. John and I have guested on any number of TV and radio talk shows regarding Diana's death; most of these interviews—though not all—were severely restricted, carefully monitored with regard to what we could or could not say, especially in the early days. On one such show, for example—the James Whale Show, on which John and I appeared in January 2002—we were told on air by the host James Whale that he had received a directive that very day warning him that our interview should be limited to certain questions or the national radio station for whom he worked would lose its licence. In other words, there were entire passages of our book that we were not allowed to refer to or speak about on air. It was like taking the witness stand and not being allowed to tell the whole truth— to give voice to those crucial bits of supporting evidence that make the rest of it make sense.

Once again, we'd been gagged.

Set Up

Given this situation, then, we were forced to find alternative ways of reaching the public, and despite the fact that it was already awash with 'Diana theories', the internet was an obvious platform. But by using this medium we were immediately laying ourselves open to association with some of the more exotic theories littering the net, which in turn, we now realize, played directly into the hands of those who were actively trying to discredit us. Following a recent conversation with one of our sources, in an attempt to try and gain a better understanding of what on earth was going on, I spent some time studying these internet theories, and in certain cases, tracing them back to their origins. OK, some were just plain crazy, and seemed to originate in the minds of those who can only be described as unstable or paranoid. But some, it turned out, unquestionably originated with someone I knew to be an MI5 plant—a freelance broadcast and tabloid journalist on the MI5 payroll. Others originated with someone I also suspected of being a plant, but have thus far been unable to confirm. But there are many other such plants in the media. It was renowned *Washington Post* journalist, Carl Bernstein, remember, famous for uncovering the Watergate scandal, who first revealed the sheer numbers of undercover intelligence agents posing as mainstream journalists. As stated in *Chapter 11*, Bernstein revealed that more than 400 journalists in the US alone were either deep-cover CIA agents, or they were on the CIA payroll. And as one of our own sources told us soon after the crash:

"The paparazzi in London and Paris are crawling with British intelligence. Some are freelancers on the MI-6 payroll, others are our own deep-cover agents."

Indeed, that the media are to some significant degree populated by both deep-cover and part-time intelligence agents is beyond question. The only question is: who are they?

We recall the words of the Queen in this regard.

"There are forces at work in this country about which we have no knowledge," she famously told Paul Burrell during their highly publicized meeting at Buckingham Palace, insinuating that those who had set Mr Burrell up on false theft charges would never be identified and brought to justice. The added insinuation, of course, was 'Keep looking over your shoulder, Paul, and be very careful what you say and do in future if you wish to avoid the wrath of the unseen "*forces*".'

Perhaps this is why, having kept Diana's letter secret for more than six years, Mr Burrell finally decided to publish it. Stepping out into the open is very often the best form of protection—the very reason John and I decided to go public with our story in the first place.

But the question remains: Who exactly are these unseen "*forces... about which we have no knowledge*"? Might they have included certain members of Charles's secret army of in-house protectors and hangers-on, one wonders? The powerful grey suits who populate the shadows of Buckingham Palace? Certainly it is clear that Diana thought this to be the case. And in light of the startling disclosures in her note, it would surely be remiss on our part not to suspect the same.

But might they also include the deep-cover intelligence agents we know to be working in the media? And might these deep-cover "*forces*" include those whose sole specific directive is to influence public opinion in favour of the 'accident theory'? We must bear in mind here that Stealth not only forewarned me of an imminent prime-target assassination—that it had been "*planned for a good many months*", that it would be "*bigger than Kennedy*" and that it would "*take place within days from now*". He also forewarned me of the carefully planned cover-up to be implemented immediately following the operation.

"Provision for public reaction has already been considered. They have good experience of how to deal with public reaction ... It's being taken care of as we speak. The media is being primed, as we speak."

So said Stealth on Saturday, August 23, 1997—one week prior to Diana's death. But what exactly did he mean? Who exactly was being "*primed*"? Who exactly are "*the media*"?

In light of a conversation that took place between myself, John Beveridge and someone who provided us with invaluable information towards the beginning of our investigation, and a second, more recent conversation with a different but equally well-placed source, both John and I have begun to wonder if we too might have been "*primed*"—if we were used as unwitting pawns in an insidious plan to disseminate, not disinformation as such, but 'conspiracy theory', as much if not all of the evidence surrounding Diana's death has come to be branded. At the time, I perhaps somewhat naively took "*the media*" to mean the national newspapers and broadcast networks. When Stealth said "*the media is being primed*" I immediately assumed he meant that MI5/MI-6 were already preparing what the mainstream media would subsequently be directed to disseminate. And in the main, we still hold this to be true.

But of course, John and I were also journalists. By our own choice we were independent journalists, true enough. But we were journalists just the same, part of the 'media', something neither of us ever really stopped to consider—until now. From the outset we were so deeply involved in our endeavours to uncover the evidence that neither of us gave so much as a second thought to the possibility that we might have been "primed" as well—that we too might have been set up, in this instance specifically to 'expose' information the authorities wanted exposed anyway; genuine information that would subsequently be associated with conspiracy theory by the media and debunked for that very reason. After all, this would serve well enough to ensure vital evidence and conspiracy theory became confused in the public mind. Which it did. Henri Paul's blood sample. The emergency operation. The Fiat Uno and its driver. The assassination technique known as 'the Boston brakes'. All of these points comprise legitimate evidence that needs proper and rigorous judicial examination. But before this can happen, of course, that evidence needs to be taken seriously. It has to be credible. If presented in a concerted campaign by the mainstream media there can be little doubt that it would indeed have been taken seriously, and thus that an independent judicial inquiry would almost certainly have been forced through long before now. When presented by independent journalists, however, so-called 'conspiracy theorists' claiming they were forewarned of Diana's death a week before it happened, it is easy to see how the 'evidence', by association, becomes confused with 'conspiracy theory', thus throwing doubt on the reliability of that evidence and, accordingly, making it less likely to be taken seriously enough that an inquiry would result—or indeed, in the event that an inquiry did result, that it would be taken seriously enough by the inquiry's presiding officials that they might be swayed in its favour.

And this is precisely what has happened. Whether we are right in our suspicions, of course, is a case to be proven. But the probability that we were set up is certainly the considered opinion of the source we recently spoke to. And in hindsight, I would have to say he has a valid point.

"I'm afraid it looks like you were set up, Jon," I was told in no uncertain terms. "It's obvious from what you've written that you conducted a very thorough investigation; most of what you've written is very solid and credible. But what you have to understand is that, so far as the mainstream media are concerned, it's all conspiracy theory. They report it as conspiracy theory because that's the directive from central office. That's how they get you. They take the weird and wacky theories about Diana, even make some of them up themselves, and [then] place them side by side with the real evidence. By association it makes the whole thing look ridiculous, and in the process I'm afraid it discredits you as well. This is how they discredit your findings; it's how they fool the public into believing what you say is nonsense."

In a separate conversation some short while later, this same source continued: "This is how we work it these days. The internet has made it very difficult ... It's become virtually impossible to control or prevent the spread of information, so we have to 'help' it out into the public arena and then set about discrediting it. It's a very effective way of doing things ... The best-kept official secrets are the ones everybody knows about, but which have been turned around to seem preposterous so that no one really takes them seriously. Generally speaking, the public believe what the media tells them, and if the media tells them that what you've uncovered is conspiracy theory, well that's what they'll believe. It's simple but very effective."

He added, wryly: "We no longer shoot people like you; we use them to our best advantage!"

Although this last statement was offered in good faith, and good humour, none the less both John and I realized its import clearly enough.

Closing Thoughts

So there we have it. Perhaps we were set up, perhaps not. But either way we have endeavoured in so much as our time and resources have permitted to proceed with diligence. We set out to uncover the facts surrounding Diana's death, and to present those facts to the public. This we have done. Now, as each day goes by, the seemingly endless stream of 'new revelations' continues to unfold, each one in turn seeming to corroborate even further the information and evidence presented in this book. Most recently, for example, we finally learned the truth about Diana's secret affair with her former bodyguard, Sgt. Barry Mannakee—indeed, that the princess not only had an affair with Sgt. Mannakee, but that she planned to run away with him and make their relationship permanent. Until this latest revelation was aired publicly on America's NBC network (December 2004), in a videotape recorded in 1992 by Diana's personal voice coach, Peter Settelen, any mention of an affair between the princess and Sgt. Mannakee was vehemently denied by the Royal Household and ridiculed in the press. Certainly when we first revealed the affair in the hardback edition of this book, we were shot down in flames by those seeking to cover it up. Now it is common knowledge. The fact that the princess herself is seen and heard on the tape to confess to the affair means it can no longer be denied and covered up. The fact that she also states on the tape that she believes her lover was "*bumped off*" means that our own evidence in this regard becomes all the more admissible. The fact, moreover, that Diana says she learned of Mannakee's death as she travelled to a premiere at the Cannes Film Festival with her then husband, Prince Charles, who turned to her and casually informed her that her former lover had been killed in a 'road traffic accident', means that Prince Charles knew about the affair, as well. And yet, following Diana's death, also by 'road traffic accident', he said nothing. Extraordinary. While the rest of us drew the obvious and inevitable comparison between the manner in which Diana and Mannakee had perished, Charles elected to sit smugly behind the Royal Household's denial of the affair as though it was idle gossip—when in fact it was admissible evidence. Indeed, it was the very basis upon which public suspicion over Mannakee's death was founded, which in turn, of course, gave rise to further suspicions over the 'road traffic accident' in which Diana herself died.

In short, knowledge of Diana's love affair with Sgt. Barry Mannakee was crucial to the investigation into the princess's death. And still Charles said nothing. Extraordinary.

Of course, there may be no substance at all to the very serious allegation made by Diana that Charles was planning to have her killed by 'road traffic accident'. But given the evidence presented in this book, together with the circumstances in which the princess died, it is none the less an allegation that needs proper and unobstructed investigation. In this regard we have to say we are dismayed to learn that Metropolitan Police Commissioner, Sir John Stevens, Britain's most senior police officer, has been appointed to head up the British investigation into Diana's death, and that, as part of that investigation, in response to Diana's videotaped confession, he has agreed to review the case regarding Barry Mannakee's death. Not that we are averse to this case being re-investigated. Just that we find it difficult to get excited knowing the outcome before the case is even opened.

And speaking of foregone conclusions ...

... As stated, Sir John has also been appointed to investigate claims that Diana was assassinated, and despite the fact that he is due to retire at the end of January, 2005, he has vowed to continue to head up the investigation until it is completed. We await his findings with baited breath. Indeed, we look forward to those unprejudiced findings being given a fair and unbiased hearing when presented to the Royal Coroner and his non-elected jury consisting of twelve hand-picked members of the Royal Household. Laughable, isn't it? Perhaps this is why the British public have already prejudged the inquest a whitewash.

FOOTNOTE I

MONDAY, FEBRUARY 14th, 2005:

The book has now been typeset and is ready to go to print. It is today, somewhat ironically, Valentine's Day. I say ironically because, just the other day, Prince Charles finally announced that he is to marry Camilla Parker Bowles in a civil ceremony to be held at Windsor Guildhall on April 8th. Since the announcement, the British press has beamed with photographs of the happy couple, wishing them well, depicting them as victims of an all too tumultuous fate: 'soul mates' who should now be permitted to live out the remainder of their lives in peace and uninterrupted happiness. While the Church hierarchy rumbles with discontent, its most senior denizens running this way and that in a slapstick attempt to smooth the way for the marriage to take place, the rest of us are expected to dutifully line the streets and wave our flags as we all sing *Rule Britannia*.

Well call me cynical, but for some reason I find it difficult to share in the celebrations. I mean, doesn't this announcement ring alarm bells in your ears, too? Isn't it all a little too convenient, in a perverse kind of way? Doesn't this fairy-tale ending read just a bit too much like a True Crime novel with a bitter, albeit predictable twist?

"This particular phase in my life is the most dangerous," Diana wrote in her now famous, chillingly predictive note. "My husband is planning an accident in my car, brake failure and serious head injury, in order to make the path clear for him to marry."

Whichever way you look at it, Diana simply could not have said it any more clearly.

Indeed, as I sit here digesting news of the announcement, I cannot help but marvel at the apathy and gullibility of the general public. I am quite simply stunned. The entire tragic scenario, it seems, has been played out before the eyes of the world, and all but the keenest of those eyes have chosen to avert their gaze from the terrible truth confronting them: the evidence, the facts. And the facts, ladies and gentlemen of the jury, suggest very strongly to me that Diana was murdered for the very reasons contained in her note—or at the very least that this possibility should be investigated with the utmost vigour within the confines of an independent judicial inquiry. I say this because, in the final analysis, either Diana was psychic, or the fulfilment of her prediction is the most chillingly pertinent coincidence I have ever come across. The only other explanation, of course, is that the princess really did know all along that Charles's protectors were planning her death by 'road traffic accident', *"in order to make the path clear for him to marry"*.

And that is why she included the allegation—the clue—in her note.

FOOTNOTE II

FRIDAY, MARCH 21st, 2006:

Incredibly a year has passed since we first completed this paperback edition and sent it off to the publisher for typesetting and printing. In that time we have been constantly communicating with our publisher about when to release the book—when would be the optimum moment to put this thing to bed, we wondered, once and for all? When would this seemingly endless saga finally draw to a close and provide us with at least some sort of meaningful conclusion, an 'ultimate verdict' that would signal the perfect time for publication? Problem is, for one reason and another, the Royal Inquest has been delayed several times in the past year or so; even though it was initially due to begin in earnest in January 2005, we are now told it will not begin until the spring of 2007, at the earliest. In consequence, the natural endpoint to our story has continued to elude us: the 'ultimate verdict' still has not arrived—which is why this paperback has taken so long to hit the bookshelves.

One of the main reasons our 'ultimate verdict' has failed to arrive, of course, is that Operation Paget, the official British investigation into Diana's death, headed up by former Metropolitan Police Chief, Sir John (now Lord) Stevens, remains ongoing. Initiated in January 2004, the investigation has certainly thrown up some surprises, and the media have shown no small amount of interest as a result. Indeed, with every new day, it seems, some or other fresh revelation has been leaked to the press, and it would appear that certain elements of the media now seem more prepared to entertain the idea that Diana might have been murdered, while some even appear to support the need to find answers.

Britain's *Daily Express* in particular has led the way in this regard, barely a week passing by without some or other new take on the story plastered across its front page (or at least what the paper *claims* is a new take). Ever since Lord Stevens shocked the nation by publicly announcing in January of this year (2006) that the case was "*more complex*" than he'd first thought, that his 'Diana Team' had thus far been unable to find answers to some of the key questions still festering at the murky heart of this mystery, and thus that he *"cannot rule out murder"*, the *Daily Express* has sensed a banquet, shadowing the investigation and its findings on an almost day-to-day basis, and serving up a veritable feast of juicy headlines as a result. 'DIANA CAR SWITCHED BEFORE DEATH CRASH'; 'DIANA WAS PREGNANT'; 'DIANA'S DRIVER WAS NOT DRUNK'; and 'DIANA: HOW SPY STARTED CAR DEATH CHASE'.

More recently the paper has even hinted at who might have been responsible for the crash, carrying such unusually bold headlines as: 'DIANA'S DEATH: SPIES FLASHED LASER BEAM AT CRASH DRIVER'. And even more specifically: 'DIANA'S DEATH: DIRTY TRICKS BY MI-6', referring to the spy agency's ongoing attempts to *"hide the truth over the death of Princess Diana"*.

'SPIES SABOTAGE DIANA INQUIRY' was yet another, even more recent and equally bold headline. Once again the accompanying story claimed that the secret services were plotting away behind the scenes to cover-up the truth about Diana's death.

And the headlines did not stop there. Following an interview on BBC Radio 2 with Mohamed al Fayed and his head of security, former high-ranking Scotland Yard police officer, John McNamara, the paper's front page proclaimed: 'DIANA DEATH DRIVER IN SECRET SPY PLOT' (*Daily Express*, Monday, May 22nd, 2006). The story proceeded to allege how chauffeur Henri Paul *"had a three-hour meeting with British and French spies on the night of the tragedy"*, that during the meeting he was paid the equivalent of £2000 in French francs and told to take a specific, pre-planned route from the Ritz Hotel so that the *"team on the ground"* would be able to *"track and eliminate"* the *"target"*. The target, of course, was Princess Diana.

A CCTV Conviction
An Autopsy Scandal
And A Royal Cover-up

Several further stories have recently come to light, the first of which casts serious doubt on the claim by French authorities that all 10 CCTV cameras lining the route from the Ritz Hotel to the Alma Tunnel, plus the 17 or so CCTV cameras alleged by the *Daily Express* to have been operating in the tunnel itself—no fewer than 27 cameras in total—mysteriously stopped working on the night Diana died. In consequence, the authorities say, no

CCTV footage of Diana's journey from the Ritz to the crash tunnel exists.

In stark contrast to this, however, it has recently emerged that a woman driving through the Alma Tunnel shortly after midnight, some fifteen minutes before the crash, was caught on camera and subsequently prosecuted for speeding. The woman in question, whose identity has not been released by the French authorities, was duly convicted on evidence provided by the very CCTV and speed-trap cameras the French claim were out of action on the night Diana died. Somewhat implausibly, they blame the failure on an alleged problem with the electricity supply, even though the electricity company in question denies this. And in any event, there would seem to have been little problem with the electricity supply fifteen minutes prior to the crash, because that is when the woman was caught on camera speeding through the tunnel where Diana's 'accident' occurred. Yet another contradiction in this seemingly endless stream of misrepresentations and mistruths comes to light, then. Indeed, each day seems to reveal its own contradiction, its own tiny piece of an emerging mosaic that spells 'cover-up'.

And speaking of cover-ups, it has more recently emerged that the pathologist who carried out the illegal embalming of Diana's body in the hours following her death has been accused of taking part in yet another, equally gruesome cover-up. Fifty-nine-year-old Professor Dominique Lecomte, who has consistently refused to speak about her involvement in Diana's autopsy, was at the centre of a second autopsy scandal some two years earlier—one that prompted the bereaved family to take legal action through the French courts in an attempt to uncover the truth.

But what makes this second autopsy scandal all the more relevant to the scandal surrounding Diana's autopsy is not only that it involves Professor Lecomte. Rather, that it also bears grisly similarities to the cover-up concealing the truth about the death of James Andanson.

Jean-Paul 'James' Andanson, we recall, a well known paparazzo and alleged MI-6 agent, was found dead in a burnt-out car in the middle of a secluded wood in southern France, four-hundred miles from where he should have been. It was Andanson, of course, who owned a white Fiat Uno identical to the one involved in the Paris crash, and whose offices at the famous Sipa press agency in Paris were raided by armed thugs shortly after his death. His photographic archive was stolen in the raid, never to be seen again, while the armed gang responsible for the raid, in which a security guard was shot, escaped and seemingly vanished, prompting many security experts to conclude that the so-called 'armed gang' was in fact a 'private security firm' working for French intelligence.

But what, in any event, is the connection between Andanson and Professor Lecomte?

In 1995, a leading French judge, Bernard Borrel, was found dead in the former French colony of Djibouti in East Africa. His charred and mutilated remains were discovered in the pit of a ravine near the country's capital. The official verdict, like that of James Andanson, who died in eerily similar circumstances, was suicide, but now lawyers for the judge's widow have unearthed new evidence that suggests Borrel was murdered.

It transpired that Judge Borrel had suspected Djibouti's president, Ismael Omar Guelleh, of being involved in the 1990 bombing of the Café de Paris, a restaurant in Djibouti. Borrel also suspected Guelleh of being involved in arms-trafficking and money-laundering, and was at the time advising Djibouti's Ministry of Justice in an attempt to bring Guelleh to trial. Evidently Guelleh was not best amused. Indeed, recently declassified documents belonging to DGSE (the French equivalent to MI-6) have revealed that Borrel was assassinated for 'political reasons' by order of Guelleh's entourage. It is hoped that Guelleh will now be forced to attend the International Court of Justice, the UN's official judicial court based in the Hague, to face questions about his involvement in Borrel's horrific death.

But that aside for the moment, comparisons must surely be drawn here, and in consequence, the question must surely be tabled: When the body of a senior judge involved in the investigation of high-level political bombings and arms-trafficking is found charred and mutilated, who on earth in their right mind would consider that he had committed suicide? Answer: Professor Lecomte, the very same woman at the centre of the scandal surrounding Diana's autopsy. It was Professor Lecomte who conducted the autopsy on Judge Borrel in 1995, and based on her autopsy report the French inquiry wrongly concluded that Borrel had committed suicide. It was also Professor Lecomte who conducted the autopsy on Henri Paul in 1997, and based on her autopsy report the French inquiry wrongly concluded that Paul had been drunk. Moreover, it was Professor Lecomte who conducted an external examination of Princess Diana, following which Diana's body was illegally embalmed. True, the order to carry out the embalming came from a higher source, but Professor Lecomte was once again at the centre of the scandal, just the same. An intriguing twist indeed.

There is an even more intriguing twist. Lord Stevens is now investigating claims that the order to prematurely embalm Diana's body originated with Sir Michael Jay, British Ambassador in Paris at the time. It has long been rumoured that the order originated with a senior British diplomat, but it is only recently that the diplomat in question has been openly identified and investigated. Of note is that Sir Michael Jay has since moved on from his post as British Ambassador in Paris to become head of Britain's Diplomatic Service—effectively the political face of MI-6. The plot not only thickens, it insinuates a sinister backstage collusion between British and French authorities in Diana's assassination and the ensuing, ongoing, high-level cover-up. In our opinion, Sir Michael Jay should be brought to account for these very serious allegations made against him.

And so, for that matter, should the Queen's former private secretary, Sir Robert Fellowes, who claimed he was on leave on the weekend of Diana's death. But new evidence has emerged that suggests Sir Robert (now Lord) Fellowes may actually have been in Paris on that fateful weekend. And moreover, that on the night Diana died he was seen at the British Embassy in Paris where he allegedly ordered a former British Foreign Office worker to leave his post and not return until told to.

The man in question, a staunch supporter of the Royal Family who at the time worked as a wireless operator at the British Embassy in Paris, was on duty at 9.53 pm when Diana and Dodi arrived back at the Ritz for dinner. Implausibly, Embassy officials have always denied any knowledge of Diana's presence in Paris that night, but this man tells a different story. All evening, he says, the communications room was abuzz with encrypted phone calls and messages relaying information on the princess's whereabouts back to Britain—Downing Street, Whitehall, the Palace. Though perhaps a little busier than usual, given Diana's high-profile presence in Paris, all seemed routine enough—until, that is, just before midnight, when the couple were preparing to leave the Ritz and head back to Dodi's apartment. It was at this point, according to the wireless operator in question, that two well-spoken Englishmen dressed in suits burst into the communications room and ordered the wireless operator to leave. The man who gave the order, the operator claims, was none other than Lord Fellowes himself, although it should be said that Fellowes denies the allegation, claiming instead that he spent the weekend at his Norfolk estate. None the less Lord Stevens and his investigation team took the allegation seriously enough that they recently questioned Lord Fellowes on his whereabouts that weekend. We will need to wait and see whether Lord Stevens pursues the matter further.

Meanwhile, the wireless operator who made the allegation remains adamant about who ordered him to abandon his post. *"It was that bastard Fellowes,"* he revealed to Britain's *Daily Mail* (Saturday, June 17th, 2006). *"He turfed me out of my own office. He was in Paris the night Diana died."*

Of course, the wireless operator could be mistaken. On the other hand, Lord Fellowes could have his dates mixed up. Either way seems a little implausible, true. But in any event, the question remains: If the Queen's private secretary truly was giving orders inside the British Embassy in Paris on the night Diana died, as alleged by the former British Foreign Office worker based in the embassy's communications room that night, then who authorized him to do so? Did someone from within the Royal Household authorize Lord Fellowes to take command of operations at the British Embassy in Paris that night? And if so, who? Fellowes, remember, was the Queen's private secretary—aside from blue-blood members of the Royal Family there were few, if any, more senior ranking officers in the Royal Household than Fellowes himself. So who had the authority to send him on a secret mission to Paris on the night Diana died? And why, in any case, would he expel a wireless operator who is bound by the Official Secrets Act? It makes little sense. Unless, of course, an 'above top secret' intelligence operation was in progress that night—an operation of such high sensitivity that the wireless operator in question was not permitted to know about it. Indeed, assuming the wireless operator is not mistaken, and Lord Fellowes actually was the one who ordered him from his post, what other explanation is there? Fellowes claims he was in Norfolk at the time, true enough, and presumably has an alibi to substantiate his claim. But even so, in light of this very serious allegation, the possibility that high-ranking officers from within the Royal Household were involved in Diana's death must surely be investigated with renewed vigour. The House of Windsor and its in-house mafia must not be immune from investigation, nor indeed, prosecution. The British public have a right to know who was behind the unlawful killing of their princess—no matter who they might be, no matter how senior their rank.

And no matter the consequences—the ramifications—should they be they are prosecuted.

A New French Inquiry
And A Feature-Length Movie

The latest offering in this seemingly endless eruption of sensationalist Diana headlines revealed perhaps the most important breakthrough to date. The front page of the *Daily Express*, Monday, August 21st, 2006, read: 'DIANA DEATH WAS NOT AN ACCIDENT—French Doctors Face Charges As New Cover-Up Evidence Emerges.'

Under pressure from Mohamed al Fayed's legal team, as well as from recent media reports and Lord Stevens's apparent desire to leave no stone unturned in his pursuit of the facts, the paper tells how the French inquiry into Diana's death has been sensationally forced to reopen. The Director of Public Prosecutions in France, it seems, has finally bowed to the welter of evidence suggesting that Henri Paul was not drunk at the wheel on the night of the crash, and in consequence, has ordered the deputy chief judge at Versailles, Thierry Bellancourt, to reinvestigate the two leading figures responsible for allegedly falsifying evidence to make it look as though Diana's death was the result of a simple 'drink-drive' accident. Leading pathologist, Professor Dominique Lecomte, together with Dr Gilbert Pepin, are to appear before Judge Bellancourt to defend the evidence they gave to the original inquiry. If it is proven that they *did* give false evidence, the paper claims, the two will face jail.

Professor Lecomte, we recall, the pathologist who conducted Henri Paul's autopsy, is also embroiled in a legal action in France regarding what appears to have been yet another sinister cover-up—that surrounding the mysterious death of Judge Bernard Borrel in 1995 (see above). But it is what went on during the autopsy of Henri Paul that has now come under the scrutiny of the French judiciary. According to the original, official French inquiry report, Professor Lecomte testified under oath that she took 3 blood samples from Henri Paul's body, but sensationally, a recently unearthed laboratory log book reveals that no less than 5 samples were actually taken, casting more than a little suspicion on the veracity of Professor Lecomte's testimony, as well as serious doubt on the validity of the blood samples themselves, in particular the two mysteriously undeclared 'extra' samples.

And moreover, shedding even further doubt on the authenticity of the blood samples taken that night, we have now discovered that, prior to the blood samples being taken, Professor Lecomte, together with her assistant,

Commandant Jean-Claude Mulés, unbelievably mistook the body of Henri
Paul for that of Dodi Fayed. In yet another bizarre twist it has recently
emerged that, on his arrival at the morgue, Commandant Mulés labelled
Henri Paul's body with the number 2146, unaware—presumably—that this
number had already been assigned to Dodi Fayed's body, making it now
virtually impossible to positively identify which blood sample came from
which body, much less how many samples were actually taken. The word
'travesty' springs to mind. Indeed, this plus the fact that Professor Lecomte is
now under investigation for an alleged previous autopsy cover-up, and the
added fact that Dr Pepin has been recalled to explain his dubious findings
regarding the inexplicably high levels of carbon monoxide found in Henri
Paul's blood, must surely call into question, not only the validity of the blood
samples, but the entire autopsy procedure. For the record, both Professor
Lecomte and Dr Pepin concluded, and gave evidence to the effect that Henri
Paul had been three times over the legal drink-drive limit at the time of his
death. While everybody else of reasonable disposition suspected at the time—
and has since come to realize—that Henri Paul was almost certainly sober
when he drove Diana to her death, the original French inquiry none the less
concluded that Paul was indeed three times over the legal drink-drive limit,
and that, therefore, Diana's death was the result of a drink-drive accident.
This conclusion was based solely on the evidence given by Professor Lecomte
and Dr Pepin—which surely makes the vigorous re-examination of their
evidence all the more critical.

        All of the above revelations and more, then, have sensationally found
their way during the course of the past year or so on to the front pages of
Britain's tabloid newspapers, as if some prohibitive order has suddenly been
lifted. Indeed, in February of this year, after years of being either suppressed
or ignored, even John and I found ourselves the centre of national media
attention, when again the *Daily Express* led the way with news that our story
is to be made into a movie. "FILM TELLS OF DIANA 'MURDER'" the
headline read (Saturday, February 11th, 2006). The accompanying story
went on to describe how the movie would be based on "*Jon King's sensational
claim*" that he was warned of Diana's assassination in advance, how this
information prompted him, together with his co-author, John Beveridge, to
fully investigate the mystery, and how the movie's producers "*promise that the
film will rattle governments, secret service agents and the Royal Family by
examining evidence suggesting that Diana was assassinated and that the
execution was covered up*". The story was even carried by Sky News, albeit on
the Showbiz interactive pages. But it made Sky News, just the same.

On the one hand, of course, these and other similar headlines have signalled good news for those of us still intent on bringing Diana's assassins to justice, not least because the resulting publicity has helped sway public opinion even further in favour of the belief that she was murdered, prompting yet another headline in the *Express* on Wednesday, May 25, 2005: '94% OF YOU BELIEVE DIANA WAS MURDERED'. The accompanying article went on to present evidence that chauffeur Henri Paul was a paid MI-6 informant, that renegade former MI-6 officer Richard Tomlinson claimed to have seen a top-secret file substantiating this very allegation, and that former MI5 officer Annie Machon—partner of David Shayler, himself an MI5 whistleblower—had become the latest in a long line of intelligence and security personnel to defy their former bosses and publicly state their belief that Diana was indeed murdered. All good publicity, then.

On the other hand, though, this sudden U-turn in media reporting has been a bit galling, to say the least. For the past nine years and more John and I have been shouting these same slogans from every rooftop and soapbox we could find, only to be shot down—or at best ignored—by the mainstream media, as well as being gagged by a government DA Notice that prevented our book gaining any kind of media publicity when it was first released. It was even banned from being serialised in the *Sunday Mirror,* who pursued John and I for months prior to the DA Notice being served. And there were other forms of official censorship and suppression—like the *Daily Express* itself, ironically enough, who several years ago refused to carry our story or promote our book because the paper's conservative hierarchy deemed it too conspiratorial. Strange how precisely the same story bearing precisely the same meat and headlines can be viewed so differently when the climate suddenly suits.

Still, I guess we should at least be grateful that the tide now seems to be turning.

BOOK TWO

OPERATION PAGET, THE OFFICIAL REPORT

II

16

AN OFFICIAL WHITEWASH

A Tragic Accident

The long-awaited, and much-anticipated, report detailing the findings of Lord Stevens' Operation Paget investigation into the deaths of Princess Diana and Dodi Fayed was finally published today (Thursday, December 14th, 2006). Needless to say, it contained few surprises. Rather than a serious criminal investigation into allegations of conspiracy to murder—which the report initially claimed to be—it instead reads like an official whitewash designed primarily to discredit the Establishment's principal antagonists, namely: Mohamed Al Fayed; former MI-6 officer-turned-whistleblower, Richard Tomlinson; and, of course, Princess Diana herself. While Diana is presented in the report as a paranoid neurotic who spends most of her time glancing back over her shoulder for signs of a government hit man, or an MI-6 'mechanic' intent on fixing her brakes, Richard Tomlinson is quite incontestably cast as a liar. I struggle to imagine what he must have been threatened with (or promised in return for completely changing his story), but virtually every word he has ever written or uttered regarding MI-6 involvement in Diana's death can now be pretty much discounted. During the course of the investigation Richard Tomlinson was twice 'interviewed' by Operation Paget detectives. He was also 'visited' by French police and security service (DST) officers who ransacked his home in southern France and confiscated, among other effects, his passport, credit cards and computer equipment. Intimidation tactics? Who knows. What we do know is that, as from today, Richard Tomlinson has a new story to tell regarding Diana's death, one far more in keeping with the Establishment spin on events; indeed, one that exonerates MI-6 entirely from any involvement in what so many still believe to have been a brutal and premeditated murder. Let's at least hope, then, that MI-6's overlords now keep their end of whatever deal they may have imposed on Tomlinson and leave the man in peace.

As for Mohamed Al Fayed, his treatment at the hands of the Paget team can only be described as despicable. True, there are those who will undoubtedly say he set himself up for ridicule, that he is an easy target for the Establishment hawks who drool over the promise of this wealthy Egyptian's demise. And in many respects, of course, they are right. But having been promised a full, vigorous and unbiased investigation into his son's untimely death, and more, that he would be granted a preview of the report before it was published in order to ensure that every avenue of enquiry had been thoroughly exhausted, the Harrods owner must have turned a triple somersault when presented with the report on the morning of its publication, only to find that Stevens had duped him. Indeed, Mohamed Al Fayed is portrayed in the report as a man of wild and unfounded accusations, a 'grieving father' whose emotions surely conspired to invent a plethora of conspiracy theories that have no basis in fact. In consequence, 'the Al Fayed theories' are easily shot down by the Paget marksmen, one by one, like stupid defenceless pigeons, while the man's character—together with those of Diana and Tomlinson—is quite simply destroyed. Case closed. The Paget team must have delivered that report from behind the most conceited smirk in town, fully believing their guile had triumphed, convinced they had at last won this unscrupulous, dirty war. After all, if those who assert their fears of a high-level assassination and cover-up can be so convincingly and publicly discredited—and thus by extension their allegations are perceived as ill-conceived, or at best unreliable—then there is no case to be had. Right?

This would certainly seem to have been the tactic decided upon by Stevens and his highly paid Establishment cronies when they first sat down to devise their battle plan. It would also seem to have been the tactic agreed upon in deciding which bits of evidence to investigate and which bits to prudently sweep aside. When dealing with possible motives, for example, no mention is made of Diana's massively successful landmines campaign, in which she single-handedly impelled then President Clinton to defy the immensely powerful US military-industrial complex by agreeing to a global ban on the manufacture, sale and deployment of antipersonnel landmines. No mention is made of the fact that her campaign threatened to expose the lucrative 'arms-for-oil-and-diamonds' deals brokered by the CIA in Angola at the time, deals that would have implicated the Bush-Cheney oil syndicate, as well as the British Royal Establishment. No mention is made, either, of Diana's unprecedented international popularity—and we do mean unprecedented—and consequently her ability to sway public opinion in her favour, against the status quo, something she was beginning to achieve with ever increasing effect. And neither is there any mention of the fact that, in the final few years of her life—in the aftermath of her infamous Panorama interview in November 1995, and her subsequent divorce from Prince Charles the following summer—Diana had become the single biggest threat to the monarchy since Oliver Cromwell. Indeed, the fact that this 'loose cannon' was in process of establishing a very real and viable 'counter-monarchy', an alternative power base within the Royal Household towards which the British public were growing ever more sympathetic and supportive, is not mentioned, either.

And there is more.

The Stevens investigation also failed to look into the very real possibility that, due to his familial connections and alleged business dealings with one of the world's most notorious arms dealers, Adnan Kashoggi—who just happened to be his mother's brother—Dodi, and not Diana, might have been the target. Or that, conversely, Diana might indeed have been the target, but not simply because of her relationship with an Egyptian Muslim, not simply because she might have been pregnant with this Egyptian Muslim's child. But because the Egyptian Muslim in question, Dodi Fayed, had an alleged business relationship with his arms-dealing uncle and other Saudi arms dealers. There is even suspicion that the reason Henri Paul was ordered to take such an unusual route from the Ritz Hotel that night was because Dodi had a prior business appointment with an unnamed Saudi arms dealer, but this allegation finds no mention in the report. It should be said that, according to our sources at any rate, Dodi had no such appointment in his calendar, and so far as we know, was not involved in any illicit arms deals, either with Kashoggi or anyone else. But that is only our conclusion based on the information we have been able to glean with our own, relatively limited resources. It doesn't mean that Lord Stevens, with a £4 million budget and unlimited resources at his disposal, should have elected to completely overlook this allegation as a possible motive, together with all the other possible motives cited above, as though they didn't exist.

But that's precisely what he did. And the reason he did—or rather, the reason he was able to cherry-pick which allegations to investigate, and which ones to brush aside—is because this report, we contend, is the product not only of a flawed and spurious investigation. But of a very cleverly veiled deception on the part of Stevens and his Establishment conspirators.

When the idea for the investigation was first tabled, its terms of reference were decided upon as follows:

"*To identify allegations which would suggest that the deaths of the Princess of Wales and Dodi Al Fayed were caused other than as a result of a tragic road traffic accident and assess whether there is any credible evidence to support such assertions and report the same to the Coroner.*" [Operation Paget Report, Page 4]

Seems straightforward enough. Indeed, it has to be said that, taken at its word, a very courageous decision would seem to have been made in setting such apparently broad and comprehensive terms of reference. "*To identify allegations which would suggest that the deaths of the Princess of Wales and Dodi Al Fayed were caused other than as a result of a tragic road traffic accident...*" would appear to us to mean that all allegations of conspiracy to murder were to be investigated. Stevens even stated, publicly, at the outset of his investigation, that he would leave "*no stone unturned*" in his efforts to discover the truth. Over the course of the past few years, however, as the investigation progressed, Stevens' resolve to leave "*no stone unturned*" would seem to have transformed into an unrivalled determination to 'whitewash the evidence'. At the same time, in order to accommodate this new ambition, the investigation's terms of reference would seem to have been somewhat revised, resulting in a far less broad and comprehensive remit. As the report's opening paragraph tells us:

"*This police report documents the findings of the criminal investigation into an allegation made by Mohamed Al Fayed of conspiracy to murder the Princess of Wales and his son Dodi Al Fayed.*" [Operation Paget Report, Page 1]

Let us repeat that.

"*This police report documents the findings of the criminal investigation into an allegation made by Mohamed Al Fayed of conspiracy to murder the Princess of Wales and his son Dodi Al Fayed.*" [Operation Paget Report, Page 1]

Suddenly, seemingly overnight, Operation Paget's remit would seem to have been narrowed down from investigating "*allegations which would suggest that the deaths of the Princess of Wales and Dodi Al Fayed were caused other than as a result of a tragic road traffic accident*" to investigating "*an allegation made by Mohamed Al Fayed*". I guess we should all have read the report's title before ploughing headlong into the contents of the report itself. "*The Operation Paget inquiry report into the allegation of conspiracy to murder,*" the front cover informs us. Not, *allegations* (plural) of conspiracy to murder, but, *the* allegation (singular) of conspiracy to murder, referring of course to the sole allegation made by Mohamed Al Fayed. No other allegations are even mentioned, much less investigated.

Our point in highlighting this deception is simply to clarify the nature of the report before we delve into its contents: *i.e.* as declared by Stevens himself, this report details the findings of a criminal investigation into an allegation made by Mohamed Al Fayed. Nothing more, nothing less. Whether or not Princess Diana and Dodi Fayed were the victims of an Establishment plot to murder them is not determined in this report. The only thing determined in this report is whether or not Mohamed Al Fayed's allegation of conspiracy to murder holds up in the eyes of Lord Stevens and his Establishment paymasters.

And there is a further deception being perpetrated here, namely: this report is not the official 'Coroner's Report' to be presented at the inquest, as it purports to be. As the small print informs us, this £4 million investigation and subsequent report was ordered simply "*to help him [the coroner] decide whether such matters would fall within the scope of the investigation carried out at the inquests.*" In other words, if the coroner decides that these matters do fall within the scope of the investigation, a further report—the official inquiry report—will be prepared by the Metropolitan Police Service specifically for the inquest process. This report, and not Lord Stevens' report, will be known as the 'Coroner's Report'.

We should of course expect that the forthcoming Coroner's Report prepared by the Metropolitan Police will concur fully with Lord Stevens' report, in essence if not entirely in detail (in particular as the now 'retired' Lord Stevens—then Sir John Stevens—we recall, was Commissioner of the Metropolitan Police at the outset of his investigation). But in any event, Lord Stevens' report should be viewed for what it is: *i.e.* the findings of a criminal investigation into an allegation made by Mohamed Al Fayed. The Stevens report does not contain the findings of a comprehensive criminal investigation into the suspicious circumstances surrounding the deaths of Princess Diana and Dodi Fayed, as we were led to believe it would. The goalposts have been moved. And it would seem for all the world the reason they have been moved is to further bolster the Establishment assertion that this was all a tragic accident.

17

HENRI PAUL

A Secret Fortune

Within the parameters of their newly concocted terms of reference, it is true to say that Lord Stevens and his Operation Paget team do seem to have conducted a fairly extensive and thorough investigation, certainly in terms of addressing what the Establishment still delights in referring to as the 'conspiracy theories'. Many of the questions raised in this book and elsewhere have indeed been investigated, and in some instances answers have been offered. But it has to be said that the general tenor of the document is such that one cannot help but feel this investigation was set up in a purposeful attempt to explain away the awkward questions rather than actually solve them. One of those questions, for example, centres on the mystery of Henri Paul's multiple bank accounts discovered after his death, and the amount of cash found on his person on the night he died.

In keeping with the evidence presented in this book, the report does conclude that, despite his approx £20,500 (approx US $41,000) a year salary, on his death Henri Paul had somehow accumulated around £170,000 (approx US $350,000) in fifteen separate bank accounts, and that £43,000 (approx US $90,000) had been deposited in those accounts during the final eight months of his life—that's about $11,000 a month, or $130,000 a year, more than six times his annual salary. Despite the report's curious assertion that, as a single, middle-aged man with no children, it should not be viewed as out of the ordinary for Henri Paul to have amassed this amount of money, we still feel that the manner in which this money was amassed, and moreover, the short period over which the money was amassed, should raise suspicion, even in the eyes of the most partisan detective. $90,000 in eight months, deposited largely in cash amounts of $8,000, seems to us not only extravagant, but without reasonable explanation, as well.

Unless, of course, as postulated in the earlier chapters of this book, these amounts were paid to Henri Paul by his intelligence handlers on a 'cash-for-services' basis, something our sources have assured us time and again would be consistent with the way in which the intelligence services work. This explanation certainly makes good sense—not only does it explain why most of the deposits were made in cash: it also explains the $2,500 in cash found on Henri Paul the night he died.

But why would the intelligence services have recruited someone like Paul in the first place? The answer to this, of course, is simple and straightforward, and has been covered extensively in the earlier chapters. A brief outline will suffice here.

Given Paul's position as Acting Head of Security at the prestigious Ritz Hotel in Paris, an establishment frequented by the business world's most powerful movers and shakers—be they arms dealers, oil tycoons, bankers, financiers, foreign diplomats, international power brokers—it is surely inconceivable to imagine that Henri Paul would not have had a working relationship with either French or foreign intelligence agencies. Or both. Indeed, his unprecedented access to information sought by these agencies would have made him a prime asset, and his rewards would no doubt have been handsome, proportionate to the highly valuable information he was able to gather on their behalf. In keeping with intelligence protocol, of course, he would have been paid for his services in cash, throwing light on the mysterious and vast amounts of cash deposited in his various bank accounts, and the mysterious sum of around $2,500 found on his person on the night he died. Of course, the Paget investigation did its level best to disprove any connection between the Ritz security man and the intelligence services, but even they were forced to admit that Henri Paul did have a relationship with at least one intelligence service, France's DST (in general terms the French equivalent to Britain's MI5). As the report states:

"Henri Paul had two telephone numbers alongside 'DST' in his telephone contact lists. The DST has confirmed that Henri Paul was known to them and was tasked with 'enquiries in hotel circles'. They denied being with him on Saturday 30 August 1997." [Operation Paget Report, Page 191]

Hmmm … now there's a surprise. Although forced to admit that Henri Paul worked for them on a part-time basis, the DST denied being with him on the night he died. And of course, Lord Stevens etched this denial in stone.

For the record, the report states that France's other main intelligence service, DGSE (in general terms the French equivalent to Britain's MI-6 and America's CIA) denied any knowledge of Henri Paul. And once again, consistent with what would appear to have been the unspoken directive behind this investigation, a pattern that reappears consistently throughout the report, Lord Stevens and his team were satisfied that DGSE was telling the truth.

The Paget team also satisfied itself that Paul had no relationship with MI-6 (or indeed, with any foreign intelligence agency). This conclusion, the report tells us, is based on the extraordinary claim that no files bearing reference to Henri Paul were uncovered by the Paget team when they were so graciously granted *"full access"* to MI-6's *"entire database"* dating back to 1990. *"Full access"*? *"Entire database"*? Please. Given that MI-6 had nine years to cover its tracks, to destroy and re-invent any such database, we can only wonder at the Paget team's apparent naivety in taking MI-6 at its word. Perhaps we should remind Lord Stevens of the MI-6 motto: 'Semper Occultus'. Which translated into modern English, means: 'Always Secret'. Which translated into any language means the same.

In any event, based on this 'evidence', the Paget team concluded that Henri Paul's secret and sizeable dollar stash was not the result of payments made to him by MI-6, or any other intelligence service.

"There is no evidence that Henri Paul ever worked for MI-6, as an informant or in any other capacity." [Operation Paget Report, Page 380]

In which case the question remains: Where did Henri Paul's not-so-small fortune come from? Incredibly, one can only assume for his own amusement, Lord Stevens came up with the most bizarre of answers.

Assertions that Paul was a paid informant of both the British and French intelligence services cursorily brushed aside, the Paget team concluded that Paul must have come by these relatively vast amounts of money as a result of receiving tips from wealthy Ritz clients. No, you are not hallucinating. Yes, you did read that correctly. Six times his annual salary in tips from wealthy Ritz clients. Bizarre

The report further informs us that, on occasion, Henri Paul would be required to run errands for some of his clients—perhaps make a purchase, for example—and would be expected to front the money. For this reason, the report asserts, it should not be considered unusual that Paul was discovered with around $2,500 in cash on his person on the night he died. OK, not conclusive by any means, but one has to accept that this explanation is at least a plausible one.

But what about his secret fortune? True, someone in Paul's position may well have received the odd bung, the odd backhander, and some of these bungs would no doubt have constituted a veritable fistful—$100 in used notes? $500? Maybe even, on occasion, $1000. But $130,000 a year? In gratuities alone? Cash? Surely Lord Stevens cannot be serious. Surely this explanation must have been dreamed up for a laugh one night, after work, in the bar, with his mates. Surely even Clouseau would have filed this one in the bin marked *implausible*, if not *preposterous*. But not Lord Stevens. On the contrary, for the vastly experienced and conscientious former Metropolitan Police sleuth, this most unlikely of explanations was the answer he'd been seeking all along. As he informs us in the report:

"Henri Paul had deposited around £43,000 [approx US £90,000] in cash / cheques / unknown method into his accounts in the last eight months of his life. Although these amounts were inconsistent with his salary, they were not so large as to be conclusive of Henri Paul's involvement in illicit or clandestine activity." [Operation Paget Report, Page 380]

Can you imagine the taxman reaching a similar conclusion if your fifteen separate bank accounts had been found to contain such a vast, untraceable sum? If you had deposited around $90,000 in multiple bank accounts, largely in cash, over a period of eight months, do you think the Inland Revenue Service or its American equivalent would swallow your story that unknown wealthy clients had filled your coffers? Indeed, do you think they would conclude that your secret fortune was *"not so large as to be conclusive of [your] involvement in illicit or clandestine activity"*, as concluded by Lord Stevens in the case of Henri Paul? No, neither do we.

The report continues:

"It is impossible at this stage to explain all of the movements of cash and finance into and between Henri Paul's accounts ... Claims that Henri Paul received cash payments from intelligence or security services could not be proved or disproved from this evidence." [Operation Paget Report, Page 380]

And that, as they say, is that. Although the report does state that: "*Claims that Henri Paul received cash payments from intelligence or security services could not be proved or disproved from this evidence...*", none the less the cleverly crafted inference is that Henri Paul amassed his fortune by way of receiving tips from mega-wealthy Ritz clients. No spies involved.

As a footnote, we would just like to add that, for the past decade, authors and journalists alike, including John and I, have written about Henri Paul as though he were fiction—a character from some or other gripping, though tragic, crime novel. He wasn't, of course. He was a real person, a human being with family and friends who must be deeply affected by what has been written. Insinuations that he was involved with the intelligence services of France and Britain are one thing. But insinuations that he was involved in the murders of Princess Diana and Dodi Fayed must be difficult in the extreme for his family and friends to deal with. For this reason we would like to take this opportunity to state, here and now, that we do not believe Henri Paul was knowingly involved in these murders. Rather, we believe Henri Paul was a man mixed up in someone else's war, and that, sadly, he caught the stray bullet. As for his secret fortune, whether or not it was the product of payments made to him by the intelligence services, we cannot say for certain. True, the evidence does suggest to us that this was probably the case, and that this line of enquiry should, therefore, be reopened and investigated by someone intent on discovering the truth, rather than covering it up. Because so far as we are concerned, whatever the truth of Henri Paul's multiple bank account fortune, the 'tips from wealthy Ritz clients' theory is plainly ridiculous. No more to be said.

The Autopsy Scandal

We have already covered, in *Footnote II*, the seeming incompetence and dubious practices of Professor Dominique Lecomte, the pathologist who carried out Henri Paul's autopsy, and the accuracy—or inaccuracy—of the tests carried out on what is alleged to have been Henri Paul's blood by independent toxicologist, Dr Gilbert Pepin. Indeed, as we speak, Mohamed Al Fayed's legal team is in process of challenging the accounts given by these two individuals regarding the taking and testing of Henri Paul's blood samples. The Fayed team is claiming that, either by error or design, both Lecomte and Pepin gave false evidence to the French inquiry, and that this evidence led Judge Herve Stephan to wrongly conclude that Henri Paul had been drunk at the wheel. Certainly there are yawning inconsistencies in their accounts, although there would appear to be a more plausible explanation fo the apparent inconsistencies in Dr Pepin's account than in that of Professor Lecomte, who seems unable even to recount how many blood samples she took from Henri Paul's body, much less from which part of the body she too them. In her autopsy report, she stated categorically that five samples were taken, although the number of samples taken according a subsequen account contained in the official French Judicial Dossier was three. And there were many other discrepancies, all of which Lord Stevens tried his leve best to explain away, as we shall see. Indeed, though the report goes to grea lengths in its efforts to validate the evidence given by these two 'experts'—to sort out the mess they left in their wake—even so, it is clear that even the Paget team found it difficult in the extreme to make a convincing case of it. The Operation Paget Summary of Sampling Issues thus states:

There was no explanation for the different weights and heights o. Henri Paul referred to by Professor Lecomte and Commandant Jean-Claude Mulés.

There was no explanation for some of the sample labels being handwritten and some being pre-printed.

There was no explanation for the different figures on documents D789/1 and D1322, for example '4 viscera' on '31/8/97' and '5+5 viscera' on '1/9/97'. There was no explanation of the word 'Andrieux' handwritten on Document D789/1.

There was no explanation for the blood samples from the hemithorax (chest cavity area—blood taken from this area is called haemothorax blood) being placed in vials labelled 'sang cardiaque'—heart blood. (Although there was only one photograph of a blood sample and this clearly showed 'sang cardiaque' there was no evidence in any documentation to indicate the other two samples were properly marked as haemothorax).

There was no apparently logical/reasonable explanation for the change in the number of blood samples taken on 31 August 1997 to be changed from '5' to '3'.

It was not possible to say with any certainty how many blood samples were taken on 31 August 1997. The evidence in the French dossier accounted for three blood samples—one went to Professor Ricordel and two to Dr Pepin for analysis. If there were two other blood samples taken on 31 August 1997 they were not referred to anywhere in the French dossier in terms of toxicological analysis or destruction. [Operation Paget Report, Page 285 and 286]

And that was just the start of it. The problems encountered in attempting to determine how many samples had actually been taken from Henri Paul's body, from which part of his body the blood had been taken, as well as the massive discrepancies that existed between the results of the two separate toxicological tests carried out by Dr Pepin; and indeed, whether or not the blood tested actually belonged to Henri Paul, were daunting, if not unsolvable. And there are further problems to consider. The report also confirms, for example, that Commandant Jean-Claude Mulés, an officer of the Brigade Criminelle who was present at Dodi's external examination, as well as at Henri Paul's subsequent autopsy, made a pretty basic *"error"* in identifying—or misidentifying—the bodies of Dodi Fayed and Henri Paul. For the record, Dodi Fayed's 'body number', assigned on arrival at the morgue for identification purposes, was 2146, while Henri Paul's 'body number' was 2147. As the report states:

"In describing his presence at the autopsy of Henri Paul and the earlier external examination of Dodi Al Fayed by Professor Lecomte, Commandant Mulés accepted that he made an error in mixing body numbers 2146 and 2147." [Operation Paget Report, Page 260]

Of note is that Commandant Mulés was present at the morgue by special request of the coroner, Professor Lecomte, something of a mystery in itself. Normal practice in the event of a fatal road traffic accident, according to the Paget report, would be for an official Judicial Police accident investigator to assist the coroner, but as Commandant Mulés himself confesses in the report, in this instance *"a decision was made at a high level to have him [Commandant Mulés] assist the Professor"*. One has to ask: why? Indeed, aside from Professor Lecomte and Commandant Mulés, the report states that only two others were present at Henri Paul's autopsy. The first was the *Identificateur* (the technician responsible for assisting in the taking of samples), one Mr Chevriers, who is now dead. Staggeringly, the identity of the second, the police photographer, remains unknown! Commandant Mulés was unable to recall his name, the report tells us, and that is that. As Commandant Mulés was also 'unable to recall' how many blood samples were taken, and could not be certain from which part of the body they were taken (although he thought maybe the "thoracic area", the chest cavity), and Professor Lecomte herself is 'unable to recall' these same, rather crucial details, one has to ask some very serious questions in respect of the entire autopsy procedure. We recall, for example, that Professor Lecomte recorded in her autopsy report that five samples had been taken, while other documentation in the official French Judicial Dossier records that three samples were taken. When questioned by the Paget team, however, Commandant Mulés said that normal practice was for two samples to be taken, and indeed, that Professor Lecomte had been directed to take two "*batches*", or samples. It is true that an added sample of 'peripheral blood' would normally be taken as well, making the total number of samples taken three. But incredibly, neither Commandant Mulés nor Professor Lecomte could recall whether any peripheral blood had been taken. Perhaps it is no surprise, then, that Professor Lecomte is again, at the time of writing, under investigation in France.

Also of note is that this same dossier (the French Judicial Dossier, the official dossier compiled by the French Inquiry) contains an unsigned form dated 31st August, 1997, with the name 'Andrieux', or 'Andreux', handwritten at the top of the page. Nobody seems to know who this mysterious character is. According to Commandant Mulés, remember, only four people were present at the autopsy: himself, Professor Lecomte, the deceased Identificateur and the unidentified police photographer. So who is this fifth character whose name appears at the top of the unsigned form discovered in the French Judicial Dossier? The janitor? A secret service agent? Agatha Christie would have been proud of this plot.

Immediately below this unidentified name is a list detailing samples taken at the autopsy, thus:

> 'Expert : Dr. Lecomte I.M.L. no. 2147
>
> Body of : X male (Scored through) PAUL Autopsy of 31 August 1997
>
> NUMBER :
>
> Blood 5
>
> Organs 4
>
> Muscle
>
> Urine 1

Bile 1

Vitreous humour 1

Gastric contents 1

Hair 1

Histology

pail 1

jar'

[Operation Paget Report, Page 271]

At first glance this list seems innocuous enough. But what we need to know, of course, is who compiled it? Professor Lecomte? Her name certainly appears at the top of the list. But again, who is the mysterious character, 'Andrieux', or 'Andreux', whose name appears at the top of the page on which this list was written? Neither Lord Stevens nor any of the French Inquiry officials are able to tell us.

But what is perhaps even more pertinent, and equally intriguing, are the entries detailed on a second list (below), which appears on an unnumbered form also contained in the French Judicial Dossier. Again, who compiled this second list? And why, when it refers to the samples taken at the self same autopsy, do the entries differ from those detailed on the first list? This unnumbered form is dated 1st September, 1997, the day after the first list was compiled.

'Expert: Prof. Lecomte Body of: X Male (PAUL Henri)

Forensic Institute No 2147 Autopsy, 31.8.97

(sheet completed 1.9.97)

NUMBER:

Blood 5

Organs 5 + 5

Muscle 0

Urine 1 + 1

Bile 1

Vitreous humour 1

Gastric contents 1 + 1

Hair 1 + 3

Histology

Pail 1

Jar'

[Operation Paget Report, Page 272]

As the Paget report notes: "*These two forms, apparently completed o* *Sunday 31 August 1997 and Monday 1 September 1997 respectively, ar* *clearly completed with differing entries.*" Indeed, except for the fact that the both bear the name "Paul", they would appear to refer to separate autopsies But they do not refer to separate autopsies. On the contrary, both ar apparent records of samples taken from Henri Paul's body, at Henri Paul' autopsy; yet their origin, together with the information they contain, remain a conundrum, even for those present, including, it would seem, Commandan Mulés. For the record, when asked by the Paget team if he could explain th discrepancies between these two documents, Commandant Mulés said h could not. Likewise, when asked if he could identify the mysteriou character, 'Andrieux', or 'Andreux', whose handwritten name appears at th top of the page containing the first list, he again said he could not. And neither, he claimed, could he throw light on yet another apparent mystery, ar altogether stranger mystery entirely than all the above combined. Namely: the measuring of the height and weight of Henri Paul.

Evidently, one of Commandant Mulés' tasks at the autopsy was to record the height and weight of Henri Paul. This same task was also undertaken by Professor Lecomte, and one would assume these two highly experienced officials would have been able to carry out this pretty basic task with at least some degree of concurrence. However, their measurements on both counts differed widely.

"*Professor Lecomte recorded [Henri Paul's] body weight as 73kg and* *height as 1.72m (French Dossier D789/11) …Commandant Mulés recorded* *the body weight as 76kg and height as 1.67m (French Dossier D90).*'
[Operation Paget Report, Page 261]

Hello? For the record, 73kg is equivalent to 160 lbs, while 76kg equals 167lbs. That makes a difference of seven pounds, or half a stone. It is of course a well known fact that being dead is probably the most effective form of weight-loss diet, but seven pounds in a few minutes?

Likewise, 1.72m is equivalent to 5ft 7ins, while 1.67m equals 5ft 5ins. Again, a difference of two full inches! Blatantly a pair of chimpanzees could have produced more accurate results. Not only did Professor Lecomte and Commandant Mulés get their measurements utterly wrong; between them, bizarrely, they somehow managed to conclude that the shorter man weighed more than the taller man! Was Henri Paul taller and leaner, we ask ourselves, or shorter and stockier? Were these two comrades-in-arms even measuring the same corpse? We must remember here that Commandant Mulés had already managed to confuse Henri Paul's body with that of Dodi Fayed, mixing up their body identification numbers on arrival at the morgue. Seriously, one has to wonder what on earth was going on in the morgue that night, because contrary to initial impressions, Professor Lecomte and her bungling accomplice are not the innocent buffoons they might appear to be. Quite the opposite: they are highly trained and well practised experts in their own fields, a fact that raises serious questions against their seemingly amateurish conduct. After all, given the apparent discrepancies regarding the amount of samples taken; from which part of the body (bodies?) they were taken; the apparent differences in height and weight of the body (bodies?); the misidentification of the bodies of Henri Paul and Dodi Fayed: indeed, the amount of apparent 'blunders' made, period, one surely has to wonder at the integrity of those concerned.

'Unknown Male'
Sang Cardique

And there were more blunders, a lot more blunders, most critically regarding the labelling of the bottles containing Henri Paul's blood samples. Thus when the first test was carried out by the French police toxicologist assigned to the case, Professor Ivan Ricordel, nobody could be certain whether the blood being tested was actually that of Henri Paul. As the report states:

"There was no photograph of this bottle. It is not known if this sample had a pre-printed or handwritten label. The label on Professor Ricordel's sample according to his account showed 'X M'. This was believed to indicate: X—unknown, M—male. Other labels that were printed at the time showed the

name as 'Paul Henry'. [Operation Paget Report, Page 299]

Confirmation, then, that the first test carried out to determine whether or not Henri Paul had been drunk was actually carried out on the blood of an "*unknown male*". In any event, Professor Ricordel found that the blood sample he tested had a blood/alcohol level of 1.87 grams per litre of blood, well over the French drink-drive limit, and perhaps more crucially, at odds with the results of the tests carried out by Dr Pepin, who found a blood/alcohol level of 1.74 grams per litre of blood. It was Dr Pepin, of course, who also tested for carbon monoxide, and surprised himself and everybody else by finding a carbon monoxide (carboxyhaemoglobin) level of 20.7%, well above the levels one would expect to find even in the heaviest of smokers. Indeed, no medical expert has thus far been able to explain such high levels, and the explanation contained in the report, though in some lame sense 'plausible', is in our opinion far from conclusive. The fact is, due to labelling blunders and a failure to DNA-test the sample in question, the Paget team cannot even be certain that this blood was Henri Paul's, much less determine how on earth it could have contained such high levels of carbon monoxide. And since this blood sample no longer exists, further tests to double-check the results, or indeed, to determine whose blood it actually was, are not now possible.

Even so, an explanation as to how the mystery of the carbon monoxide came about is offered in the report, albeit with some trepidation The carbon monoxide levels found in Henri Paul's blood were so high, we are told, because the blood sample that rendered these results was taken from the chest cavity, and thus would have been affected by contaminants such as mangled blood tissue and bone marrow. Quite how bone marrow translates to carbon monoxide would seem to be a mystery in itself; this process is not clearly explained in the report. But what is clearly explained is the fact that the bottle containing this sample was not only labelled "*XM*", or "*unknown male*". It was also labelled "*Sang Cardiaque*", or 'Heart Blood', suggesting to us at any rate that the blood in question had been taken from Henri Paul's heart and was thus 'pure blood': uncontaminated. Somewhere down the line, however, we are assured by the Paget team that Professor Lecomte had made a "*mistake*" in labelling the sample bottle; the blood had actually been taken, not from Henri Paul's heart, as the label clearly states, but from his chest cavity. Evidently the hapless Professor, who claims she cannot remember how many blood samples she took, much less which one came from which part of Henri Paul's body, had wrongly labelled the bottle. Her report, designated in the official French Judicial Dossier, D4412 and D1323, states:

"The post mortem examination was conducted at eight o'clock in the morning on 31 August 1997, in other words, a few hours after the accident. The blood was taken from the left hemithorax area..." [Operation Paget Report, Page 269]

The left hemithorax area would indeed be best described, in layman's terms, as the chest cavity, and not the heart. Problem is, can we believe a word written or spoken by Professor Lecomte? If, as she claims in her autopsy report, the blood was taken from Henri Paul's chest cavity, then why did she label it *"Sang Cardiaque"*, or 'Heart Blood'? Indeed, when interviewed by Operation Paget detectives some eight years later, in response to the question: *"From where did you take the sample of blood?"*, why did she clearly reply:

"As I have just said, I took the sample from the heart..." [Operation Paget Report, Page 270]

Confused yet? Hang in there; it gets worse!

According to Professor Lecomte's latest testimony, then, she did take the blood sample from Henri Paul's heart. But if this is true, why in her autopsy report did she record that the *"blood was taken from the left hemithorax area"* [chest cavity]? Indeed, why did Lord Stevens, quite arbitrarily, it would appear, elect to *"believe"* Professor Lecomte's autopsy report, in which she claimed to have taken the blood from the chest cavity, rather than her sworn statement, in which she stated, quite unequivocally, that she took the blood from the heart?

Professor Lecomte's Statement

"As I have just said, I took the sample from the heart..." [Operation Paget Report, Page 270]

Operation Paget Comment

"Operation Paget believe the blood was actually taken from the hemithorax, 'chest cavity'." [Operation Paget Report, Page 277]

There would seem to be no basis for this belief, other than it supports Lord Stevens' apparent ambition to quash any evidence that might suggest foul play.

In any event, these contradictory claims made by Professor Lecomte surely demonstrate the highly unprofessional manner in which she acted, especially when we take into account the fact that she was autopsying the Princess of Wales's chauffeur, and that, in consequence, she should have been aware that her work would almost certainly be scrutinized far more closely than if she was autopsying anyone else. The fact that Operation Paget expressed a discretionary 'belief' that Professor Lecomte's initial claim was true, even though she contradicted herself on numerous occasions, surely betrays the level of professionalism demonstrated by Lord Stevens and his team, as well.

That said, the upshot of all this is that, for an incredible eight years, we are told, the world's most eminent medical experts were led to believe that the blood containing the abnormally high levels of carbon monoxide was heart blood, when all along—if Lecomte's initial claim is true and Stevens' 'belief' is thus vindicated—it was chest-cavity blood. So far as the Paget team are concerned, anyway, this explains the mystery of the carbon monoxide found in Henri Paul's blood, as we shall see.

But firstly, let us clarify a further mystery that arose as a result of Lecomte's alleged labelling error. Namely: why, according to the Paget report, it was eight years before anybody realized that the sample bottle had been wrongly labelled, if indeed it had been.

Evidently, in 2005, when Operation Paget arrived on the scene, detectives discovered that for some strange reason Professor Lecomte's report detailing the areas of the body from where the blood had been taken had been replaced in the official French Judicial Dossier by another report referring to samples of Henri Paul's spinal chord. As the Paget report explains:

"*The original document in the French Dossier numbered D1323 describing the blood sample sites at the autopsy of Sunday 31 August 1997 had been replaced with another document referring to spinal cord samples. The following explanation of the detail of how this was discovered is, by its very nature, complicated.*" [Operation Paget Report, Page 277]

Complicated, indeed. In the first instance, the Paget report tells us, Professor Lecomte's autopsy report was designated the number D1323, but at some later date it was collated along with various other documents and re-designated the number D4412, at which point it would seem to have disappeared. Until 2005, that is, when—just when they needed it most—it was magically conjured up by the Paget team and produced as evidence to explain the mystery of the carbon monoxide. For eight years, the Paget team claims, pathologists and toxicologists alike remained baffled by the high levels of carbon monoxide found in Henri Paul's blood because they were under the impression it had come from his heart, when all along, of course—according to Professor Lecomte's exhumed autopsy report—it had actually been taken from the chest cavity and would therefore have been contaminated. As stated, taken at face value this would seem a plausible enough explanation, if it were true. But it was not true. In fact it was clearly a lie, a desperately overstated one at that. Check this:

"Until 2005, discussion on carboxyhaemoglobin [carbon monoxide] levels had assumed, not unreasonably, that the label on the blood sample vial from the autopsy of 31 August 1997, 'Sang Cardiaque', was correct and that the 20.7% carboxyhaemoglobin [carbon monoxide] level related to pure cardiac blood." [Operation Paget Report, Page 328]

And again:

"It was clear at this time, i.e. November 1998, the three professors [Professors Patrice Mangin, Thomas Krompecher and Professor Vanezis] still believed the blood samples on 31 August 1997 were taken from the heart i.e. cardiac blood 'Sang Cardiaque' - and were not aware that the sample was chest cavity blood. Their points are therefore naturally based on this premise." [Operation Paget Report, Page 329]

And again:

"In February 1999 the experts were still under the impression that the carboxyhaemoglobin reading of 20.7% related to Henri Paul's heart and not the hemithorax." [Operation Paget Report, Page 333]

And again:

"In December 2001 it was again clear that various experts were discussing the levels of carboxyhaemoglobin in Henri Paul's cardiac blood." [Operation Paget Report, Page 334]

One more time:

"This sample of blood was labelled as 'Sang Cardiaque', (cardiac blood) rather than chest cavity blood. Errors in the French judicial dossier meant that those looking at these issues on behalf of Mohamed Al Fayed and Operation Paget did not identify this labelling error until 2005." [Operation Paget Report, Page 374]

Lord Stevens goes to great lengths to establish his point, then. However ...

...If in November 1998, February 1999 and December 2001, it was *"clear that various experts"* still believed the blood sample in question had been taken from Henri Paul's heart, then what are we to make of this comment made by one of those *"various experts"* referred to by Lord Stevens, Professor Peter Vanezis, Regis Professor of Forensic Medicine at Glasgow University. [Quote: Daily Telegraph, Wednesday, September 10th, 1997— less than two weeks after the crash.]

"Prof Peter Vanezis, of Glasgow University, told a press conference called by Michael Cole, the Fayed spokesman, that it was 'unsafe and unfair' to rely on the initial sample, taken from near the heart, as it could have been contaminated after rupture of M Paul's organs."

It is clear, then, that as early as ten days after the crash, on September 10th, 1997, Professor Vanezis was under the impression that the sample had been "taken from *near* the heart" [our italics], and thus that the sample "could have been *contaminated*" [our italics]. And in support of this comment, it is worth reproducing a further comment from Professor Vanezis, which he made together with Professors Patrice Mangin and Thomas Krompecher a little over a year later, in November 1998. This comment is contained in Chapter 4 of the Stevens report, and is immediately followed by a comment from Operation Paget. These two comments are reproduced here exactly as they appear in the report.

(i) November 17 1998

Professors Patrice Mangin *and* **Thomas Krompecher** (supported by **Professor Vanezis***) commenting on a report by Professor Lecomte and Dr Pépin relating to carbon monoxide in the blood, stated:*

'The cardiac blood sample was taken on the 31 August 1997 whereas the femoral vein sample was taken on the 4 September 1997 (four days later). It is not surprising therefore that it shows a level of 12.8% as one would expect such a reduction over this period of time from a level of approximately 20% down to approximately 12%.'

Operation Paget Comment

"It was clear at this time, i.e. November 1998, the three professors still believed the blood samples on 31 August 1997 were taken from the heart i.e. cardiac blood—'Sang Cardiaque'—and were not aware that the sample was chest cavity blood. Their points are therefore naturally based on this premise." [Operation Paget Report, Page 329]

We take issue with this Operation Paget reply, in particular with Lord Stevens' interpretation of the professors' use of the term *"the cardiac blood sample"*. We contend that the professors' use of the term *"the cardiac blood sample"* is technical rather than descriptive—that it refers to the sample's labelling rather than its site of origin. Technically speaking, at this time the correct term to use when referring to this sample was indeed *"the cardiac blood sample"*, as the sample was labelled *"Sang Cardiaque"*. To have used any other term would have been misleading. That the professors referred to the sample as *"the cardiac blood sample"* meant everyone in the loop knew which sample was being referred to; it had become the given name for that particular sample at that particular moment in time. Professor Vanezis, we recall, already knew that the sample had been taken form *"near the heart"* and thus that it *"could have been contaminated"*. We can safely conclude, therefore, that he and his colleagues used the term *"the cardiac blood sample"* purely in a technical context, and that Lord Stevens deliberately misinterpreted the use of this term in a flagrant and cynical attempt to bolster his own case.

And there is further evidence to support the view that, years earlier than Lord Stevens claims, the *"various experts"* he refers to believed that the blood was not pure heart blood.

In February 1999 Professors Vanezis, Mangin and Krompecher, together with a fourth expert, Professor John Oliver, Professor of Forensic Toxicology: B.Sc, PhD, Chartered Scientist, Chartered Chemist and Fellow of the Royal Society of Chemistry, produced a joint report. In it they stated:

"It appears from the report that the heart blood was taken by use of a ladle. This means that it was not taken specifically from the left ventricle but was a mix of blood originating from both sides of the heart." [Operation Paget Report, Page 330]

Once again, these four experts concluded that the blood sample had been made up of blood which had, in all probability, spilled from both sides of the heart into the chest cavity as a result of Henri Paul's thoracic aorta rupturing on impact. Indeed, this probability was further supported by one of Stevens' own 'experts', Dr Robert Forrest, speaking in an interview for *Diana: The Paris Crash—A Special Inquiry*, an ITV documentary on the results of the French Inquiry report, screened in Britain on Friday, 3rd September, 1999. In this documentary, screened six years before the date cited by Lord Stevens as being the date when the *"various experts"* finally realized that the blood was actually chest-cavity blood, we were informed that the first blood sample taken from Henri Paul's body had indeed been taken from the 'chest cavity', and that consequently it was likely to have been contaminated. When interviewed in the documentary, Dr Forrest confirmed to senior British barrister and former Chairman of the Bar Council, Anthony Scrivener QC, who co-presented the program, that Henri Paul's aorta had been ruptured as a result of the crash impact, and that consequently blood had spilled into Henri Paul's chest cavity and that this was the blood scooped out by the French pathologist and labelled *"Sang Cardiaque"*, or 'Heart Blood'. For the record, Dr Forrest also confirmed in the 1999 TV documentary that the four-day time-lapse between the taking of the first sample from the chest cavity, and the taking of the second sample from the femoral vein, could have accounted for the difference in results regarding the carbon monoxide levels found in Henri Paul's blood, as the amount of carbon monoxide would have decreased over this period, a conclusion supported by Professors Vanezis, Mangin, Krompecher and Oliver. Dr Forrest also stated in the 1999 TV documentary that, in his many years as a forensic pathologist and assistant coroner, he had never witnessed such high levels of carbon monoxide as those found in Henri Paul's blood.

So, it would seem, despite this 3-year, £4 million investigation, the questions still remain:

Was Henri Paul drunk when he drove Princess Diana and Dodi Fayed to their death? Lord Stevens seems convinced he was. But the only evidence to support this belief is the 1.74 g/l blood/alcohol result obtained from tests carried out on a blood sample marked "*XM*", or "*unknown male*", and wrongly labelled "*Sang Cardiaque*" by a pathologist whose practices, if not indeed her character, must surely be called into question. The fact that this same blood sample was never DNA-tested, of course, means there is no way of knowing for certain if it even belonged to Henri Paul, much less whether it was taken from the heart or the chest cavity. Thus there is no evidence whatever in the report that alcohol was the cause of Princess Diana's death. Indeed, the evidence suggests otherwise.

Unsolved Mystery
of the Carbon Monoxide

With regard to the abnormally high level (20.7%) of carbon monoxide found in this same unidentified blood sample, and the equally abnormal level (12.8%) of carbon monoxide found in the second test carried out by Dr Pepin, we have to conclude that Lord Stevens is no nearer the truth four years on than he was at the outset of his investigation. Or at least that he refuses to see the truth when it stares him in the face. Perhaps this is due to his seeming determination to champion the opinions of the 'experts' he employed, while at the same time disregarding the opinions provided by other 'experts', whom he did not employ. For example, while the Paget team, somewhat arrogantly, it has to be said, presumes to disregard the results of the initial blood test entirely (which found a 20.7% carbon monoxide level), citing a labelling error allegedly made by Professor Lecomte as their reason, other experts are less hasty to follow suit. This is of course understandable in that the Paget team found it difficult to explain this one away, at least in any convincing manner. Other experts, though, feel they can offer a perfectly reasonable explanation for the seeming discrepancy which appears to exist between the two carbon monoxide readings. As Professors Mangin, Krompecher and Vanezis agree, it is due to the four-day time-lapse between the taking of the two blood samples.

But the real problem facing the Paget team here is that both figures— 20.7% and 12.8%—are considered excessively high, even for the heaviest of smokers. Again, as Professor Vanezis and his colleagues state:

"*We query also the statement that Mr Paul had [a high] level of carboxyhaemoglobin as a result of being a heavy smoker. Our experience and based on published research on the issue shows that one could not expect a figure higher than 5%-8%. There is also no confirmatory evidence to support the statement that he was a heavy smoker.*" [Operation Paget Report, Page 331]

This opinion is also upheld by eminent forensic pathologist, Dr Robert Forrest, who stated in a TV documentary screened in Britain in August 1998, entitled *Diana: Secrets Of The Crash*, that a person who smokes around 20 cigarettes a day would expect to have no more than 5%-8% carbon monoxide in their blood. 10%, he said, would be deemed excessively high. Indeed, though stated with duly adjusted emphasis given his new position as Lord Stevens' 'expert', he none the less reiterates this opinion in a report compiled for Operation Paget, in which he declares:

"*Heavy smokers can have base line carboxyhaemoglobin concentrations of certainly up to 10%.*" [Operation Paget Report, Page 323]

But as we have seen, and certainly according to his closest friends, Henri Paul was not a heavy smoker; best estimates suggest he smoked only a few cigarillos a day, not nearly sufficient to account for 20.7% carbon monoxide poisoning, nor even for 12.8% carbon monoxide poisoning. As the Paget report informs us:

"*A sample of Dodi Al Fayed's blood, taken at his post-mortem examination in Hammersmith and Fulham Mortuary on Sunday 1 September 1997 was tested in February 1998 for carboxyhaemoglobin levels. The level was 2.5%. As the blood sample was refrigerated it is believed that this is a reliable indicator of the figure at the time of the crash. This level is not considered unusual, especially as Dodi Al Fayed was a cigar smoker.*" [Operation Paget Report, Page 378]

The last line of the above quote is particularly interesting. Lord Stevens notes that 2.5% carbon monoxide in the blood "*is not considered unusual, especially as Dodi Al Fayed was a cigar smoker*". One wonders if Lord Stevens realizes what he is saying here. It is well known, of course, that cigar smokers are likely to have higher concentrations of carbon monoxide in their blood than cigarette smokers, and yet the relatively low level of 2.5%, he says, is "*not considered unusual*". Well if 2.5% is not considered unusual for a cigar smoker, then by definition 12.8%—not to mention 20.7%—must surely be considered highly unusual, in particular for someone who only smoked a few cigarillos a day. Indeed, as corroborated by Professor Vanezis and his eminent colleagues, 12.8% is excessively high, especially as this figure was obtained four days after Henri Paul's death, and that, unlike Dodi Fayed's body, Henri Paul's body was not refrigerated following his autopsy. Yet another blunder by Lecomte and her team which meant any carbon monoxide present in Henri Paul's blood at the time of the crash would have diminished considerably. Which it obviously had.

But even after four days there still appeared to be 12.8% carbon monoxide in Henri Paul's blood, a figure, according to Professor Vanezis and his colleagues, which can only be described as excessively high. In a report prepared for Operation Paget, they revealed:

"The second, lower figure of 12.8% was obtained by testing blood taken 4 days following the crash. Whilst we accept that figures this high have been achieved in some circumstances from tests on smokers, to put the figure in context, another study obtained an average of 8.6% from smokers who smoked 20 cigarettes in succession without interruption and were then tested within 15 minutes of the last cigarette. Out of many studies reported, only one of which we are aware has produced a figure as high or higher than that found in the 4 September sample tested by Dr Pepin [12.8%], and even in that study less than 0.6% of more than 7500 people tested apparently reached those levels." [Operation Paget Report, Page 378]

To our mind, then, the evidence speaks for itself. In a controlled experiment, a group of smokers chain-smoked 20 cigarettes in succession, *"without interruption"* , and were subsequently tested for carbon monoxide within 15 minutes of smoking the last cigarette. Even so, despite this highly intensive smoking session, 8.6% was found to be the average level of carbon monoxide found in their blood, and yet we are expected to believe that, after four days of being very dead, and having smoked considerably less than *"20 cigarettes in succession without interruption"* within fifteen minutes of his death; and further, that his body was not refrigerated following his autopsy, Henri Paul still had 12.8% carbon monoxide in his blood. A very unlikely scenario. Indeed, as Professor Vanezis, Professor John Oliver and Professor Atholl Johnston jointly concluded:

"We are satisfied that in all likelihood Henri Paul took only half/one

breath between the point of impact and death (at most it could not have been more than two breaths). This would exclude any possibility of intake of carbon monoxide from the airbag, broken manifold or anything similar occurring at the time of the crash. We remain sceptical about any explanation which attributes the two levels of 20.7% and 12.8% to smoking, and we have been unable to identify any other rational explanation for the very high carbon monoxide figures. This leaves only two other possible explanations. The first is that this is an error. We consider it unlikely that those involved in the process would have made major errors in dealing with a very high profile and important event, and we therefore tend to discount this possibility. That leaves an alternative which is that the blood tested was not that of Henri Paul." [Operation Paget Report, Page 323]

Of course, conclusions such as these are loaded. They set off alarm bells, especially when presented not by a gaggle of ribald conspiracy theorists, but by a group of the most eminent and respected experts in their field. The bottom line here is that, if these experts are right in their conclusions—that the abnormally high level of carbon monoxide found in Henri Paul's blood is not the result of a faulty manifold or a split airbag; that it is not the result of smoking; that it is not the result of an error on the part of Dr Pepin; but that it is indeed the result of tests carried out on blood that did not come from Henri Paul—then there can be only one explanation. And that is, whether by design or error, the blood sample was switched. No wonder Lord Stevens is reluctant to accept the facts as they stand. He concluded:

"This level of 12.8% carboxyhaemoglobin is not unusual, and provides no evidence that would support a claim of swapped bodies or blood samples." [Operation Paget Report, Page 376]

And there we have it, the official verdict, not for the first time entirely at odds with the evidence.

18

CCTV

A Culture of Privacy

Over the years, widely varying accounts regarding the number of CCTV
cameras lining the route from the Ritz Hotel in Paris to the Alma Tunnel,
plus those supposedly situated in the tunnel itself, have been reported in the
press. *The Daily Express*, for example, claims there were 10 cameras en
route and 17 inside the tunnel, 27 in total, while the *Independent* claims
there were *"more than 14 CCTV cameras in the Pont d'Alma underpass,
yet none have recorded footage of the fatal collision"*. Other guesstimates
fall more or less in the same ballpark, but the astonishing thing is, no one
seems able to offer a definitive number. Needless to say, the Operation Paget
report disagrees with all of them. (These figures, remember, refer to the amount
of cameras operating in 1997.)

The truth of the matter, so far as we can ascertain (as documented in
Chapter 5 and *Footnote II*) is that there are—or were in 1997, at the time of
the crash—at least 10 CCTV cameras situated along the route, and one
traffic-monitoring camera situated on the flypast directly above the tunnel
itself. Photographs and TV images of the crash and immediate aftermath,
despite media claims to the contrary, would seem to support the Paget view
that there were no cameras inside the tunnel itself, that is unless a very
efficient team on the ground went to work within minutes of the crash and
ripped all 17 cameras alleged by the Daily Express to have been operating
inside the tunnel off their mountings, which even to us seems an unlikely
story. But in any event, according to the Paget report, no matter how many
CCTV and speed-trap cameras were actually operating on the night Diana
died, none returned any images of either the fateful journey or of the crash
itself. This, at least, is the conclusion of Lord Stevens' 3-year investigation.

So the question remains, then: why are there no CCTV/video images of the
journey or the crash?

According to Lord Stevens, the answer to this question is straightforward: it is due, he says, to France's unique privacy laws, which effectively restrict the number and location of cameras. Evidently, as Dr Eva Steiner, Doctor of Criminal Science and former member of the Paris Bar, informed Operation Paget:

"Distrust of CCTV cameras by the general public accounts for their installation being subject to very strict rules."

And further:

"The French public are easily exasperated by systems such as video cameras which they perceive as an uncalled for intrusion into their daily private lives." [Operation Paget Report, Page 406 and 407]

Poor things. Kind of makes you wish you were French, doesn't it?

"We really dislike all those CCTV cameras everywhere, Mr President. We find them so intrusive!"

"No problem, citizens. I'll have them removed immediately."

Meanwhile MI-6 realizes that France is the ideal place to assassinate princesses as there are no cameras to witness the blood-letting! *Click click!*

Joking aside, that the French government is indeed reported to be less fanatical about filming everybody would seem, at least, to go some way in offering a reasonable explanation with regard to the lack of CCTV images of Diana's final moments. As asserted in the Paget report, we do tend to assume that CCTV and security cameras exist in equal quantities in every major city in the western world, and based on this assumption, we further assume that there must have been images of either the journey or the crash (certainly of the journey) caught on camera. Hands up: we are as guilty of making this assumption as anyone. And before you start to fear the worst, no we are not going soft. There are still gaping holes in the report's lame explanations and smoothing over of the CCTV anomalies, and we will tackle them in a moment. But when a reasonable explanation is offered as to why no CCTV images of the incident have been forthcoming, then we have to accept that maybe there is some truth in that explanation. Certainly it is difficult to imagine ourselves driving through the streets of New York or London without being caught on film. Big Brother's eyes seem to be watching from every corner, every junction, and it is perfectly reasonable for us to assume that this would also have been the case in Paris in 1997. But as the Paget report argues, there is "*a culture of privacy prevailing in France*", and one of the consequences of this culture is that the number of CCTV cameras in Paris is restricted compared to that of other major metropolises. As Dr Eva Steiner further explains:

"*In France, video surveillance is regulated by a law of 21 January 1995. Under article 10 of this law the usage of CCTV cameras is only permitted for the protection of public buildings and their surroundings, the safeguard of national defence installations (also including nuclear power stations), the regulation of road traffic flows and the discovery of offences related to road traffic violations, and to prevent any infringement to people's personal safety and to that of their belongings in places, including public places, where there is an increased risk of attack or theft.*" [Operation Paget Report, Page 406]

Point taken.

Speed Trap

But this still does not explain why the cameras that were operating that night failed to capture any footage of the Mercedes as it sped along the riverside highway on its way to the Alma Tunnel. Even Lord Stevens admits that "*Lieutenant Gigou's report identified cameras at ten locations along the route taken by the Mercedes on its final journey to the Alma underpass*". However, Lieutenant Gigou then informs us that "*none of the cameras along the route would have been in a position to record the passage of the vehicle or any of the events connected with it*". For the record, Lieutenant Gigou was the Brigade Criminelle officer tasked by Judge Stephan to identify the CCTV cameras operating between the Ritz Hotel and the Alma underpass on the night in question.

According to some reports, of course, the reason no footage has surfaced is because all the cameras had been deliberately turned off. As most of the cameras are owned and operated by private companies, however, this claim, unless supported by evidence of a massive conspiracy involving all of these companies, would seem to hold little water. Other reports claim that the electricity supply was switched off just before midnight, and that therefore the cameras stopped working a few minutes before the Mercedes arrived at the crash tunnel. Again, the involvement of a private French power-supply company in the assassination of a British princess seems somewhat implausible—unless, of course, the company had been penetrated by secret service operatives who were able to isolate the supply to the cameras and turn it off, leaving the rest of the city on full power. Once again, this seems so unlikely it is hardly worth a mention. And in any event, according to a report carried by several British newspapers (see *Footnote II*), approximately fifteen minutes prior to the crash a woman driving through the Alma Tunnel was caught by a speed-trap camera and subsequently prosecuted, which, if true, not only means that the cameras must have been working fifteen minutes before the crash. It also means that someone complicit in the assassination of Princess Diana must have been very careless. After all, who would want to draw attention to the fact that a speed-trap camera was working fifteen minutes before the murder, when the entire operation had been planned on the basis that no cameras lining this particular route were in a position to film the Mercedes as it entered the crash tunnel? Think about it. Indeed, it is actually a recognized fact that, in 1997, there were no fixed speed-trap cameras in the centre of Paris, another solid reason for MI-6 to have chosen the French capital as its killing field. MI-6 knew as well as anyone that the only speed-trap cameras deployed in the vicinity of the Alma Tunnel in 1997 were mobile, which in itself is a very interesting point, especially when considered against the testimony of a French paparazzo by the name of Pierre Suu, who was one of the rat pack stationed outside the Ritz Hotel, and who subsequently made his way, via Dodi's apartment, to the crash tunnel. As the Paget report states:

"*Pierre Suu claimed that Pierre Hounsfield, a fellow paparazzo, had witnessed police removing a portable radar camera from the Cours Albert 1er about 300 yards from the entrance to the underpass shortly after the crash. He stated that this camera was well known and was deployed mainly on weekends.*" [Operation Paget Report, Page 399]

Curiously, the paparazzo alleged by Pierre Suu to have witnessed the mobile camera, Pierre Hounsfield, declined on legal advice to be interviewed by Operation Paget. He did, however, speak to the Paget team by telephone and confirmed his story that he had seen a mobile speed camera being dismantled and removed by police. The camera, he said, had been positioned near the entrance to the Alma Tunnel, "*by the trees separating the slip road from the embankment expressway*".

In an interview conducted on September 18th, 1997, for the original French inquiry, Hounsfield told his story.

"*Us three, Suu, Cardinale and myself got into our vehicles and headed for l'Alma. I took the place de l'Etoile, then avenue Marceau. Once at l'Alma, I parked in rue Debrousse. There was already a police vehicle parked at the Alma Tunnel exit in the Paris-Suburbs direction and another one in the same place but in the opposite direction of traffic flow. Police officers prevented us from looking over to see the tunnel entrance.*" [Operation Paget Report, Page 400]

Lord Stevens assures us that, because of the route Hounsfield had taken, as described in his interview (above), he could not have seen the camera as claimed. Evidently Hounsfield had stated that he had seen the camera *en route* to the crash tunnel, but his route did not take him past the site where he claimed the camera had been. A detailed map showing Hounsfield's route is provided in the Paget report, and true enough, to all intents and purposes it would seem that Lord Stevens was right. Unless, of course, Hounsfield had seen the camera when he got out of his car and walked the few hundred yards to Place de l'Alma. Or maybe even he had seen the camera, as he clearly stated he did, but in a different location, perhaps the other side of the tunnel. Hounsfield did, after all, reportedly admit to Lord Stevens that he "*wondered if his memory was playing tricks*". Stevens, of course, took this statement as confirmation that Hounsfield had either been lying or mistaken—that he had not seen the camera after all, and that, therefore, there was no camera at the Alma Tunnel that night. Case closed. But, we wondered, what if his memory had been "*playing tricks*" in a way different to that interpreted by Lord Stevens—that he had seen the camera, but not where he thought he'd seen it? We should bear in mind here that he had just arrived at the scene of Princess Diana's fatal car crash. Would *your* mind have been calm and collected in this situation? Would *your* recollections of your immediate surroundings have been clear and unaffected by events going on around you? Or do you think maybe your mind might have played tricks on you, too? We'll leave you to decide for yourselves whether Pierre Hounsfield saw the camera or not, but there would seem little reason for him to have told his fellow paparazzo that he had seen it if he hadn't. Indeed, so far as we know, there is no reason at all for him to have made the story up, and if true, it would certainly go a long way in helping to corroborate the claim that an as yet unidentified woman had been caught speeding, on camera, at the entrance to the Alma Tunnel some fifteen minutes before the crash, as this mobile camera could well have been the camera that captured her. Certainly in our opinion this possibility is worthy of more serious investigation than Lord Stevens seems to have given it. Indeed, we could find no mention of this speeding violation in the Paget report. Of course, this does not mean the claim is without substance, only that Lord Stevens failed to include it in his report. When questioned by reporters at the press conference on the day the Paget report was published, the former police chief brushed the claim aside as *"speculation"*. Whether this means he failed to investigate the claim, or that he did investigate it but was deflected by dismissals from the French police, we do not know. Lord Stevens did not comment further. Perhaps he should have, but he did not. Maybe the newly designed 'terms of reference' discussed earlier, that he need only investigate *"the allegation made by Mohamed Al Fayed"*, let him off the hook. We will have to wait and see if this claim is brought up at the Inquest.

Blind

There is one other claim we should consider, in our opinion the most plausible claim thus far tabled, namely: that all the cameras that could have caught Diana's last moments were mysteriously turned inwards, towards the buildings that housed them and away from the road, thus rendering them 'blind' and making it impossible for them to record the Mercedes as it drove past. Indeed, as dubious as this explanation might seem, the Paget report claims that this was indeed the case—that the only cameras operating were privately owned security cameras, and that all of them pointed inwards towards the buildings that housed them, thus:

"Lieutenant Gigou of the Brigade Criminelle explained the work undertaken to identify CCTV images. Those private CCTV systems were not recording the public carriageway but were focused on the buildings to which they were attached." [Operation Paget Report, Page 409]

Don't know about you, but most private security cameras we've ever seen point away from the buildings that house them, if only to capture unwanted intruders who might be thinking about breaking in. True, some might well point inwards in order to film the interesting brickwork that holds them up. But in our experience most do the job they were put there to do: film intruders. And that means they point outwards. After all, when an intruder breaks into a property in order to steal some of its contents, is it not fairly common practice for that intruder to make his getaway in a car? Parked nearby? Or maybe even directly outside? And isn't the purpose of the security camera to capture an image of that intruder, firstly as he approaches the building, then as he departs and jumps into his waiting car? Wouldn't it be helpful if the camera was positioned such that it captured not only the intruder, but the car as well, its size, make, number plate? Apparently not. Not in Paris. In Paris, we are told, the cameras are turned inwards to face the buildings they are supposed to protect.

As stated, no wonder MI-6 chose Paris as its killing field.

19

THE MERCEDES

S280 Limousine

There is a very brief, almost cursory chapter in the Paget report regarding the team's examination of the Mercedes S280 limousine in which Diana died. This puzzled us. Not so much that the report should have contained this chapter, but more that its sole purpose was to investigate the claim that the Mercedes' speedometer had stuck on 192 kilometres (approx 120 miles) per hour at the moment of impact. And there we found our answer. The Fayed camp, we recalled, had alleged that the media had used the story to further bolster claims that Henri Paul had been drunk, and in consequence, had been driving way too fast, recklessly even, as he entered the Alma Tunnel. The Paget report, we once again reminded ourselves, was all about refuting allegations made solely by Mohamed Al Fayed, and not about investigating all of the facts relating to Princess Diana's death. Hence this chapter was so short. Remaining dutifully within the bounds of its cleverly contrived 'terms of reference', the Paget team was able to skirt around many of the questions that still exist regarding the Mercedes—questions that should have been more vigorously investigated. Who stole the car in April 1997, four months prior to the crash? Who carried out the repairs? Is it true, as reported in the press, that the car's EMS (effectively a microchip that controls the steering and the brakes) was the only component stolen from the car? If so, who replaced it? Was the new EMS chip found and examined after the crash? If so, by whom?

And further: Why was this particular Mercedes "*the only suitable vehicle available*" for the journey from the Ritz that night, as stated in the report? Why had the car been left unattended in "*the Vendome underground car park*" for three and a half hours prior to the journey? How secure is that car park? Are there any CCTV or security camera images of the car during this period? Is it possible the car could have been tampered with during this period? In this regard, why was former SAS officer Sir Ranulph Fiennes not questioned on his knowledge of deniable operations, in particular the 'Boston brakes' method of 'car crash assassinations'? Why was former Equerry to the Queen, Air Marshall Sir Peter Horsley's testimony not considered in this same regard? Etc. Etc. Etc. True, in addition to the 'speedometer claim', the Paget team did also bullet-point the results of its examination of the car, in order *"to give a full picture of the technical aspects of the Mercedes car"*. But why were the results of a previous examination carried out by the Institut de Recherche Criminelle de la Gendarmerie Nationale (IRCGN), the official French police research team that examined the Mercedes for the French inquiry in October 1998, not included in this chapter? Was this because, in particular with regard to tests carried out on the brakes, tyres and seat belts, the IRCGN results disagreed with the Paget results?

Indeed, not only did the French team find an intermittent problem with the brake warning light. Not only did they find that the front right tyre had been cut. They also claimed that the seat belt Princess Diana should have been wearing was in proper working order, a claim curiously disputed by the Paget team, as we shall see.

The Speedometer
And The Rear Right Seat Belt

But firstly, as expected, the Paget team concluded that all press reports claiming that the speedometer had stuck at 192 kilometres per hour on impact were unfounded, and thus, untrue. The report concluded:

French Dossier D2729

"A photograph of the vehicle in its post-impact position clearly showed the speedometer needle at the zero position." [Operation Paget Report, Page 417]

And further:

"When examined by Police Capitaine Francis Bechet on 1 September 1997 the speedometer needle of the Mercedes car was at zero." [Operation Paget Report, Page 418]

And that was the extent of it. No big deal.

What was a big deal, though, is this.

"David Price's examination of the seat belts showed that they were in a good operational condition with the exception of the rear right seat belt, which was found to be jammed in the retracted position because part of the internal mechanism had become displaced." [Operation Paget Report, Page 421]

For the record, David Price, a Forensic Accident Investigator at Britain's Transport Research Laboratory, was employed by Lord Stevens as his 'crash expert'. As stated, Mr Price found on examination of the Mercedes that all the seat belts were working properly, *"with the exception of the rear right seat belt"*, which, he said, was *"jammed in the retracted position"*. In a feverish and somewhat unconvincing attempt to brush this finding aside, the report goes on to say that *"the evidence strongly supports this displacement occurring after the collision"*. Evidently, *"French expert, Serge Moreau"* of IRCGN, had assured Operation Paget that the seat belt in question was *"in proper working order at the time of his examination in October 1998"*. Strange how Lord Stevens, when the shit comes down, calls on the French experts for help. On other issues, where their findings and opinions disagree, he dispenses with them.

In any event, what is particularly significant about this finding, of course, is that *"the rear right seat belt"*, had it been working, would have been the seat belt worn by Princess Diana. *Wo!* One more time. *"The rear right seat belt"*, had it been working, would have been the seat belt worn by Princess Diana. Yet Lord Stevens fails even to allude to this crucial detail, much less investigate it further. Why? Surely even the Establishment's favourite snoopdog must have found this a tad suspicious. From the minute news of Diana's death broke, those who knew her best constantly questioned why she was not wearing her seat belt. She always wore a seat belt, they said; fears for her own safety had made it an obsession with her, if not a religious observance. *We cannot understand why Diana was not wearing her seat belt!*

Well now you know. Tucked away in Chapter Six of the Paget report we find that, on this night, Diana was unable to follow what had become for her an instinctive, compulsive routine because her seat belt was *"jammed in the retracted position"*. Yet Lord Stevens fails even to consider this point as being in the least significant. While his actions in calling on the 'French experts' for backup clearly betray his desperation in attempting to explain this one away, no allusion is made to the possibility that the seat belt might have been tampered with prior to the fatal journey. Instead, true to his apparent ambition to uphold the Establishment viewpoint at any cost, the great man simply called on *"French expert, Serge Moreau"* of IRCGN to bail him out, and the Frenchman duly complied. Moreau assured him that the seat belt had been *"in proper working order at the time of his examination in October 1998"*, and Lord Stevens gratefully accepted this statement as fact. No explanation of how the seat belt might have become *"jammed"* in the intervening years, as the crumpled Mercedes sat idle in a French police lockup, was forthcoming. Indeed, the only other reference to this smoking-gun anomaly was Lord Stevens' cursory conclusion, thus:

"There was no defect in the seat belt system. The seatbelts were not used. There were no signs of any interference with the vehicle." [Operation Paget Report, Page 426]

Unbelievable, especially as every crash expert this side of the asteroid belt has stated, quite unequivocally, that had Diana been wearing her seat belt she would almost certainly have survived the crash. We recall the opinion of Britain's foremost crash expert, Professor Murray MacKay, for example, who told us that the right rear seat should have been the safest seat in the car, the *"most survivable"* seat, and that had Diana been wearing her seat belt she would in all probability have survived. But as we have seen time and again, this faithful Knight of the Realm and newly ennobled Lord of the United Kingdom seems to listen only to those 'experts' whose opinion supports his agenda, no matter how unsafe that opinion might be. Dr David Kelly killed himself, right? JFK was gunned down by a lone gunman. There are weapons of mass destruction in Iraq.

And Diana died in a tragic road crash, because she wasn't wearing a seat belt.

Brake Failure

In January 2004, Britain's *Daily Mail* ran an article in which it claimed to have gained possession of the official French Judicial Dossier containing the results of the French inquiry. This in itself was interesting, as nobody else, not even the Royal Coroner at the time, Michael Burgess, had seen the document. It is even more interesting to note that author, broadcaster and journalist, Martyn Gregory, an aggressively outspoken champion of the 'accident theory', also mysteriously claimed to have gained access to this top-secret document while researching material for his TV documentary, *Diana: The Ultimate Truth*, screened on Britain's Channel 4 on 5th February, 2004. Quite how a mid-level British broadcast journalist gained access to such a highly sensitive document has never been explained. One might imagine the following:

Judge Stephan: *"The French inquiry is now complete. The Judicial Dossier containing the results of our investigation are top-secret and will remain under lock and key indefinitely."*

Mohamed Al Fayed: *"May I see the document, please, as it might contain vital evidence of a conspiracy to murder my son and his future wife?"*

Judge Stephan: *"No."*

Professor Peter Vanezis, Regis Professor of Forensic Medicine at Glasgow University: *"May I see the document, please, as it might contain valuable forensic evidence that would help us determine whether or not Diana was pregnant at the time of her death?"*

Judge Stephan: *"No."*

Professor Peter Vanezis: *"But it might also contain information that would help us determine whether or not Henri Paul was drunk."*

Judge Stephan: *"No."*

Daily Mail: *"Can we have a look at the document, please? We'd like to publish your top-secret findings in the pages of our British tabloid."*

Martyn Gregory: *"Oh yes, me too. I'd like to make a TV documentary."*

Judge Stephan: *"No problem, gentlemen. Bon voyage!"*

Makes you wonder.

In any event, not unlike Lord Stevens' Paget report, Gregory's documentary set out with one intention in mind, and one intention only: to dispel the 'conspiracy theories'. And in a banal kind of way, that is precisely what it laboured to do.

But the difference between Gregory's attempt to discredit the evidence, and a similar attempt made two weeks earlier by the *Daily Mail*— the newspaper that had serialised Gregory's book, *Diana: The Last Days*, some five years earlier—was that the *Daily Mail*, one can only assume inadvertently, let slip a very interesting fact. Having gained access to the 6,000-page French report, it revealed that the brakes on the Mercedes in which Diana died had failed as Henri Paul entered the Alma Tunnel (see *Footnote II*). Quoting from the French dossier, the article went on to explain that, according to the official French police research establishment that examined the car for the French inquiry, IRCGN, Henri Paul was forced to try and slow the vehicle by ramming the automatic gear lever into neutral. Realising the brakes had failed, the paper claimed, Paul committed this stupid mistake in a moment of drunken panic, the insinuation being, of course, that Paul was over the limit and thus was solely to blame for the 'accident'. Remarkably, the question of what had caused the brakes to fail in the first place was never raised, much less explored.

However, in printing this story the *Daily Mail* revealed to an astonished nation that the brakes had indeed failed on the Mercedes as it entered the Alma Tunnel. This information had been sourced from the official French inquiry report, the paper said.

Enter Lord Stevens and the Paget team. Perhaps not surprisingly, David Price, who examined the car for Operation Paget, found nothing untoward when he examined the brakes, brake pipes, brake sensor pads and brake fluid. According to Mr Price there was nothing wrong with the brakes. Although a defect that caused the brake warning light to come on intermittently had mystified the French team, Mr Price put Lord Stevens' mind to rest when he discovered that "*the rear right brake pad wear sensor was out of position and had wear not associated with its normal function*". He concluded that this was the likely culprit for the intermittent fault with the brake warning light. Case solved.

Or is it? Indeed, if the brakes were working properly, as the Paget report maintains, then what are we to make of the *Daily Mail* story? If, as claimed, they gained access to the official French report in 2004, and indeed, sourced their material from that report, how is it that this same report now appears to state something entirely different? And there is one further, extremely crucial point that seems to have been overlooked here. Namely: if the brakes were working, then how is it there were no skidmarks found at the scene of the crash? Tyre marks, yes. Skidmarks, no. As the Paget report confirms:

"The condition of the tyre treads was also consistent with the lack of skid marks found at the scene of the crash." [Operation Paget Report, Page 423]

The Mercedes did not skid, then. The white Fiat Uno, having been clipped by four tons of speeding Mercedes at the entrance to the Alma Tunnel, did not skid either, implying that the Uno's driver made no instinctive correction manoeuvre following the glancing blow from the Mercedes, or indeed, on witnessing the Mercedes slam into a concrete pillar just a few yards in front of him (see *Chapter 5*). According to Britain's leading crash expert, Professor Murray MacKay, this would appear to demonstrate what he referred to in our interview with him as *"abnormal driving"* on the part of the Uno driver, further implying that the driver in question was no ordinary driver, but a highly skilled driver who showed the presence of mind to regain control of his vehicle after being struck by the Mercedes, and subsequently avoid the wreckage of the Mercedes as it slammed into the concrete pillar and spun back out across the road in front of him, all without using his brakes. For the record, Professor MacKay, who visited the Alma Tunnel in an official capacity soon after the crash, and employed state-of-the-art computer-simulated reconstructions of the crash to enhance the accuracy of his findings, confirmed the Paget conclusion that tyre marks belonging to the Mercedes were discovered at the crash scene, but that no skidmarks were found, indicating to us, at least, that Henri Paul, for some strange, inexplicable reason, failed to apply the brakes as he careered head-long into a concrete pillar at more than 60 miles per hour. Either that, or he *did* apply the brakes but they did not respond, which is why he was forced to ram the automatic gear lever into neutral to try to slow the Mercedes down.

Verdict? The *Daily Mail* was right: the brakes failed. We can think of no other logical explanation for the lack of skidmarks at the scene of the crash, and moreover, according to the Paget report, neither can Lord Stevens. No explanation whatever is offered in this regard, only assertions, which in the end we are left with little choice but to accept. Indeed, due to conflicting evidence, plus the fact that the official French findings have never been published for the consumption of us mere mortals, we are left with little choice but to accept Lord Stevens' word that "*both the French and British examinations of the Mercedes have shown that there were no mechanical issues with the car that could have in any way caused or contributed to the crash*". We are left with little choice but to accept Lord Stevens' word in this regard for the simple reason that he is one of only a select few who have ever seen the 6,000-page French inquiry dossier, and thus only a select few know for certain what it contains. For the record, those select few include the Operation Paget team, of course; the Royal Coroner; the *Daily Mail* ... oh, and Martyn Gregory, the man who not only makes it his business, curiously, to so vociferously and publicly defend the Establishment position with regard to Diana's death. But interestingly, the man who is also alleged by Mohamed Al Fayed to have collaborated with bodyguard Trevor Rees-Jones in the writing of his book, together with MI5. More on this later.

Slashed Tyre

One final anomaly—or discrepancy—we should highlight with regard to the Paget report's chapter on the Mercedes refers to tests carried out on the vehicle's tyres. As the report informs us:

"*There was a contradiction in the reports of Capitaine Francis Bechet* (French Dossier D568) *and the French technical experts, Jacques Hebrard, Gilles Poully and Serge Moreau.* (French Dossier D5651)

And further:

"*Capitaine Francis Bechet reported that the front right tyre was deflated when he examined the vehicle at Nord Garage, Boulevard MacDonald on 1 September 1997 whereas Jacques Hebrard, Gilles Poully and Serge Moreau reported that the tyre was inflated to 2.1 bar (30 psi) at the time of their examination in October 1998.*" [Operation Paget Report, Page 423]

Capitaine Francis Bechet was the senior French police officer in charge of the team that first examined the Mercedes following the crash. Indeed, Capitaine Bechet's examination took place on September 1st, 1997, the day after the crash, and one would imagine that because he examined the car so soon after the crash his results would be the most reliable, in particular in terms of the general, cosmetic state of the vehicle immediately following the crash. OK, perhaps Capitaine Bechet's examination was less thorough than subsequent examinations carried out by IRCGN and Operation Paget, but in this instance we are only talking about the state of the tyres, and not some specific, technical problem that might well have required a more thorough examination to identify. In any event, Capitaine Bechet's report regarding the state of the tyres was clear and straightforward enough: the front right tyre was flat. No rocket science required.

Of course, one might expect that the vehicle had been severely damaged in such a violent collision, especially as the Mercedes collided with a steel-reinforced concrete pillar, head-on. The fact that the front right tyre was found to be flat should not in itself raise too many alarm bells, then.

But what is of note is that, when the vehicle was examined for the French inquiry by IRCGN some 13 months later, the same front right tyre was found to be inflated to 2.1 bar (30psi). In other words, it was found to be inflated to more or less the correct tyre pressure. Very strange, and yet nobody seems to have asked the obvious question: who inflated the tyre? Or perhaps more to the point: why? No explanation is given, even though this would appear to indicate that someone did not want the rest of us to know that the tyre had been flat following the crash. Perhaps there is a clue in this further discovery, made by David Price.

"*David Price found a small penetrating cut in the side-wall of this tyre, as a result of which it was no longer airtight.*" [Operation Paget Report, Page 423]

Of course, as with every other anomaly associated with this case, bar none, Lord Stevens assures us that the "*small penetrating cut*" discovered by David Price was not man-made. Thus:

"*The nature of the cut indicated that it had been caused by damaged bodywork during the crash and had not been caused by any malicious means.*" [Operation Paget Report, Page 423]

Thank heaven for Lord Stevens and his team, then. We were just beginning to suspect foul play!

In all seriousness, we do not in good conscience contend that Lord Stevens' conclusion is anything but reasonable. As stated, one might expect to incur a flat tyre in such a violent collision. But what we do find anomalous is that no questions were asked regarding the discrepancy between the results of the two examinations. Either the tyre was flat following the crash, or it wasn't. Capitaine Bechet certainly found it to be flat, and Operation Paget's subsequent assertion that a *"small penetrating cut"* was discovered during David Price's examination would certainly appear to corroborate the Capitaine's conclusion. So why, when the car was examined by IRCGN some 13 months after Capitaine Bechet's examination, did the so-called 'French experts' find then that the tyre was not flat, but *"inflated to 2.1 bar (30psi)"*? The IRCGN team, remember, specifically *"French expert, Serge Moreau"* of IRCGN, was the very 'expert' upon whom Lord Stevens relied to help him explain away Diana's seat belt mystery. This time around, however, Serge Moreau would appear to have become the villain of the piece; this time around he would be disregarded, surely evidence in itself that Lord Stevens mistrusted his findings. How then could he assert with such confidence that Diana's seat belt had been *"in proper working order at the time of his [Serge Moreau's] examination in October 1998"*, especially as his own 'expert', David Price, found that it was *"jammed in the retracted position"*? The facts just do not stack up. It is glaringly obvious that someone must have tampered with the car during the 13-month period between Capitaine Bechet's examination and that of Serge Moreau and the IRCGN team, otherwise the IRCGN team could not possibly have found that the front right tyre was *"inflated to 2.1 bar (30psi)"*. As Lord Stevens himself asserts in his report:

> *"The tyre could not have been inflated to 2.1 bar (30 psi) as reported by the French technical experts unless it had been re-inflated shortly before then."* [Operation Paget Report, Page 423]

And if someone had indeed *"re-inflated"* the tyre *"shortly before"* the car was examined by IRCGN, then surely this is evidence of tampering. There can be no other explanation. There is no explanation, at least, offered by Lord Stevens in his report, and in consequence, we can only assume that he failed to investigate this very serious and possibly significant incident. Indeed, the former police chief, who has been commended on no fewer than 27 occasions for outstanding detective ability, seems to simply acknowledge this anomaly with what can only be considered a dangerous degree of nonchalance, like one might nonchalantly acknowledge some other trivial fact. Was there evidence of tampering? Yes. How do we know? The tyre had been pumped up. By whom? We do not know. *Why* had the tyre been pumped up? We do not know. Why? Because Lord Stevens failed to ask the appropriate questions. Either that, or he *did* ask the appropriate questions but failed to include the answers in his report. How then can we trust the conclusions of the Paget team with regard to the brakes, seat belts and tyres? We cannot. Yet again we can only take Lord Stevens at his word, and as honourable and conscientious as this Knight of St John might be, his word alone is not evidence, much less *conclusive evidence*.

Verdict: anomalies regarding the Mercedes' brakes, seat belts and tyres need further, more vigorous investigation.

20

THE CRASH

The Journey From The Ritz
The Unidentified Motorcycle(s)
And A Bright Flash In The Tunnel

At the beginning of Operation Paget Report, Chapter Seven, we are told the following:

"Subject of course to the Coroner's direction, the events immediately preceding and following the fatal incident in the Alma underpass are likely to be examined in some detail at the inquest(s).

Operation Paget holds evidence that is relevant to both the conspiracy allegation and the inquest(s). This chapter examines evidence in terms of its relevance to the conspiracy allegation [made by Mohamed Al Fayed] only. It is not intended to examine evidence, particularly eyewitness evidence, in order to show how the crash occurred. That is a matter for the inquest(s) to decide in due course." [Operation Paget Report, Page 430]

In light of this declaration, we decline to comment on the above points (the journey from the Ritz, the unidentified motorcycle(s), and the bright flash in the tunnel). We have covered these points in some detail in earlier chapters anyway. And until all the evidence is published, we stand by the evidence presented in those chapters.

21

EMERGENCY

The Doctors And Paramedics

Debate regarding the efficiency—or otherwise—of the emergency operation has raged since news of the crash first reached Britain. Certainly within days, as details of the operation and Diana's medical treatment emerged, doubts over the length of time it took to get her to hospital—the amount of time it took to get her in the ambulance, the amount of time it took the ambulance to get from the crash scene to the hospital, the decision to bypass at least one fully equipped hospital en route to Pitie-Salpetriere Hospital, where Diana was eventually treated; plus the fact that the ambulance stopped for 10 minutes just a few hundred yards from the hospital entrance—raised suspicions that fester to this day. Certainly to us it seemed inconceivable, even if it did take 46 minutes to extricate Diana from the Mercedes and get her into the ambulance, as the Paget report claims, that it should then have taken a further 26 minutes to get Diana to hospital, 3.25 miles from the crash scene. Again, the Paget report confirms these statistics.

However, it is true to say that, with the publication of the Paget report, we now have a far better understanding of the emergency operation and those who played a role in it. In this light it is difficult in the extreme for us to question the integrity of the SAMU doctors and paramedics involved in the rescue operation. For many years after the crash, nobody outside of the French judicial inquiry knew who these paramedics were, and as their identities were protected by Judge Stephan and the French inquiry, speculation that they might have been undercover intelligence operatives grew. True, details of what happened at the crash scene and who might have been present during the 10 minutes or so prior to the arrival of the emergency services remain sketchy, and in our opinion require far more vigorous investigation. But with the release of the Paget report, at least we now know the names of the doctors and paramedics involved, and in consequence, must accord them due respect. It is the easiest thing in the world for us to sit back in our armchairs and criticize others who, after all, dedicate their working lives to saving the lives of others. As stated previously, we remain convinced Diana was murdered, and the contents and general tenor of the Paget report have achieved little in changing our point of view in that regard. But when a reasonable explanation regarding some of the questions and anomalies surrounding this case is presented, then we must at least consider that explanation as a viable possibility. This does not mean, of course, that the explanation is necessarily right. Just that it might be. Or at least that it might contain some greater degree of truth than we would previously have accorded it.

This, at least, is our opinion based on the evidence contained in the Paget report regarding the rescue operation. While we remain wholly uneasy with the idea that it should have taken so long to ferry Diana to hospital, we do have to take into account the fact that the French emergency services work differently to those of most other nations. Again, while this may well have been a factor in MI-6 choosing Paris as its killing field, as indeed the known lack of CCTV cameras operating in Paris in 1997 might also have been, none the less we should perhaps be less full-blooded in firing off accusations of either negligence or incompetence at the paramedics who attended the scene. These are real people doing a very difficult and worthwhile job, and it is hard to reconcile this fact with accusations of deliberate neglect, or worse. None the less, there remain one or two points that really have not been satisfactorily resolved, and we should scrutinize those points here.

The Paget team has gone to great lengths to interview all those involved on the night, from the doctors and paramedics on the ground to the doctors and nurses at the hospital. It is difficult for us to question their statements. Though we may well, and rightly so, view the more senior figures involved in the rescue operation with some suspicion, we have to ask ourselves why an ordinary, day-to-day Parisian paramedic would knowingly participate in a conspiracy to murder a British princess. And not just one: there were several doctors, paramedics and ambulance drivers involved that night, which means the entire crew would had to have been involved. True, given that we are talking about an event unprecedented in modern times— the assassination of a princess; and more: the assassination of the most famous and loved princess in the world—the possibility that the French ambulance and fire services had been penetrated by undercover operatives cannot, we concede, be ruled out. Not entirely. But at the same time we surely have to err on the side of realism and concede that the paramedics in question were probably just that *paramedics*—and that their reasons for taking so long to get Diana to hospital, while still not entirely convincing to anyone who lives outside France and who is thus unaccustomed with the way they work, are none the less, for the most part, plausible. As Dr Jean-Marc Martino, specialist in anaesthetics and intensive care treatment and the doctor in charge of the SAMU ambulance that took Diana to hospital, states in the report:

"She was stuck in a 'medically abnormal' position, between the back of the right hand passenger seat and the rear seat, and with some difficulty we got her out, taking every precaution, with the assistance of the Fire Brigade. Despite this, during this operation she went into cardiac arrest and I had to intubate and ventilate her and [cardiac] massage in order to resuscitate her." [Operation Paget Report, Page 514]

According to Dr Martino, then, extricating Diana from the Mercedes was not straightforward, and naturally this contributed to the length of time it took to get her in the ambulance. Once they did remove her from the car at around 1.00 am, we are told, Diana suffered a heart attack. As the Paget report further states, referring to Dr Martino's treatment of Diana at the scene:

"She was removed from the car at around 1am with the assistance of the Sapeurs-Pompiers [Fire Service with paramedic capabilities]. She then went into cardiac arrest. Following external cardiopulmonary resuscitation the Princess of Wales' heart started beating again. She was moved to the SAMU ambulance at 1.18am." [Operation Paget Report, Page 514]

And further:

Ω*"Dr Martino then made a more detailed examination. He noted a right side chest trauma that had not been obvious initially. There was an apparent fracture to the right upper arm and right wrist and a wound to her right thigh. He also noted an injury to her face."* [Operation Paget Report, Page 514]

At this point, the report continues, Diana's blood pressure started to fall, indicating that she might be suffering from internal bleeding. Dr Martino thus realized the need to get her to hospital, we are told. The time was now 1.18 am; the paramedics had been at the scene for a full forty-six minutes, yet they had only just realized the necessity to get Diana to hospital. We can only put this down to the manner in which French doctors and paramedics are accustomed to working.

None the less it has to be said that, according to paramedic experts we interviewed—most notably British Paramedic Supervisor Andy Palmer—the first assumption in such an horrific crash as this must be that the victim might have suffered internal bleeding. We accept that French paramedics work differently, and that in any case, it is impossible to be certain that the victim is bleeding internally until they are opened up in theatre. We also accept that as soon as Dr Martino realized Diana's blood pressure was falling, a sign that she was probably bleeding internally, he took measures to get her to hospital. But it was not until this point that the hospital was even contacted and told to expect delivery of Diana. Once again, we can only accept that the doctor was following standard French procedure, and thus that no blame should be laid at his feet with regard to the amount of time it took to get Diana in the ambulance. What happened next, though, must surely come under far closer scrutiny.

"Drive Slowly"

"At 1.41am, once the Princess of Wales' blood pressure was stable enough for the journey, Dr Martino gave authority to the SAMU ambulance driver to move off, instructing him to drive slowly as the effect of acceleration and deceleration could be harmful." [Operation Paget Report, Page 514]

We are no medical experts, and we do not wish to question Dr Martino's wisdom in instructing the ambulance driver to *"drive slowly as the effect of acceleration and deceleration could be harmful"*. But the fact remains that it is now 1.41 am, a full forty-one minutes since Diana was extricated from the Mercedes and twenty-three minutes since Dr Martino realized Diana's blood pressure was falling and that, consequently, he needed to get her to hospital. Surely when he then instructed the ambulance driver to *"drive slowly"*, he could not have meant *that* slowly. True, the decision to bypass Hotel Dieu Hospital—which was a mile closer to the crash scene—and take Diana to Pitie-Salpetriere Hospital—which was better equipped, the report claims—had already been taken, and it should be stated that Dr Martino was not involved in the making of that decision. One would, in any event, normally calculate an extra mile to be fairly negligible; at an average speed of, say, 40 mph, the extra mile would add only a minute and a half and the entire journey of 3.25 miles should take less than 5 minutes. But we are told in the report that the ambulance did not arrive at Pitie-Salpetriere Hospital until 19 or 20 minutes later, at approximately 2.00 am, indicating that the ambulance travelled at approximately 10 miles per hour. A further mile at 10 miles per hour adds 6 minutes to the journey, and we contend that this extra 6 minutes could have been crucial, especially as we are then told that the ambulance stopped for a further 5 minutes (other reports state 10 minutes; Dr Martino confirms he is only estimating 5 minutes and that it could have been 10 minutes) just across the road from the hospital entrance. This amounts to an extra 16 minutes in total. As the Paget report informs us, it was Dr Martino who ordered the ambulance driver to stop.

"I took that decision because the arterial pressure was dropping and I feared there would be another cardiac arrest. I had the vehicle stopped in order to re-examine the Princess. There was something abnormal going on, and the vehicle had to be stopped so that I could understand that abnormality. I did not do any cardiac massage at that moment but it is not easy to do cardiac massage or resuscitation with a vehicle moving." [Operation Paget Report, Page 514]

Again, we are no medical experts, and thus we do not know if Dr Martino's actions in deciding to stop the ambulance at this point should be called into question. To us it seems a somewhat controversial, if not dubious decision to have made. Did the ambulance really need to stop for Dr Martino to *"re-examine the Princess"* when she was just a few hundred yards from the hospital entrance? As he tells us, he did not perform a further cardiac massage during these five or ten minutes, so what *did* he do that required the ambulance to be stationery for this amount of time, when the hospital was just across the road? What *did* he do that was so important it couldn't have waited a further minute or two, by which time Diana would have been in theatre? It is true that all the medical experts interviewed by Operation Paget claimed that Diana was too badly injured to have survived anyway. The debate rages on. In this regard, we can only hope that independent medical experts are called to the inquest to offer their own professional opinions on this matter, because we are simply not sufficiently qualified to comment.

For the record, the crash occurred at 12.23 am. Diana was finally taken into the hospital at 2.06 am, one hour and forty-three minutes later, and one hour and thirty-six minutes after the emergency services arrived at the crash scene just over 3 miles from the hospital. By this time, however, it was too late to save her.

She was pronounced dead at 4.00 am.

22

ILLEGALLY EMBALMED

Allegations

If the doctors and paramedics who treated Diana at the crash scene and at the hospital were, in our opinion, for the most part vindicated in their actions, then those involved in her embalming clearly were not. Indeed, they should have been far more rigorously questioned with regard to who actually ordered the embalming and why it was performed without proper authorization. The somewhat lame reason given is that Diana was embalmed for purposes of "*presentation*"—evidently Prince Charles, the French President and his wife, plus other French dignitaries and members of Diana's family were on their way to view the body and pay their respects. But we cannot accept this as a valid reason for Diana's body to have undergone a full embalming process. Normal procedure in this situation would have been either for dry ice to have been applied, or for a process known as 'mortuary cleansing' to have been performed. The latter involves general cleaning of the body, suturing of the mouth, closing of the eyes and the application of make-up in order to make the body presentable. As the official reason given for Diana's embalming was indeed "*to make her body presentable before viewing*", then there seems no legitimate reason why this option should not have sufficed. True, Jean Monceau, in charge of the embalming process, argued that because Diana's body, curiously, had not been refrigerated, and due to the extent of her injuries, a full embalming was the only appropriate course of action. We will explore these claims in due course.

For now, it has to be said that, certainly in our opinion, the chapter in the Paget report that deals with Diana's embalming is a prime example of how Lord Stevens cherry-picks bits of evidence that support his 'accident directive', and then deftly weaves them together in order to reinforce his case. He seems to do this not with any noticeable degree of stealth or underhand intention, but openly, as a matter of course, as if like some schoolyard bully this is the way he has always worked, and got away with it. As if nobody has ever challenged him. As if, with the full might of the Establishment at his back, nobody has ever dared.

Essentially, the main allegations investigated in this chapter of the report are whether or not Diana's embalming was illegal under French law, and whether there was any evidence that Diana had been embalmed in order to cover up the fact that she might have been pregnant with Dodi's child. With regard to the first allegation, these are the facts as we have them:

Was Diana embalmed?

Yes.

Fully embalmed?

Yes.

Illegally embalmed?

In our opinion, yes. According to Lord Stevens, on the other hand, it would seem to depend on how one interprets the facts, together with the statements of those involved. See what you make of it.

French Law

In the first instance we are told that, according to French law:

"*The embalming of a deceased person cannot proceed without an authorisation given by the Mayor of the area where the death took place or the area where the embalming takes place.*" [Operation Paget Report, Page 531]

The report goes on to explain that, in the absence of the Mayor, this duty falls upon "*the representative of the State in the Department*", usually the local police chief, or "*Prefet*". If, however, the *Prefet* is not available either, the report states, then the most senior police officer who is available will do. Seems straightforward enough.

In the case of Princess Diana, then, as in any other case, we have to ask the question: did the Mayor, or in his absence, the *Prefet,* or in his absence, the most senior police officer available, authorize the embalming? Answer: no. Well did some other senior French official authorize the embalming on their behalf,? No. A junior police officer, then? No. The janitor? No, not even his pet poodle.

The fact is that the authorization was given not by any French official, but by the British Consul-General in Paris at the time, Keith Moss of the British Embassy, effectively the headquarters of MI-6 in Paris. We are told that Jean Monceau, Assistant Commercial Director in 1997 for the French embalming company BJL, which was responsible for the embalming, received authorization from this senior British Embassy official and acted on that authority and that authority alone. Don't know about you, but from where we are sitting this means that the embalming was clearly illegal under French law, as authorization had come not from the Mayor or one of his representatives, nor from the city police chief or one of his subordinates, but from a very senior figure based at the British Embassy in Paris. A British diplomat. An Englishman. Media claims that the embalming had been ordered by the British authorities, then, would seem to carry some considerable weight. Indeed, if the Paget report is to be believed, further claims that the embalming had been carried out without the appropriate authorization would also seem to be true. The evidence speaks for itself.

In the Paget report, however, Lord Stevens interprets this evidence in his own inimitable way. Accustomed over many years to carrying out the letter of the law, he argues that:

"*Jean Monceau believed that, in the person of the Consul-General, he had the consent of 'those having authority to proceed with funeral arrangements'.*" [Operation Paget Report, Page 539]

And that, in a nutshell, is the substance of Stevens' argument that Diana's embalming was not carried out illegally. Jean Monceau, he assures us, "*believed*" he had the authority to proceed, and that puts him in the clear.

"*Hey buddy, you're under arrest for forced entry and burglary.*"

"*But I believed I had the authority to enter these premises and take whatever I wanted!*"

"*You did? Oh. Well have a nice day!*"

It really is very disturbing that someone who has been knighted and elevated to the peerage for his work as Britain's top police officer should be able to get away with this kind of claptrap. Jean Monceau "*believed*" he had authorization to embalm the Princess of Wales, and that, it would seem, was good enough for Lord Stevens.

But it was not good enough for us, nor should it be good enough for anyone else with a sincere desire to find the truth. We delved deeper, scrutinizing the report, line by line, name by name, word by spurious word. It soon became clear enough to us, when reading through Monceau's statement and the circumstances that led to him performing a full embalming, that something just wasn't right. We began to smell a rat. Allegations that a senior British diplomat had been instrumental in ordering the embalming came flooding back to us. More recently that senior British diplomat, we recalled, had been named in the press as Sir Michael Jay, British Ambassador in Paris at the time. According to the Paget report, Sir Michael denied any involvement in the decision making, and once again, of course, this oligarch's denial was good enough for Lord Stevens. Sir Michael Jay was off the hook.

But what of Keith Moss, we wondered, Consul-General at the British Embassy in Paris at the time? Unlike Sir Michael Jay, Keith Moss was unable to deny involvement as he had been named in Jean Monceau's statement. Keith Moss, of course, denies giving the order for the embalming to be carried out; indeed, according to Jean Monceau, it was the other way around. It was he who suggested to Keith Moss that Diana's body should be embalmed, but it was none the less Moss who gave Monceau the authorization to do so. Certainly Monceau claimed he "*believed*" Moss had authorized him to carry out the procedure, but bizarrely, Moss claims that because some of their conversation was held in French, "*he believed he was agreeing to a less intrusive form of treatment in order to make the Princess of Wales presentable for her family when they arrived at the hospital*". Unbelievable. Now we are faced with a Consul-General, the most senior British consul in France, who has trouble holding a conversation in French!

In any event, from this conversation, we are told, Monceau "*believed*" he now had "*verbal authorization*" to commence the embalming procedure. But this is not entirely correct. In his statement to Operation Paget, Monceau clearly affirms:

"*However, he [Keith Moss] told me that he must first resolve the problems surrounding the authorisations.*" [Operation Paget Report, Page 539]

Having agreed in principle to the embalming, then, Keith Moss concludes his conversation with Monceau by telling him he must first *"resolve the problems surrounding the authorisations."* In other words, whatever Monceau's understanding of the conversation, Keith Moss had not yet given authorization to proceed with the embalming. As he clearly told Monceau, he first needed to gain permission from one of Diana's next of kin or someone else with authority to give the green light. And this is where the question of authorization, specifically with regard to Diana's embalming, becomes a little blurred at the edges.

As previously stated, French law is quite specific with regard to gaining authorization for embalming. One must gain authorization from either the Mayor, the local police chief or the most senior police officer available. There is nothing ambiguous about that. But as we have seen, Jean Monceau took his authorization from the British Consul-General in Paris at that time, Keith Moss. Violation number one.

In order to obtain authorization from one of the above-mentioned officials, one is required under French law to produce, as the Paget report declares:

"A *written notice expressing the wishes of the deceased or a request from any person having authority to proceed with funeral arrangements, justifying his position and home address.*" [Operation Paget Report, Page 531]

Clearly there was no "*written notice expressing the wishes of the deceased*", which left Moss, Monceau *et al* to seek authorization elsewhere. As the second part of the above statement tells us, authorization now would have to be gained in the form of "*a request from any person having authority to proceed with funeral arrangements*", and it is this clause that would seem to have been interpreted by the Paget team in a very interesting way. As we have seen, Lord Stevens seemed content that Jean Monceau "*believed that, in the person of the Consul-General, he had the consent of* 'those having authority to proceed with funeral arrangements'." But even if Jean Monceau did believe this, the fact is that Keith Moss alone did not have the authority, even as Consul-General, to give Jean Monceau the green light with regard to Diana's embalming. First he had to gain permission from someone who did: Prince Charles, for example, or perhaps a member of Diana's immediate family. Perhaps even from Diana's Private Secretary at the time, Michael Gibbins. But so far as we know, and certainly as the Paget report affirms, Keith Moss did not receive permission from any of these people, not directly. Rather, Keith Moss acted on the instruction of one of Diana's security guards, a relatively unknown ex-Metropolitan Police copper by the name of Colin Tebbutt, who informed Keith Moss that Prince Charles was due to arrive at the hospital later that afternoon and thus they needed to prepare Diana's body for his arrival. As Mr Tebbutt recounts in his statement to Operation Paget:

"The Funeral Directors were also in the room and I said 'Would you kindly do whatever you do to prepare the body for when the family arrives'. Mr Moss who had been present, standing next to me in the office when I was speaking to Mr Gibbons [on the telephone], then spoke to the Hospital Funeral Directors in French, and as far as I am aware he asked the Funeral Directors to prepare the body for when the family arrived.'" [Operation Paget Report, Page 543]

Keith Moss, then, received his authority to give Jean Monceau the green light to embalm the princess from Colin Tebbutt, who had travelled to Paris with Diana's butler at that time, Paul Burrell, in order to help organize the repatriation of Diana's body. Mr Tebbutt in turn claims he received authority from Michael Gibbins, Diana's Private Secretary in 1997, which, if true, would surely have resolved the problem, once and for all. But Gibbins refutes this claim. He says he gave no such authority to embalm the princess, only to have her cleaned up for presentation purposes, as is clear from his statement to Operation Paget:

"I have been asked if the word 'embalming' was ever used. I can't remember, I had so many calls. I can however state that I never gave Colin Tebbutt directions to have the Princess embalmed. I was never aware that the Princess had undergone or was about to undergo any form of embalming process. The issue was to make the Princess look presentable for the arrival of the family." [Operation Paget Report, Page 544]

The chain of command, it seems, ends with Michael Gibbins, but Mr Gibbins says he gave authority only for Diana's body to be cleaned up. Indeed, Mr Tebbutt in turn, according to his statement, claims he also gave authority only for the princess's body to be made ready for presentation. Which can only mean one thing: Keith Moss, when he spoke to "*the Hospital Funeral Directors in French*", must have given the order for Diana to be embalmed, as we shall see.

Panic And Confusion

Clearly Jean Monceau, identified in the Paget report as the person Colin Tebbutt was referring to when he spoke of the "*Hospital Funeral Directors*", was under the impression that Keith Moss had given him the green light. But if this is true, we have to ask the question: who, in truth, might have instructed Keith Moss to green-light the embalming? Indeed, who had the authority? Sir Michael Jay, the most senior British Embassy official in Paris at the time, certainly had the authority to instruct Keith Moss in this regard. Michael Gibbins? Doubtful. His statement concurs wholly with that of Colin Tebbutt, in that his instructions were for Diana to be prepared for viewing, not embalmed. Colin Tebbutt, then? No. It would appear from his statement that Mr Tebbutt acted in good faith, on instruction from Michael Gibbins, even though his instruction to 'clean up the princess' seems to have been mistranslated somewhere down the line. Whether or not he was acting on orders from someone other than Michael Gibbins, of course, we do not know. But certainly on his own merit Colin Tebbutt would not have had the authority to grant Jean Monceau permission to embalm the Princess of Wales. He was nothing more than an ex-copper running an errand.

Attempts to establish exactly who gave authorization for Diana's body to be fully embalmed, then, as evinced by the chain of events described above, seemed only to create its own paper trail. To some greater or lesser degree, we put this down to the climate of panic and confusion that seemed to prevail in the aftermath of Diana's death. But not entirely. The more we scrutinized the statements of those involved, even if only to conceal their own mistakes, the more we began to realize that someone was not telling the whole truth. The reason given in the Paget report for Diana's immediate and full embalming, remember, was for presentation purposes only. Yet there seemed to be a very evident element of desperation driving Jean Monceau's ambition to embalm the princess, so much so that a series of frantic phone calls between France and Britain were logged, as well as a number of meetings between various authority figures in Paris, resulting in the embalming taking place before proper authorization was obtained. Not only does this make the embalming illegal in French law, it also raises suspicions as to who was *really* behind this seemingly desperate drive to embalm Diana's body as quickly as possible, even if it did mean breaking the law. Did Consul-

General Keith Moss take it upon himself to ensure that the princess was embalmed? Exactly what did he say to Jean Monceau "*in French*" while Colin Tebbutt was in the room? Certainly Jean Moncèau seemed to become obsessed with embalming the princess following his conversation with Moss, while Moss claims his conversation in French must have been misunderstood by Monceau. Not altogether convincing coming from someone who, given his position of Consul-General, must surely have spoken fluent French.

But even if Keith Moss is our culprit, and this clearly seems to be the case, it is doubtful he would have been acting of his own volition. This man was a British Embassy official, and as such he took orders from those higher up the chain-of-command than he. So we have to ask the question: where, in truth, did this chain-of-command originate? Who sat at the top? Who really wanted Diana embalmed, and why? It is apparent from the report that *someone* did, and that this someone was undoubtedly British. As the report informs us, even if Monceau had failed in his ambition to gain the necessary authorization to embalm the princess, Levertons, the Royal Undertakers, were already on their way from Britain, and the British posse had every intention of embalming the princess just as soon as they arrived. As Jean Monceau states in the report:

"*I was told that Prince Charles was coming to Paris and that he was bringing with him some British embalmers. This led me to believe that he wanted the Princess to be embalmed.*" [Operation Paget Report, Page 539]

Who told him this? Who told Monceau that "*Prince Charles was coming to Paris and that he was bringing with him some British embalmers*"? Who led Monceau to believe that Prince Charles "*wanted the Princess to be embalmed*"? It can only have been Keith Moss, during their conversation "*in French*", a fact that would explain why Monceau had become almost religious about wanting to get the job done, soon as. Indeed, in his seemingly frantic efforts in this regard, he contacted the Superintendent of the Brigade Criminelle, one Martine Monteil.

"*I explained what was happening to her. She told me not to worry, and that everything would be in order and the authorisations would be given.*" [Operation Paget Report, Page 540]

And further:

"Superintendent of Police Madame Monteil also told me not to worry when I asked her if I might have problems in respect of the documents required to proceed with Embalming ... The law says that you need the request for authorisation from the family or their representative and the authority from the Prefecture of Police. On that day I had verbal agreements." [Operation Paget Report, Page 540]

But according to French law, *"verbal agreements"* do not amount to lawful authorization. Verdict: the embalming of Princess Diana was illegal under French law.

Prince Charles
And The British Embalmers

We need to interject one further relevant point here in order that everyone is seeing the entire picture.

Aside from his belief that Prince Charles wanted Diana's body embalmed, the other reason for all the apparent panic was that, evidently, both Keith Moss and Jean Monceau were concerned about the state of Diana's body as it had not been sent to the hospital mortuary and refrigerated. While this seemed to us a somewhat lame, indeed, convenient excuse, the explanation given in the Paget report for this highly unusual situation none the less stated that: *"The body of the Princess of Wales was in a room in the main hospital for security and control reasons."* Evidently Professor Bruno Riou, the surgeon who received Diana on her arrival at the hospital, decided that it would be inappropriate to transport such a high-profile person as Diana to either the hospital mortuary, which he claims was at the other end of the building, or the nearby IML (Institut Medico-Legal) mortuary, where Henri Paul's autopsy was carried out, as it might attract unwanted attention from paparazzi. But this is sheer nonsense. While Professor Riou may well have requested that Diana's body be left in the hospital room for the very reasons cited, by now some very senior British Embassy officials, as well as Diana's Butler and Private Secretary, were involved, and their word would have overridden that of Professor Riou. No doubt about that. The plain fact of the matter is, if the British contingent wanted Diana's body refrigerated, then it would have been refrigerated, no questions asked. That it was left in the hospital room to slowly decay, on the other hand, speaks volumes: the British wanted her embalmed.

Indeed, the very fact that Prince Charles was *"bringing with him some British embalmers"* is evidence enough to this end. And more than this: it surely suggests that the heir apparent might himself have been behind the stampede to have his former wife embalmed. If that were the case, of course, we can only wonder what might have been the prince's reasons for having Dodi Fayed's new lover daubed in formaldehyde, a solution that corrupts the results of toxicological tests, including those for pregnancy. We'll leave you to your own conclusions.

Pregnant?

In our opinion, then, based solely on the evidence presented in the Paget report, and in contrast to Lord Stevens' rather bizarre conclusion, the embalming of the Princess of Wales was indeed carried out illegally. No proper authorization was obtained for the embalming and, moreover, the question of who actually authorized the embalming is still to be fully resolved. There is no question that the embalming was illegal under French law.

But there is one further question to be resolved: was the embalming carried out in order to cover up the fact that Princess Diana might have been pregnant with Dodi's child?

We have, in the course of this book, touched on this subject, but as explained in earlier chapters, any hopes of finding concrete evidence that Diana might have been pregnant were dashed the day she was embalmed; the formaldehyde solution used in the embalming process would have corrupted any toxicological tests to the extent that any tests for pregnancy would not have produced a reliable result. For this reason, we have never pursued this allegation with any real vigour. And in any case, contrary to Mohamed Al Fayed's reasoning, to us the fact of whether or not the princess was pregnant is not at all relevant in citing a motive for her murder. Indeed, we feel that all the endeavours to this end are actually missing the point. If it could be proved that Diana was pregnant, of course, then Mohamed Al Fayed's allegation that the princess was murdered for this reason would assume far greater significance. But the fact is this allegation can never be proved one way or the other. And anyway, as stated, we feel the real motive here is not whether Diana was pregnant, but whether she *might* have been pregnant. If indeed the Royal Household and the Establishment bore any fears in this regard, then those fears would not have centred on the *fact* of Diana's pregnancy, which they could not have known for certain before her death, but on the *possibility* that she was pregnant or that she might have become pregnant in the future. This is motive enough. It is solid. The fact that Diana might have become engaged, possibly even married, to Dodi, and subsequently might have born his children, is a stonewall fact. It does not need to be proved. She did not need to be pregnant when she died for this motive to hold up, and for this reason we feel that all the attention focused on the question of 'was Diana pregnant?' serves only to detract from the real motive here, which is that, whether she was pregnant when she died or not, she might, at some stage in the future, have born Dodi's children. And this possibility, we contend, would have been motive enough for the Establishment to act.

That said, the possibility that Diana was pregnant when she died would still have been considered by her assassins as they would surely have plotted to cover every possible eventuality. In this light, we must assume that her premature and illegal embalming might well have been the result of Establishment moves to conceal her pregnancy. Even though, in our opinion, she did not have to be pregnant to win the attentions of her assassins, none the less they would had to have made certain that, if she was pregnant, the fact was never discovered. And what better way to conceal that fact than to daub her body in a solution that destroys all evidence to this end. As we now know, even if the French had failed to embalm her, Prince Charles and his "British embalmers" were already on their way to Paris with the full intention of carrying out the procedure themselves. Someone wanted Diana embalmed, and it stands to reason, therefore, that this someone must have had good reason for wanting her embalmed. Whether or not this reason was to conceal any possibility that she might have been pregnant, we do not know for certain. But what we do know for certain is that a full embalming was not at all necessary simply to make her presentable for viewing. Thus, in our opinion, there must have been an ulterior motive. We'll leave you to decide for yourselves what that ulterior motive might have been.

New Evidence

One snippet of information we received from an anonymous source some years back, but never published, might just be worth a brief mention here. The reason we never pursued this information further, and thus never published it, is twofold.

Firstly, as previously explained, the question of Diana's pregnancy has always seemed something of a red herring to us. It can never be proved, one way or the other. Indeed, as we have already said, in our opinion it does not *need* to be proved in order to establish a motive for her death, as the real motive lies in Establishment fears that, at any time, Diana *could* have become pregnant, and thus that, at any time, the future King of Britain *could* have become, in the eyes of the Establishment, 'lumbered' with an Arab-Muslim half-brother. That this outcome existed even as a possibility was motive enough, of this we remain convinced.

Secondly, unlike other protagonists in this ever-unfolding saga—Lord Stevens, for example, Mohamed Al Fayed—our resources are far from unlimited. We do not, and never have had, the £4 million expense sheet afforded to Lord Stevens, never mind the seemingly bottomless pit available to Mohamed Al Fayed. We have, it should be said, over the past ten years travelled far and wide and spent sizable sums of our own money investigating this case; indeed, we have spent far more than we have ever earned from this all-consuming project. But then, contrary to what some may believe, our goal in investigating this case and writing this book was never money. Rather: justice, in some shape or form. In any event, suffice to say here that our relatively limited resources have sometimes prevented us from pursuing leads as thoroughly as we would have liked. And this was one of those leads.

That said, we did receive information that might further support the fact that Diana was pregnant when she died. Or at least that she thought she *might* have been pregnant. If Diana was pregnant with Dodi's child, of course, then it could only have been by a few short weeks, as she had only become Dodi's lover during the final few months of her life, even though the couple had been friends for some time. Thus the early signs may have been there, even though the pregnancy may not yet have been medically confirmed. This point will become relevant in a moment.

The story, then.

When the hardback edition of this book first came out, it was sold and distributed via numerous wholesale and retail outlets in America and Britain, as well as a number of websites, such a Amazon. But it was via the discussion forum on one of a number of other websites that stocked the book, a site called *50Connect*, that we received the following information.

The forum in question had been set up specifically in relation to our book, and was therefore dedicated to discussing issues surrounding Diana's death. Over the years we did receive a few snippets of information from one or two subscribers, but for the most part the forum was there for discussion and for interested parties to express their opinions, of which there were many. But one message in particular, posted by someone who wished to remain anonymous and relating to the question of Diana's suspected pregnancy, caught our eye immediately. As always, when dealing with anonymous sources, we treated the information with caution. But it none the less turned out to be really quite interesting.

In précis, the subscriber informed us that he was a medical student, and that his tutor was a personal friend of someone he referred to as 'one of Diana's Harley Street specialists'. He went on to say that, over a drink one evening, his tutor had told him something he felt might be relevant to our investigation, but added that he did not wish to name the 'specialist' concerned or post his disclosure on a public discussion forum. Accordingly, we emailed him and gave him a secure address at which to send his information.

He emailed back by return, stating that his tutor had confided in him a very interesting story regarding the above-mentioned 'specialist'. In the email he named the specialist as Harley Street naturopath, Roderick Lane ND, claiming that Mr Lane was Princess Diana's nutritional guru. He further claimed that Diana had visited Roderick Lane for nutritional advice prior to her Mediterranean holiday with Dodi, and that the reason for her visit, his tutor had told him, was due to her suspicion that she was in the early stages of pregnancy. Our ears pricked up immediately. But there was more to come. The young medical student went on to reveal that, according to his tutor, following Diana's visit to Roderick Lane's exclusive clinic, the naturopath's office was broken into and his computer stolen. He concluded by informing us that, again, according to his tutor, Roderick Lane feared his computer had been stolen because it contained a record of Diana's visit, in which she confided to him that she suspected she might be pregnant. It also contained details of the special diet he had prescribed for her, he said.

Of course, at this time, in 2001, all manner of claims and rumours were doing the rounds, and in consequence, as stated, we knew we had to treat this information with some caution. If it turned out to be true, of course, then we realized we truly had stumbled on something of significance. But we also realized it was not for publication unless we could dig up at least some corroborative evidence. Who was Roderick Lane? Did he even exist? And if so, was there any truth in our informer's claim that he was Diana's nutritional guru? We set ourselves to work.

As it turned out, unlike some of the painstaking research we had undertaken, identifying Roderick Lane was a relatively simple task. Indeed, our research turned up more than sufficient evidence proving that Roderick Lane was indeed who our mysterious medical student had claimed he was. Not that it proved anything other than this, of course. But we knew, at least, that in the following review of a book he had evidently co-authored with Sarah Stacey, we had at least found our Harley Street naturopath.

"A detailed juice programme for optimal health - and also a 7 day weight loss plan - is given in Sarah's book The Adam & Eve Diet, co-written with naturopath Roderick Lane who looked after the late Princess Diana."

And again, in a review carried by Britain's *Daily Mail*, January 10th, 2002, we found:

"Devised, after years of research, by Roderick Lane, the man who transformed Princess Diana's physique, our Lifeplan divides people into five different BioTypes ..."

And finally, in the *Irish Independent*, Tuesday, November 14th, 2000, in an article entitled, 'Shaping Up To A Figure Like Diana's':

"How to get the perfect body for you by the man who shaped Diana. Sherron Mayes talks to Roderick Lane who takes us through a diet fit for a princess."

We were suitably intrigued. Whoever the medical student that offered us this information was, he had certainly been right about one thing: Roderick Lane was indeed Diana's nutritional guru. Next, we decided to talk to the man himself.

Having tracked him down at his London clinic, we telephoned Mr Lane and asked him if indeed Princess Diana had visited him during the summer of 1997, prior to her Mediterranean holiday with Dodi Fayed. Mr Lane, quite naturally, seemed reluctant to proceed with the conversation, except to assure us that our information was incorrect: his office had not been broken into, he said, and his computer had not been stolen. The answer to our question regarding Princess Diana's visit, he affirmed, was confidential. He was not prepared to talk about it. We pressed him further about the alleged break-in at his office, explaining that the information he might be able to furnish us with could, after all, prove extremely significant in establishing the truth about Princess Diana's death—at which point he made his excuses and rang off. We called him again a few days later but this time Roderick Lane was 'unavailable'. We did not call him again.

Instead we turned out attentions to "Professor X" (name on file), our medical student's mysterious tutor and the source of this intriguing claim. But evidently, we discovered, the professor had left the country, was now living in France, and unless we were prepared to travel there to meet him he was not prepared to talk. Which was a bit of a blow. In all honesty we did not have the available funds at that time to simply up camp and chase our man across Europe—not, at least, in the uncertain hope that he would turn out to be a willing, reliable and, perhaps most of all, reputable source. We decided we would at least check him out first: due diligence.

Other than he appeared to be who our medical student claimed he was, there seemed to be a noticeable dearth of information on this man. But one interesting thing we did discover was that he'd experienced something of a run-in with a fairly well-known British journalist, who we will call "David" (real name on file). With little else to go on we decided to give David a call. Over the years David had built something of a reputation as an investigative journalist, in particular in signals communications and medicine, and we figured he might be able to enlighten us further regarding the source of our information. He was indeed able to enlighten us further, and what he told us proved a bit of a disappointment.

In short, David claimed that Professor X was something of a charlatan and that his information could not, therefore, be relied upon. Somewhat surprisingly, though, David also told us that he knew Roderick Lane personally, and that although we were correct in that he seemed to recall the naturopath's office had indeed been broken into, possibly during the summer of 1997, and that his computer had been stolen, he did not, on the other hand, believe that Diana had been murdered and therefore suspected no connection between the break-in and Princess Diana's alleged pregnancy.

But you can confirm that Roderick Lane's office was broken into?
Yes.
And that his computer was stolen?
I believe so, yes.
But Roderick Lane never mentioned anything to you about the princess being pregnant?
Most certainly not. That's confidential information anyway.

We thanked David for his time and left it at that. What else could we do? At least we had managed to confirm some of our medical student's story: that Roderick Lane actually existed; that he *was* Princess Diana's nutritional guru; that, despite his denial, his office *had* been broken into and his computer *had* been stolen. On the other hand, we were unable to confirm whether Diana had visited Mr Lane immediately prior to her Mediterranean holiday with Dodi, whether her visit might have been due to her alleged pregnancy, or indeed, whether the break-in might have been carried out to conceal the fact that she had visited Roderick Lane and requested a special diet. Roderick Lane was not talking. David seemed guarded. Professor X had fled the country, and we did not have the means—nor, frankly, the inclination—to chase him down only to find that his reputation was indeed tarnished and that, when push came to shove, he might deny the story anyway and we would end up with egg on our faces. We really were left with nowhere else to go. True, we could have informed the police, but before they would do anything we knew we would first have to convince them that Diana had actually been assassinated and thus that our evidence regarding a motive for her murder was something they should act upon. Some chance. We might just as well have informed MI-6.

Thank you, Mr King and Mr Beveridge. Your information is safe with us.

We could also, one might say, have informed Mohamed Al Fayed's team, who at least would have had the resources to perhaps pursue the case more thoroughly, but in all truth we really did not think there was much of a case to pursue. If Roderick Lane refused to cooperate, and Professor X decided likewise, or indeed, was perceived as a 'charlatan' whose story could not be relied upon, then we were running up a dead end street. In the final analysis, we really felt we had little choice but to leave this story on the back burner, where it has remained until now. If anybody—Lord Stevens, Mohamed Al Fayed—feels they might be able to take it any further, let us know. We have all the information on file.

23

JAMES ANDANSON

Mysterious Anglophile

It has to be said that reading through the chapter in the Paget report dedicated to Jean-Paul 'James' Andanson was strangely difficult. Indeed, it was a soul-searching and somewhat uncomfortable experience. The case against this larger-than-life French photojournalist—that he worked, on a part-time basis, for MI-6; that he owned a white Fiat Uno identical to the one known to have been involved in the crash; that he was found 'murdered' in his burnt-out car in May 2000; that, a few days later, his office at the Sipa photographic agency in Paris was raided by an unidentified armed gang who stole his photographic archive and computer equipment—though circumstantial, had always seemed so cogent. So much so, in fact, that even the popular press had begun to refer to Andanson as a 'part-time MI-6 agent', rather than an '*alleged* part-time MI-6 agent'; the 'owner of the Fiat Uno involved in the crash', rather than the 'owner of a Fiat Uno *similar to the one* involved in the crash'. Speculation, it seemed, even for the mainstream, had become stone-cold fact.

But as anyone who has read Chapter Fourteen of the Paget report will agree, the 'stone-cold facts' according to Lord Stevens are very different to those reported by the press. Indeed, we have to confess that, on first reading, this chapter was a heart-sinker. Or at best a series of telling body blows that left us wondering how the press, as well as our own sources, could have got it all so wrong. We read the chapter again, and then several times more. Something just didn't ring true. Somehow, strangely, Lord Stevens had managed to overturn what, until now, on paper at least, had seemed to us such a compelling case against Andanson, and we couldn't help feeling that we, along with everybody else, had, quite frankly, been duped. But what was it that made us feel this way? Clearly it wasn't the evidence itself, but more perhaps the way it was presented, and perhaps more crucially still, the way Lord Stevens elected to view it. We constantly had to ask ourselves the question: why, when comparing two equally compelling statements, did this ex-London police chief so brazenly appear to support the one and not the other? Indeed, the sense that throughout his investigation Stevens had been out to prove a predetermined outcome, rather than determine the truth, was never more evident than in this particular chapter of the Paget report. Perhaps not surprisingly, then, it wasn't long before we found ourselves concentrating not so much on the contents of the various statements and the glaring discrepancies evident in them, but on the particular manner in which they had been presented and the credibility, or otherwise, Stevens had accorded them. In short, we realized that if we stood any chance at all of undoing Stevens' spurious conclusions, then we needed to read *between* the lines, rather than rely solely on their literal, verbatim content. While we remained convinced that this mysterious anglophile, Andanson, had indeed been in Paris on the night Diana died, we were forced to acknowledge that Lord Stevens had somehow managed to compile an extraordinarily powerful case to the contrary. And that if we were to credibly challenge his case, we needed to become as devious and wily as he.

Dubious Alibis

Firstly, we should draw your attention to Andanson's dubious alibis for the night of the crash, and the several differing stories that accompany them.

According to the report, James Andanson was first contacted by the French police in February 1998, five months after the crash. It was discovered that he owned a white Fiat Uno, and police wanted to interview him about his whereabouts on the night in question. Of note here is that, on being contacted by the police, Andanson became agitated and defensive, and refused permission for police officers to visit him at his home. As the Paget report tells us:

"The initial contact between the French police and James Andanson was by telephone on 11 February 1998. Lieutenant Eric Gigou of the Brigade Criminelle tried to arrange an appointment to interview him. This was as a result of the police becoming aware of his ownership of a white Fiat Uno. The exchange was somewhat terse. Lieutenant Gigou reported that James Andanson said 'He does not have the time to waste with the police' *and that he* 'Refuses to receive policemen in his manor and that he has no time to give.'" [Operation Paget Report, Page 694]

Significantly, the report goes on to say that, during the telephone conversation, Andanson claimed that he was in the south of France on the night of Diana's death.

"During this telephone call Lieutenant Gigou recorded '...on the day of the accident he [Andanson] was in Saint-Tropez and that he therefore had nothing to do with the case.' (French Dossier D4546-D4547)." [Operation Paget Report, Page 694]

But as we will see, this is the first of four widely differing locations cited in the report with regard to where James Andanson was on the night of the crash. Indeed, the very next day, when he reported to the local police station, Andanson's story had already dramatically changed.

"On Saturday 30 August 1997 I was at Le Manoir in the company of my wife and my daughter Kimberley." [Operation Paget Report, Page 695]

Le Manoir, or *The Manor*, is the name of Andanson's home.

This statement is significant for several reasons, the most obvious reason being that, only the day before, Andanson had clearly told police he'd been in Saint-Tropez on the night of Diana's death. Now, twenty-four hours later, he was claiming he'd been at home with his wife and daughter. Given the weight of evidence already hanging over this man, we surely have to ask the question: why did James Andanson claim he had been in Saint-Tropez, some 450 miles away, on the night Diana died, if in fact he'd been at home? Fair enough, in any other circumstance we could perhaps forgive him this fairly minor memory blip. But we're talking about the day Princess Diana died. Like JFK, or 911, the death of Diana had such monumental impact on us all, indeed, to the extent that everybody remembers exactly where they were, what they were doing, why they were doing it, and even who they were doing it with, when they heard the news. This applies even more so with Andanson, who had by his own admission spent the summer months stalking the princess in the hope of obtaining that elusive photograph. He followed her to Saint-Tropez. He followed her to Monaco, and back to Saint-Tropez. He followed her to Sardinia, where he photographed her aboard the Fayed yacht, the *Jonikal*. Like the rest of his celebrity rat pack, Andanson must have lived, breathed and dreamt Diana during the two months leading up to her death. Indeed, he must have had an image of the princess burned permanently on his brain throughout the summer of 1997, and must surely, then, have been impacted even more than the rest of us when he learned of her terrible fate. Yet we are expected to believe that he failed to recall whether he was at home with his wife and daughter when news of the tragedy broke, or in the glitzy billionaire resort of Saint-Tropez, some 450 miles away. This seemingly curious memory-loss, plus the "*terse*" and defensive attitude shown by Andanson towards the police during his initial telephone conversation with them, must surely raise suspicions as to whether he was telling the whole truth with regard to where he really was on the night Diana died.

In any event, during this subsequent interview with the French police, Andanson claimed he had spent the night of August 30th 1997 at home with his wife, before leaving for Orly Airport at around 3.45 the following morning. He was on his way to Corsica, he said, where he had a photographic assignment with a well-known French musician called Gilbert Becaud.

"*Before leaving at 4 o'clock in the morning, by car, to get to Orly and catch a plane at 7.20 am for Corsica (Bonifacio), I went to bed at 10.30 pm. I listened to the News on Europe No. 1, as every day. I took my vehicle at about 3.45 am and took the motorway at Bourges, exit No. 7.*" [Operation Paget Report, Page 695]

For the record, Andanson's statement was corroborated by his wife, Elisabeth.

"*I remember perfectly coming back from Paris on 30.08.97 at 9.00 pm at the latest, and finding my husband there. He left during the night, to be very precise, on Sunday 31.08.97 at 4.00 am, when he left in his car to catch a plane at Orly to take him to Corsica. He was to do a report at the home of Gilbert Becaud. I am absolutely positive about the times I have given you.*" [Operation Paget Report, Page 696]

At this point, at least, then, the story would seem to be clear. The two different accounts have been melded into one coherent account which has been corroborated by Andanson's wife. Sorted. Or it would have been had Andanson's 18-year-old son, referred to in the report as James junior, not entered the frame. Because James junior had yet another version of events for us to ponder. Having accompanied his father on his annual celebrity shoot in the south of France during the summer of 1997, he says, and having returned home to Ligniéres with him on Thursday, August 28th, two days prior to Diana's fatal stopover in Paris, James senior, according to James junior, then left for Bordeuax.

"As for my father, he had to go to Bordeaux for the grape harvest, as he does every year. I think I remember that he telephoned us, my mother and me, at about 4.30 am or 5.00 am on 31.8.97." [Operation Paget Report, Page 697]

According to James junior, then, his father was neither at home nor in Saint-Tropez on the night of Diana's death, but at the annual grape harvest in Bordeaux, some 250 miles or so south-west of his home and 470 miles north-west of Saint-Tropez, where Andanson initially claimed he'd been. Even further away, of course, in entirely the opposite direction and around 175 miles north of his home in Ligniéres, is Paris, and according to some accounts this is where Andanson actually was on the night Diana died, as we shall see. No wonder the French police struggled to pinpoint with certainty the whereabouts of this elusive paparazzo, although it should be said that James junior's recollection that his father was at the Bordeaux grape harvest is unlikely to be correct as the annual event did not start until the weekend of September 6th that year—the weekend following Diana's death. We can only conclude in this regard that James junior got his weekends mixed up. In any event, he was clear about one thing:

"I do not remember where my father was, but one thing is certain, he was not at home." [Operation Paget Report, Page 697]

Admittedly, James junior may have been wrong about the grape harvest, but he seemed certain enough that his father was *"not at home"* on the night of Diana's death. For the record, Operation Paget argued, somewhat lamely, that because James junior had spent the evening of August 30th with a friend and did not arrive home until around 1 am, by which time his father was already in bed, *"there was no reason for James Andanson junior to be aware of his father's presence in the house"*. But this is absolute nonsense. By his own account, James senior had been at home all day, and we must presume that James junior would have noticed his father's presence at some point during the day, even if only that his car was parked in the drive. This assuming, of course, James senior was telling the truth.

In any event, perhaps not surprisingly, Operation Paget chose to 'believe' Elisabeth Andanson's account—that in fact her husband was at home that night. And it has to be said that toll road receipts for James Andanson's credit card do appear to show that, on Sunday, 31st August, 1997, the paparazzo made an early morning trip from his home in Ligniéres towards Orly Airport in Paris, as claimed. Or at least that *someone* using his credit card made such a trip. However, as stated in the Paget report, there are other, more mysterious 'toll road receipts', also paid for by Andanson's credit card, dated Saturday, August 30th, 1997. These receipts show that, for some inexplicable reason, Andanson was driving along these same toll roads between 4 am and 5 am on that morning, as well—the day *before* his Corsican trip. Do these receipts reveal James Andanson's secret journey to Paris on the morning of Saturday, 30th August, 1997—the day of Diana's arrival in that city?

"There are toll road receipts for James Andanson's credit card, showing an early morning drive, around 5am, on Saturday 30 August 1997 in the area of his home. The vehicle entered the toll road at Bourges and travelled 26km, leaving at Vierzon Est at 4.55am. The vehicle then appeared to have retraced its route arriving again at Bourges 13 minutes later at 5.08am." [Operation Paget Report, Page 699]

And further:

"There was no explanation for this trip or how it was connected to the Bécaud assignment—James Andanson claimed this particular expense against that assignment (French Dossier D4573). Elisabeth Andanson had no knowledge of these tollbooth tickets and can shed no light on their relevance." [Operation Paget Report, Page 699]

OK, there may be a perfectly harmless and logical reason for Andanson to have left his home at around 4 am on the morning prior to his Corsican trip, and then driven for two hours or so to nowhere in particular before returning home. There may be a perfectly logical reason why Mrs Andanson is unable to shed any light on why her husband should have acted in this seemingly peculiar manner. But it has to be said also that, if she was able to so accurately recall the times concerning her husband's alleged movements later that same day—*"I am absolutely positive about the times I have given you"*—and later still, in the early hours of the following morning, it seems to us strange that she *"had no knowledge of these tollbooth tickets and can shed no light on their relevance."* Or indeed, that she was unable to recall or explain anything of this mysterious early morning jaunt whatever.

In any event, one thing is clear. The toll road receipt dated Sunday, 31st August, 1997, is Andanson's sole evidential alibi, but it does not prove he was at home on the night Diana died. Paris is 175 miles from Ligniéres, Andanson's home in central France, a distance covered on France's toll roads easily in two and a half hours, as stated in the Paget report. Which means Andanson could have been at the scene of the crash until 1 am and still have been home by 3.30 am, giving him half an hour before having to leave once again, this time for Orly Airport bound for Corsica, as he claims. The toll road receipt 'proving' he left home at 4 am on Sunday 31st August, 1997, then, might well be genuine. But as an alibi it is meaningless.

The Mysterious Media Source
And The Crash-Scene Photographs

So was James Andanson at home on the night Diana died? Before we attempt a definitive answer to that question, there are other accounts to consider.

The somewhat perfunctory though intriguing account of French journalist and Deputy Editor in 1997 of *Paris Match* magazine, Christophe Lafaille, for example. Evidently the Paget team received information from an undisclosed *"media source"* claiming that Lafaille could provide evidence of Andanson's presence in Paris on the night Diana died. Not so, apparently. On being questioned by the Paget team, Lafaille refuted this claim head-on.

"On Saturday 30 August 1997 I was on holiday near Biarritz. It must have been the night of Friday 29 August 1997 when I travelled there. I was therefore neither in nor near Paris on the night Diana, Princess of Wales and Dodi Al Fayed died."

He underlined:

"I didn't meet with, or see Andanson on 30th/31st August 1997; as previously mentioned, I was away on holiday near Biarritz.../... as I have already said, I was on holiday at the time and not in Paris and therefore could not have seen him." [Operation Paget Report, Page 701]

And that, as they say, was that. No explanation is given as to who the *"media source"* was who tipped Operation Paget off, or what had led them to believe that Lafaille could have offered evidence of Andanson's presence in Paris. In the end we came away wondering why on earth this statement had even been included in the report. It was pretty pointless, after all. Except, of course, that it added just a tad more weight to the theory that Andanson was actually at home with his family on the night Diana died. And that suited Operation Paget.

But as we read on we discovered something else of interest, something relating to Andanson's own mysterious death nearly three years later. On the day of his alleged 'suicide', the report tells us, instead of driving the 240 miles or so south to where he eventually burnt himself to death, Andanson was supposed to have driven 175 miles north, to Paris, for an appointment with a French journalist. And the French journalist he was supposed to have met in Paris that day was none other than Christophe Lafaille. Make of that what you will. In no way do we wish to insinuate that Lafaille was in any way connected with Andanson's death. But we do wish to make the point that his somewhat guarded, almost mechanical denial seemed to us conspicuous, as if something had been left unsaid. Indeed, as if someone knew something, even if that someone was not Lafaille himself. Who was this anonymous *"media source"* who claimed that Lafaille *"could provide evidence of James Andanson being in Paris"*? Why didn't Operation Paget more vigorously question both Lafaille and the media source? Why, anyway, did the media source suspect that Lafaille knew something of Andanson's whereabouts on the night Diana died? Where did he get his information? Questions. Denials. Gaping holes. It all leaves such an empty, sinister taste.

Thankfully, there was nothing so covert or sinister about this next account. On the contrary, try as they might—and they did—the Paget team were unable to sweep this one under the floorboards. Which is just as well. Because in many respects this account was to prove the most telling account of all.

Frederic Dard, who died in June 2000, was one of France's best loved and most prolific novelists, having sold in the region of 200 million books in his long and successful career. He was survived by his wife Françoise and daughter Josephine, both of whom knew James Andanson well. Indeed, by account, Andanson visited the Dard household two or three times a year on photographic assignments, and it was during one such visit, over Christmas 1997, almost four months after the crash, that the photographer boasted of having been in Paris on the night Diana died.

In the report, Françoise Dard tells her story.

"*Having been informed of their arrival, James was at the airport where the aircraft arrived in which Dodi Al Fayed and the Princess of Wales had been travelling landed. I do not know how he got that information. Using his motorbike he followed them to a private address in Paris occupied by the couple. Whilst waiting in situ, James followed them to the Ritz. Very cleverly he waited for a convoy to leave the hotel. Having positioned himself at another location, he saw another car with the Princess of Wales and Dodi Al Fayed in it, leave. He followed them by motorbike and witnessed the crash of which he took photographs. This is in no way an interpretation on my part, it is what he told me. Perhaps he was bragging I don't know.*" [Operation Paget Report, Page 702]

An astonishing statement. Not only was Andanson at Le Bourget Airport to greet the couple on their arrival from Sardinia, as our sources have always assured us he was. But according to Mrs Dard, he was also at the Alma Tunnel later that same evening, where he "*witnessed the crash of which he took photographs*". As stated in previous editions of this book, according to our sources, James Andanson was murdered in May 2000 for the very reason that Diana's assassins, whoever they might have been, discovered that he had taken or otherwise acquired incriminating photographs of the crash scene, and that he had secretly retained those photographs with the intention of one day publishing them. Hence his murder. And hence the subsequent break-in at the Sipa photographic agency in Paris, where some of Andanson's photographic archive was stored (more on this later). Needless to say, Lord Stevens attempted to play down Mrs Dard's statement in the report, claiming that she was moving "*in and out of the room*" while Andanson related his story to her husband and thus insinuating that she probably misheard or misunderstood. But Mrs Dard clearly stated that "*This is in no way an interpretation on my part, it is what he told me*". Indeed, according to the report, there would seem to have been no doubt at all in Mrs Dard's mind that Andanson had not only told her he was in Paris on the night Diana died. But that he possessed a secret stash of crash-scene photographs, as well.

Mrs Dard concluded:

"*He told us the photos of the crash were located somewhere and that it would cause a real stir when they were published.*" [Operation Paget Report, Page 702]

No doubt. Regrettably for James Andanson, however, it would seem the same sinister forces that caused the crash were on hand to ensure the photographs were destroyed before they ever saw the light of day. And that the man who secretly retained them was destroyed along with them. Leastwise this scenario becomes all the more plausible when considered in light of Josephine Dard's astonishing testimony, below.

Despite Lord Stevens' somewhat insidious—and explicitly unfair— attempts to persuade us that Mrs Dard's statement should be read with caution, then (indeed, that Mrs Dard's statement should not be taken as seriously as other statements supporting the claim that Andanson was at home on the night of the crash), both Françoise Dard *and* her daughter, Josephine, none the less stood resolute in their account. Josephine, in fact, who was also present when Andanson related his story, not only confirmed the details precisely as described by her mother. She further explained that Andanson had told the family his secret because he intended to publish a book about the incident, and he wanted her father, Frederic Dard, one of France's most successful ever crime writers, to assist him in creating the text to accompany the photographs. According to Josephine Dard, Andanson made a future appointment with her father at which to continue planning the proposed book, but due to Andanson's subsequent arrest and questioning by the Brigade Criminelle, the scheduled meeting never took place. We must remember, here, that Andanson revealed this story to the Dard's over Christmas 1997, some six weeks before he was first contacted and questioned by the police. At this point his name had never even been mentioned in connection with Diana's death, so there was little reason for him to fear any consequences of revealing his secret, or indeed, of publishing his story in a book. Some six weeks later, however, James Andanson's name was suddenly added to the list of other paparazzi suspects under investigation by the French inquiry, and it would be a further eighteen months before Judge Stephan would conclude that inquiry and finally clear his name. By this time, as the report states, Frederic Dard had fallen gravely ill, and was unable to work, so the proposed collaboration between Andanson and Dard never happened. But what if James Andanson approached someone else regarding his idea, we wondered? In light of Frederic Dard's illness and, consequently, his incapacity to work, what if James Andanson approached someone else regarding his plans for such a unique and explosive book? For more than eighteen months following his initial arrest, while the French inquiry was in process, one can understand why he would not have wanted to develop his idea or talk to anyone else about it, if for legal reasons alone. But once the French inquiry was concluded and Andanson's name officially cleared in

September 1999, he would once again have been free to pursue what would, without doubt, have proved a very lucrative, even if controversial project. In this regard, one can only wonder who else might have found out about this project, then, who else Andanson might have approached to help him create the text for his proposed book. A journalist colleague, perhaps? An editor he might have known well? In any event someone with connections in the literary world and someone he figured he could trust. But who *could* he trust? Many of his paparazzi colleagues, remember, as well as his journalist buddies, would likely have had relationships with the French intelligence and security services. Many others would have been running scared anyway, having only recently managed to clear their own names with the completion of the French inquiry. Might Andanson have spilled the beans to the wrong colleague, we wondered? Might word of his secret stash of crash-scene photographs and his plans to publish them in a book have been filtered through to the wrong person? This would certainly explain, judging from the statements of some of his fellow journalists and paparazzi in the Paget report, why no one seemed keen to even talk about, much less associate themselves, or their name, with James Andanson. We recall to mind, for example, the anonymous "*media source*" who alleged that former *Paris Match* Deputy Editor, Christophe Lafaille, could shed light on Andanson's whereabouts on the night Diana died, and Lafaille's seemingly wooden, almost scripted rebuttal. While reluctant at this stage to speculate further, we had to concede the possibility that someone—or perhaps more than one person—within the closely knit press and paparazzi fraternity might have found out about James Andanson's stash of crash-scene photographs. And that this was the reason, not only that his colleagues had sought to distance themselves from him, but that he was murdered, and that his archive of incriminating photographs was destroyed along with him. We'll return to this point a little later.

Andanson's Fiat Uno

By now we have to say we were beginning to question whether Andanson was directly involved in the operation that killed Diana. Certainly it seemed to us that, despite the 'toll road receipt' mystery, he almost certainly was in Paris on the night of the crash—every paparazzo in France was in Paris that night, for obvious reasons, and there is no reason at all to suspect that Andanson would not have been there as well, particularly as he was in process of compiling a photographic record of Diana's journey that summer, as we shall see; and that, as we now know, he later planned to publish that record in the form of a book. We also now know that Andanson himself claimed that he was in Paris that night: he was at Le Bourget Airport to witness and photograph the couple's arrival, he claimed, and later that same evening he was at the Alma Tunnel to witness and photograph their demise. But this does not necessarily mean he was there to participate in the operation that killed them. He was, first and foremost, a photographer, and as we have already explained, there is every reason to suspect he would have been in Paris for that very reason: to photograph Princess Diana. Certainly according to Françoise and Josephine Dard, Andanson had openly confessed to being in Paris on the night of the crash, something surely only a fool would have confessed to if he'd been there on ulterior business. If he'd been there on regular business, on the other hand, then why not admit it?

One other point raised in the report, and indeed, something we have never quite been able to get our heads around, concerns the mystery of the white Fiat Uno. True, Andanson did own a Fiat Uno identical to the one involved in the crash. But so did someone else, who we will come to in a moment. True, forensic investigations carried out by the French inquiry did confirm that paint and plastics found at the scene matched those belonging to Andanson's car, and even Lord Stevens had to concede that, forensically, Andanson's Fiat Uno could have been the vehicle that collided with Diana's Mercedes. But that being the case, what has always seemed to make little sense to us is this: if Andanson was involved in the assassination operation to the extent that he was actually stationed at the entrance to the tunnel, waiting there in his Fiat Uno in order to ensure the Mercedes crashed, would he really have used his own vehicle? Would he not have used a surrogate vehicle rather than one that could be traced back to his own front door? Considering this as a possibility, at least, does not necessarily preclude Andanson from being a French and/or British intelligence asset. And neither does it necessarily preclude him from passing back information on the couple's whereabouts that weekend. Far from it, we believe sufficient evidence exists to suggest that this may have been the case. But there is, none the less, a considerable difference between a 'hired assassin' and a 'paid informant', and we have to say there is little evidence to suggest that Andanson was the former. As stated, this is not to say he was entirely the innocent party. By his own confession he was in Paris on the day Diana arrived and in the crash tunnel later that same evening, although he did say he was on his motorbike and not in his car. Pause for thought: has anyone considered that the 'unidentified motorcycle' reported by several eyewitnesses to have been present at the crash scene might have belonged to Andanson, and that, in this event, the whole question of James Andanson and the white

Fiat Uno might be little more than a red herring? Again, this is not to let James Andanson off the hook. Quite the opposite. As prominent British barrister, former Chairman of the Bar Council and forensic expert in criminal crash investigations, Anthony Scrivener QC, concluded when responding to the evidence published by the French inquiry in September, 1999:

> *"We have to ask ourselves whether enough was done to identify that motorcyclist. Because in my judgment—in French law, or British law for that matter—there's enough evidence to charge him with manslaughter."*

No, we are not saying we believe James Andanson was the motorcyclist in question. We are saying he *could* have been, and that, therefore, the possibility needs to be investigated. If we are to point the finger then we need to be clear about the role Andanson might have played that night, if indeed he played a role at all. We still need to consider the gruesome manner of Andanson's death, true enough, as well as the fact that his office at the Sipa photographic agency in Paris was burgled, and both of these events undoubtedly suggest a more sinister edge to this enigmatic paparazzo. Indeed, clearly there was more to James Andanson than a tripod and a telephoto lens, evinced even further by his alleged dubious connections to former French prime ministers, other senior politicians and wealthy French businessmen, several of whom also died in very suspicious circumstances, as we shall see. But whether or not the white Fiat Uno involved in the crash belonged to James Andanson, or that, even if it did, Andanson was stationed at the tunnel entrance as part of an MI-6 assassination plot, remains questionable. On balance, and based on the latest available evidence, we have to say we are not convinced this is the case. Here's why...

There can be little doubt that Diana's Mercedes clipped a white Fiat Uno as it entered the Alma Tunnel, and that, therefore, the Uno in question, either intentionally or otherwise, must have played at least some significant part in causing the Mercedes to crash. The only question is: who owned that Uno, who was driving it and where is it now? Despite the biggest, most expensive search operation in French history, the French police assure us they still cannot answer that question with any degree of certainty. This fact in itself has, over the years, fuelled suspicions that the Uno was being driven not by a regular French citizen, not even by a part-time intelligence informer recruited from the ranks of the local paparazzi: but by a member of the K-Team—one of the team of hired professional assassins deployed at the entrance to the tunnel that night. And we have to say this remains a very high possibility. The fact that the multi-million-dollar French inquiry failed to identify the Uno or its driver, and that the multi-million-pound British investigation led by Lord Stevens seems also to have failed in this same regard, only serves to bolster fears that the Uno was indeed part of an MI-6 operation to assassinate Diana, and was, therefore, being driven by a professional hit man. Questions is: was James Andanson a professional hit man?

It has been known since February 1998 that Andanson was the owner of a white Fiat Uno, but what still needs to be proved is whether this was the Uno spotted by eyewitnesses at the entrance to the Alma Tunnel. Certainly our sources have confirmed to us that the use of such a vehicle *"weighed down low to the ground, probably with bags of cement or concrete blocks, so that it held the road when it collided with the bigger vehicle... so that it didn't roll on impact"* would have been consistent with this kind of deniable operation. But this information, ten years on, has also to be tempered with the latest evidence. When we first interviewed former SAS Sergeant, Dave Cornish, who furnished us with this information back in 1998, the name James Andanson was unknown to us. Dave Cornish was simply explaining that, in his opinion, and based on his experience of *"deniable ops"*, the Uno would have been used to assist in forcing the Mercedes to crash. And we still believe this could well have been the case. But the question has moved on since then. It is no longer: 'Was the Uno involved in the crash, and if so, was it being driven by a hired assassin?' Rather it is now: 'We know that the Uno was involved in the crash, but who did it belong to and who was driving it?' James Andanson, by his own account, was riding his motorbike in Paris that night, and it has to be said that statements from Andanson's family, plus those from the boss of his local car dealership, would seem to support Andanson's own claim that his Fiat Uno was in no fit state to be driven in August 1997. In his interview with the French police on Februray 12th, 1998, Andanson stated:

"I was in fact the owner of a white Fiat UNO model 60 diesel … I used this car a lot and I did 372,000 km [231,160 miles], and stopped using it in 1995, the year after which I stopped paying my insurance. I think I remember that at that time, having made a success of my career, I passed to the BMW stage." [Operation Paget Report, Page 706 and 707]

He went on: *"Afterwards this vehicle remained parked opposite my Charolais shed, and in October 1997, wanting to buy a vehicle for our heir, my son, the*

Fiat dealers (Mrs Langlois) offered to take our Fiat UNO for 5000 francs, [Paget Note: Approx £500] as it stood. The Fiat Punto at that time was worth 47,000 francs secondhand, we bought it for 42,000 francs. The Fiat UNO thus put "on the scrapheap", [illegible] battery, and no one used it." [Operation Paget Report, Page 707]

In support of Andanson's statement, both his wife and son corroborated his story, stating that the Uno had been out of service for at least a year in August 1997 and that the insurance policy for the Uno had thus been terminated. These claims were further corroborated by Jean-François Langois, Managing Director of part of the Chateauroux car dealership that part-exchanged Andanson's Fiat Uno in November 1997.

French Dossier D4584
Interviewed in the French Inquiry on 12 February 1998

"As regards the Fiat Uno vehicle registration 7704 RC 18, it is indeed a car which we have had since 04.11.1997. As you can ascertain from the garage's police register, the vehicle was registered under order No. 97112027, on 04.11.97, with the following particulars: 'FiatUno/25.03.88/ ZFA14600004307879/6CV/Andanson J Paul Le Manoir 18 Lignières/ 7704RC18/200.00/97112027'. As regards the sum of 200.00, this is the price we hope to get from the sale of this car. I can say that it was destined for scrap." [Operation Paget Report, Page 709]

Not looking good, then. Indeed, according to Andanson's local car dealer boss, it is unlikely the Uno could have made the 350 or so mile round trip to Paris in August 1997, never mind take part in an intelligence operation planned to such precision that any vehicle involved would surely have needed to be in tip-top condition. Once again, we perhaps should reassure you that, no, we are not going soft on James Andanson. But once again, we do need to remind ourselves that, where applicable, we need to take into account new evidence and fit that new evidence into the jigsaw. We need to remind ourselves that we are endeavouring to discover the truth, not prove our own theories. Indeed, we have to be honest and concede that, based on the evidence presented in the Stevens report, it is unlikely that James Andanson's Fiat Uno was the Fiat Uno involved in the crash. No, it is not impossible that the Andanson family is lying and that they have somehow managed to recruit the boss of their local car dealership as a willing accomplice in the cover-up. But the fact of the matter is that James Andanson's presence in Paris on the night Diana died, the fact that he might have been a conduit for information on the couple's movements and the added fact that he might have either taken or acquired certain compromising photographs of the crash and those involved in it, does not at all depend on whether or not it was his Fiat Uno that collided with the Mercedes. As stated, it has always bothered us that he would have been foolish enough to have used his own vehicle in such an operation. So far as we are concerned, James Andanson was almost certainly in Paris on the night Diana died. But we are not convinced it was his Fiat Uno that was involved in the crash that killed her.

A Second Fiat Uno

Here's another detail to consider. According the Paget report, a second Fiat Uno was identified by the French police, although the Paget team were strangely coy about telling us much about the owner of this vehicle. Fortunately the British press were one step ahead in this regard, naming the man as Vietnamese-born Le Van Thanh, a 22-year-old night security guard in Paris in 1997. Evidently Le Van's father told Britain's *Daily Mail* he was concerned that his son was involved in the crash and that he feared he might have fled the scene in panic, but that he couldn't be certain as Le Van had always refused to talk about the incident. And if what he told the *Daily Mail* bears any material truth, it is easy to understand why the young Vietnamese has remained tight-lipped since 1997.

"All kinds of things have happened over the past nine years and I just want the whole thing to go away. I am a father with children now and have had enough of this saga."

And further: *"I don't want to say exactly what happened. It would cause too many complications. The police have been involved and so have many other powerful people. My family and friends have been badly affected. It has to stop now, but I fear that it never will."*

One wonders exactly who the *"powerful people"* Le Van refers to might be, or indeed, exactly how they *"have been involved"*.

For the record, the newspaper also claims that Le Van's brother, a mechanic, helped him re-spray the Uno red and replace the broken tail light, a fact noted in the Paget report. Staggeringly, however, this man has not been interviewed since 1997, because neither the French nor Lord Stevens have been able to ascertain whether Le Van's Fiat Uno was re-sprayed prior to, or after, the crash. While Le Van maintains he re-sprayed the vehicle on the day of the crash, both his father and a close friend have stated that the re-spray occurred the day after the crash. Evidently, Brigade Criminelle Commissioner, Martine Monteil, elected to take Le Van at his word.

Other reasons given for letting this suspect off the hook are that the so-called French experts *"could find no trace of collision damage at the likely point of impact"*; and that the *"rear light fittings (believed smashed in the collision with the Mercedes) showed a date of manufacture which matched the vehicle"*. But as Lord Stevens states in the report, Le Van could easily have acquired a second-hand light fitting that *"showed a date of manufacture which matched the vehicle"*. He could then have had his brother fit it for him. Indeed, no consideration at all seems to have been given for the fact that Le Van's brother was a mechanic at the time.

What is also of note is that Le Van owned a black and tan Rottweiler in 1997, and he confessed that the dog was in the car with him that night. This is of particular note for the fact that, in their original statements to the French inquiry, eyewitnesses Georges and Sabine Dauzonne recalled seeing a large dog in the back of the Uno, and that the dog was wearing an *"orange muzzle or bandana"*.

According to Georges Dauzonne:

"As I was getting ready to move onto the embankment on the Right Bank, I saw a white, two door Fiat Uno motor vehicle. It was an old model, quite grimy, and had either a Hauts de Seine (92) or an Yvelines (78) registration. I think that this white Fiat Uno had a black rear number plate.

"I noticed that the car was zigzagging as it came out of the tunnel, going from the right hand to the left hand lane, so much so that it almost touched my left hand side as we were travelling side by side.

"I said to myself that the driver must be drunk and I was afraid that he would hit me, so I sounded my horn. The man, who was adjusting to his rear view mirror as he drove, slowed down enough for me to be able to overtake him. He was driving really slowly, because I approached the embankment at roughly 30 kilometres [18.5 miles] per hour."

Georges Dauzonne continued:

"*As far as the driver of the vehicle is concerned, it was a male, of European appearance, with white skin, possibly 40 to 50 years of age, with short brown hair, and he may have been tall. A large dog was on the rear seat and, although it was sitting, I could see its head, it must have been an Alsatian or a black Labrador. It was wearing an orange muzzle or "bandana".*" [Operation Paget Report, Page 704]

In her statement, Sabine Dauzonne agreed largely with Georges Dauzonne, and interestingly, also described the driver as approaching middle-age, thus:

"*The driver was European-looking, fair-skinned but a bit Mediterranean, I think his eyes must be dark, his hair was dark brown and short, he must be between 35 and 45. I don't know if I could recognise the man if he was shown to me.*

"*In the boot of the car, not on the back seat which it has, there was a fairly big dog with a long nose. It might have been a German shepherd. I remember one colour detail, a muzzle going round its face but not down to its nose or just a bandanna around its neck. Anyway this was brightly coloured, red or orange.*" [Operation Paget Report, Page 705]

Two points. Firstly, both eyewitnesses described the driver of the Fiat Uno as approaching middle-age, both concurring on a mean average of around 40-45 years old, although Georges Dauzonne estimated that he could have been as old as 50. As we know, in 1997 Le Van was only 22 years old. While we appreciate, under the circumstances, precise descriptions might be too much to expect, even so it would appear that both witnesses were left with the distinct memory of a man in his late 30s or 40s, or even in his 50s, but certainly not his early 20s. (Perhaps we should remind ourselves here that James Andanson would have been 51 years old in August 1997, a fact that should not be overlooked.) To us, this must be considered a significant detail, and in any event, based on these testimonies we must surely question whether the Vietnamese-born, Asian-looking 22-year-old Le Van was the driver of the Fiat Uno, especially as Sabine Dauzonne described the man she had seen as middle-aged and "*European-looking, fair-skinned but a bit Mediterranean*". True, other details would certainly appear to put Le Van in the frame, but we surely cannot convict a man on the mere fact alone that he happened to own a vehicle similar—or even identical—to the one described by these two eyewitnesses. And neither, we contend, should we convict a man out of sheer desperation, simply because we have thus far failed to identify and catch the real culprit. Was Le Van the driver of the Fiat Uno? We do not know, is the honest answer to that one. Certainly there would seem to be sufficient grounds for the French police to interview him again, if they can be bothered. In the meantime, let us consider 'point two', and see if that throws any further light on the mystery.

Both eyewitnesses reported seeing a large dog in the back of the Uno, and perhaps more significantly, that the dog was wearing an "*orange muzzle or bandana*". When questioned by French police towards the end of 1997, Le Van admitted that his dog, a black and tan Rottweiler, was at work with him that night, and moreover, that it was wearing a muzzle. Bizarrely, no mention is made in the report regards the colour of the muzzle, a minor detail that just might have been hugely significant, if not enlightening. Perhaps we should assume from the omission of this detail, then, that the colour did not match the eyewitness descriptions, and therefore did not support the Paget case.

But there is another dog mentioned in the report, and much to Lord Stevens' dismay, no doubt, the colour of *this* dog's bandana *did* match the eyewitness descriptions. And moreover, this dog belonged to the Andansons.

It turns out that the Andansons owned a 2-year-old golden Labrador in 1997, and that, moreover, the Andansons' Labrador sported a red bandana. True to form, Lord Stevens seemed to afford this fact little significance, and indeed, made a point of informing us that "*The dog rarely left Lignières and her [Mrs Andanson's] husband never took the dog on assignments. It was rare for it to be taken out in any of the cars apart from being taken to the vet*". We must of course note that neither Georges nor Sabine Dauzonne described seeing a golden-coloured dog, but then neither did they describe seeing a Rottweiler, the breed of dog owned by Le Van. Georges Dauzonne, however, did describe seeing "*an Alsatian or a black Labrador*", and at that time of night we all know that a light coloured or golden Labrador could easily have appeared dark or black, particularly as it was sitting in the back of the vehicle.

But what is most significant here is that Mrs Andanson admitted to Operation Paget that her dog was indeed the proud owner of a red bandana.

"*At one point, having seen dogs wearing bandanas in magazines, I*

bought him a red one. They were in fashion, but it turned out to be impractical because after a short while it got very dirty and I decided to remove it. I do not know when I bought the bandana, but the dog was already an adult."
[Operation Paget Report, Page 705]

So who *was* driving the Fiat Uno that collided with Diana's Mercedes at the entrance to the Alma Tunnel? We have to say the jury's out. We simply do not know. Based solely on the available evidence, of course, surely neither suspect, not Le Van, not Andanson, would face conviction in a fair and unbiased trial. But as we have said, perhaps we are attaching too much importance to the Fiat Uno. It is beginning to feel like a giant red herring, not dissimilar to the question of Diana's pregnancy or Henri Paul's inebriated state. Too much emphasis on whether or not the Uno belonged to James Andanson undoubtedly has the effect of pulling us in, so that other factors appear less important, indeed, to the extent even that we start to believe everything hangs on this one, crucial detail. In the end, quite subconsciously, we find ourselves willing to accept that if the authorities can prove that Henri Paul was drunk, or indeed, that the Uno was being driven by someone other than Andanson, it's as good as them proving that Diana's death was the result of a tragic though simple accident. Likewise with Diana's pregnancy: if the authorities can prove she wasn't pregnant when she died then it's every bit as good as them proving there was no motive for her murder. Which is nonsense. All this attention on Andanson and the Fiat Uno, if by association alone, serves only to shift the emphasis away from the real killers and on to what could, after all, be a meaningless and irrelevant detail. Was James Andanson driving the Fiat Uno that caused the Mercedes to crash? No? Then MI-6 played no part in Diana's death. Case solved. The possibility that the Uno could actually have been driven by an innocent party who just happened to be in the wrong place at the wrong time, and that, whether Henri Paul was drunk or not, the Mercedes crashed solely as a result of the 'Boston brakes' technique, no Fiat Uno required, is totally disregarded. It is totally disregarded because we're all so hung up on proving that James Andanson, and not MI-6, was actually the culprit. Yes, Andanson could have worked for MI-6, but it is far more likely that he would have worked for them in the capacity of a 'paid informant' rather than a 'hired assassin', and that his role that night—if indeed he played a role that night—would have been passing back information on the couple's movements rather than getting involved down at the messy end. But we must also accept that it is equally likely Andanson was in Paris that night solely in his capacity as a photojournalist, as part of the celebrity rat pack, and that the whole deal regarding his ownership of a Fiat Uno and the fact that a Fiat Uno collided with the Mercedes at the entrance to the tunnel is nothing more than a giant red herring, a coincidence—one that has served the real assassins well enough. Indeed, until now they have played that coincidence like a trump card.

As stated, we now know that Andanson claimed he was planning a book about Diana's death and that he had stashed some very compromising photographs of the incident which he intended to include in the book. Is this not motive enough for someone to have wanted Andanson dead, and then to have hired a gang of thieves to raid his office at the Sipa photographic agency in Paris to ensure the compromising photographs never saw the light of day? Clearly it is. In fact it would seem the jigsaw is slowly beginning to piece itself together. Or rather, perhaps, define itself as two distinct jigsaws which everybody has always assumed was one, single puzzle. For the past seven years or so, ever since the paparazzo's death, what we might term the 'Andanson jigsaw' has been presumed integral to completing the 'Diana jigsaw'. But of course this is merely presumption; it is not necessarily the case. James Andanson may have had nothing whatever to do with Diana's death. It might well be that he just happened to be pursuing her in his capacity as a photojournalist on the night she died. True, the fact that he owned a white Fiat Uno similar to the one later identified as being involved in the crash, quite by chance, announced him as a prime suspect in her assassination, and in consequence, everybody since then has presumed a link between Andanson's death and the operation responsible for Diana's death. But as we have seen, there is easily sufficient motive for Andanson's murder—indeed, more so—in the simple fact that he would have needed to talk to someone about his secret stash of crash-scene photographs if his intention was to publish them in a book. Which it was. We already know that he discussed the proposed book with Frederic Dard prior to the late author's death, and as the Paget report informs us, he had already begun work on a photographic record of Princess Diana prior to her death, which means there is every chance he might have been planning to publish this record in book form even before the princess perished. As the report reveals:

"James Andanson's diary for Saturday 30 August 1997 showed him at home and used the phrase 'Rapport sur le voyage de Lady Di' [Paget Note: Translated as 'Report on the voyage of Lady Di'.] [Operation Paget Report, Page 698]

The report goes on to say that "Operation Paget understands this *expression to mean that he was completing his report on the work undertaken that week involving the 'Jonikal'."* But there is nothing in that phrase to suggest he was *"completing his report"*, only that he was still working on it. Why, if he was working on a *"Report on the voyage of Lady Di"* would he have wished to complete it on the day she landed in Paris to collect her engagement ring? Why would he have wished to complete it when her voyage was not yet complete? And her voyage was not yet complete, a fact every other paparazzo in France seemed well enough informed about and one Andanson himself would certainly have been aware of. So why would he have wished to end his *"Report"* half-baked?

We contend that he did not wish to end his report half-baked, that in fact this reference in his diary was simply that: a reference to the photographic record he was compiling of Diana's voyage that summer, and that he did not complete that record until later that same night, when Diana's Mercedes crashed in the Alma Tunnel. We further contend that, by his own admission, Andanson was in Paris that night, at the crash scene, most likely on his motorbike, and that in any event he captured on film events that occurred in the immediate aftermath of the crash, including those *'unidentified faces'* who might have been in the tunnel prior to the arrival of the emergency services. Thus the man who was destined to become, in death, the most famous paparazzo in the world, recorded the death of the most famous princess in the world, and consequently, in the most bitter twist if irony, found himself in possession of the hottest, most sought-after material in the world. Perhaps we should not be surprised, then, that when word got round that he owned this material, and worse, that he intended to publish it, James Andanson was murdered, and his photographic *"Report"* destroyed.

Suicide

If Lord Stevens went to great lengths in his attempts to convince us that James Andanson was at home on the night Diana died, he went to even greater lengths in his attempts to convince us that the paparazzo's death was suicide. Though many of the points raised here by Lord Stevens are lame and unconvincing, contrived even, it has to be said that others are very persuasive. In this latter category, for example, are the so-called *"preparatory steps"* allegedly taken by Andanson on the day of his death, which Lord Stevens takes great delight in highlighting, as follows:

"James Andanson seemed to have taken a number of preparatory steps.

When he left home during the morning of 4 May 2000 he left behind his wallet, Cartier watch, mobile telephone and his attaché case, objects that he would normally keep with him." [Operation Paget Report, Page 721]

And further:

"At some point during the day James Andanson posted a letter to Sipa Press agency asking for all of his photographic royalties to be put into his wife's name. The letter was stamped at the Ligniéres Post Office on 4 May 2000 and arrived at the agency the next day." [Operation Paget Report, Page 721]

Impressive. Certainly on the face of it, while by no means conclusive evidence that James Andanson killed himself, these actions would none the less appear consistent with someone who was about to commit suicide. Indeed, we do have to ask ourselves why, if this information is genuine and not part of a cover-up to obscure the truth about Andanson's ownership of incriminating, crash-scene photographs, a man who would by habit carry with him his mobile phone and attaché case might decide, on this particular day, to leave them at home. That he left behind his Cartier watch is not, in our opinion, particularly significant. But that he left behind his mobile phone and attaché case, if indeed he did, is a point of note. No doubt about that.

Also of note, though somewhat less so, is that Andanson reportedly left his wallet at home, as well. To us this seemed more puzzling than telling. Why, even if he did intend to commit suicide later in the day, would he purposely choose to leave his wallet at home? Seemed odd, unnecessary, convenient even, as though whoever was trying to make this story stick had gone one step too far in their efforts to win us. That he left his mobile phone and attaché case at home was compelling enough; that he left his Cartier watch and wallet at home as well only served to arouse our early warning system. For one thing, we are told Andanson made a purchase of approximately £60 (608 FF, around US $120) at a filling station in Millau, close to where he would later lose his life. We are further told that the purchase was made at 3.36 pm., and that, more significantly, it was made on his bankcard. This tells us, of course, that he made a point of taking his bankcard out of his wallet before leaving home. Not that this is a major deal. Just seems a little odd. Do suicide victims leave their wallets at home on the day they plan to die? And if so, do they remove their bankcards first? Maybe.

In any event, we are also informed with regard to this purchase that "the French investigation concluded the value of the transaction was more than was necessary to fill the fuel tank of his car". In other words, the official conclusion argued that Andanson must also have filled a spare container or two of fuel at this filling station, which he later used to kill himself.

"James Andanson was known to carry fuel containers in his car." [Operation Paget Report, Page 720]

So far everything fits, then. Everything points to suicide. Everything, even the fact that he posted a letter to the Sipa photographic agency in Paris on the day he died, instructing that the royalties on his photographs be transferred into his wife's name. Surely this can only be the action of a man who is about to commit suicide, right? And there is still worse to come.

The report also presents statements made by some of Andanson's associates, in which they claim the paparazzo had become depressed and had even talked of killing himself by setting fire to his car while he was still in it. You couldn't write a better script.

"Jean-Gabriel Barthélémy, a photographer who had known [Andanson] since 1972, stated that when they were in Gstaad, Switzerland together, ten years before he died, James Andanson had told him that if anything happened to his wife he would kill himself by pouring petrol from a canister in his car boot and lighting it with the end of his cigar." [Operation Paget Report, Page 721]

"Franck Doveri, a friend of twelve years, saw James Andanson in Klosters in April 2000. He recounted a conversation that took place amongst a group of photographers whereby one stated that his wife had left him. James Andanson laughed at this man saying that he had the perfect wife, but he later said to Franck Doveri that if his wife ever left him he would lie in bed next to her and put a bullet in his head." [Operation Paget Report, Page 721]

"Sophie Deniau, who used to buy photographs from James Andanson, recalled a conversation with him on 18 April 2000 during which he said that if anything were to happen to a member of his family he would not be able to live with himself and he would commit suicide by sitting in his car with a good cigar and setting fire to himself." [Operation Paget Report, Page 721]

"Christian Maillard from Sipa Press and a friend of James Andanson *since 1988 stated that during a conversation with him, only about ten days before his death, James Andanson had told him that he was thinking of committing suicide by creating an explosion in his motor vehicle."* [Operation Paget Report, Page 722]

Perfect. James Andanson may just as well have placed an advertisement in France's best-selling tabloid and announced to the world that he was about to commit suicide by burning himself to death in his car. The image would have been spectacular, up there, on the billboards of Paris—a cigar, a BMW and an exploding fuel canister, James Andanson waving goodbye through the flames. But strangely, James Andanson did not place such an advertisement. Indeed, he never even left a suicide note, an odd occurrence in an otherwise meticulously planned suicide. And there are other oddities to consider—why, for example, James Andanson would have chosen this particularly horrific method of suicide above other, less painful ways to die. It will surely come as little surprise to learn that, statistically, burning yourself to death accounts for less than 0.1% of recorded suicides, and almost every known instance has been religiously or politically motivated. The only exception to this we were able to find, in fact, was the murder— oops! Sorry, suicide—of senior French judge, Bernard Borrel, whose charred remains were discovered in the pit of a ravine in the former French colony of Djibouti, East Africa, in 1995. Of note is that, as recounted in *Footnote II*, the pathologist who carried out the autopsy on Judge Borrel, and whose testimony thus persuaded the presiding coroner that Borrel had committed suicide, was none other than Professor Dominique Lecomte, the very same pathologist who autopsied Henri Paul. It seems the French are no strangers to cases of self-inflicted incineration, then. Which is a curious fact in itself. Because so far as the rest of the world is concerned, more than 93% of recorded suicides are achieved by firearms, suffocation or poisoning (including overdoses). The remaining 6% or so is largely made up of people launching themselves off high buildings, bridges or cliffs, or throwing themselves under heavy vehicles, trains mostly. Burning to death, on the other hand, seems the unique speciality of the French.

Or perhaps more accurately: the French secret service.

As for the above statements claiming how Andanson had admitted to feeling depressed and that he'd bragged about committing suicide, it is interesting to note a similar story with regard to one of the paparazzo's close friends, former French Prime Minister, Pierre Bérégovoy, whose suspicious death in May 1993 was, like that of Andanson, officially ruled a suicide. Evidently, according to statements submitted by so-called 'friends' and 'family', Bérégovoy had also been feeling 'depressed' in the months leading up to his death, which might explain why, according to the classified account, he shot himself in the head: *twice*. He must have been feeling very depressed indeed, while at the same time incredibly fit and strong. Because the story goes that this 67-year-old less than robust politician, who'd spent most of his life sitting behind a desk, grappled with his fit, young bodyguard, overpowered him and wrestled his gun from him. He then proceeded to shoot himself twice in the head, though the official account assures us that the second shot was a reflex. Indeed, there are conflicting accounts with regard to how many bullets were recovered, but witnesses say they clearly heard two shots, and Bérégovoy's family have always been denied access to the autopsy report. In any event, it should be noted that, like Elisabeth Andanson, Bérégovoy's wife flatly denied her husband had been feeling depressed, and she also questioned the verdict of suicide, partly because, like James Andanson, Bérégovoy did not leave a suicide note.

But then, murder victims seldom do.

However, he did leave behind something of a mystery regarding who might have been with him in the moments immediately prior to his death. Interestingly, French investigator Dominique Labariérre wrote in 2003 that all the evidence pointed to the fact that Bérégovoy had been assassinated, and moreover, that his assassination had occurred immediately following an appointment with someone in his home town of Nevers. That someone, according to Labariérre, was none other than James Andanson, who had photographed Bérégovoy on several occasions in the past, was a personal friend, and was indeed known to have travelled to Nevers on the day Bérégovoy died. Food for thought.

In any event, officials revealed that Bérégovoy's personal notebook containing many highly secret state details together with high-profile name associations had gone missing. Many commentators have since expressed their agreement that Bérégovoy was assassinated, not only because of his involvement in the numerous financial scandals surrounding then President François Mitterrand, but also because the former French Finance Minister knew too much about Mitterrand's secret involvement in illicit arms deals, specifically the sale of component parts for the Condor II long-range ballistic missile to CIA-sponsored Iraqi president, Saddam Hussein, as well as other, similar deals involving the DST and the French oil giant Elf Aquitaine (later Total-Fina-Elf—see *Chapter 13*). It is little wonder, then, that Bérégovoy's death would be mirrored by the 'suicides' of other high-ranking Mitterrand cronies, all of whom, it is alleged, knew James Andanson personally:

The death of former Mitterrand cabinet minister and *conseiller du président*, François de Grossouvre, who was found dead in his office at the Elysée Palace in April, 1994, following allegations of French government involvement in arms-for-oil deals in Rwanda, Congo-Brazzaville and Angola. Unlike Bérégovoy, there is no disagreement with regard to how many times de Grossouvre shot himself: *twice*, in the head. Quite the fashion for high-ranking French politicians in the 90s, it would seem. For the record, de Grossouvre was Mitterrand's right-hand man, and together with high-ranking executives of the French oil giant, Elf Aquitaine, as well as the French security service, DST, he was accused of helping to protect and sponsor one of Europe's biggest and most notorious arms dealers, Jacques Monsieur, the middleman responsible for shifting the hardware in return for huge rewards. Of note is that Jacques Monsieur's neighbour in Ligniéres in the 1990s was none other than James Andanson. Like Andanson, and Bérégovoy, de Grossouvre did not leave a suicide note.

The death of former high-ranking French police officer, Pierre-Yves Guézou, who was found hanged in his office in December 1994. Guézou was Mitterrand's pet mole, in charge of illegal wiretap operations unlawfully set up by Mitterrand with the cover of investigating terrorist organizations. In secret, however, Mitterrand was wiretapping politicians, journalists and other high-profile personalities and effectively using the operation to cover up his numerous extra marital affairs, most notably his long-term affair with Anne Pingeot, which produced a daughter, Mazarine. When the scandal broke, Guézou hanged himself, or so the story goes. He did not leave a suicide note.

The death of former Director of French Social Security in the early days of Mitterrand's presidency, René Lucet, allegedly involved in fraud and money laundering; in any event complicit in Mitterrand's financial improprieties. Lucet was found dead in March 1982; evidently he too had shot himself in the head: *twice*. Not an easy feat, to be sure, but one, it would seem, destined to become uniquely popular among close associates of President Mitterrand, as well as friends of James Andanson. René Lucet did not leave a suicide note.

Inclusion of these above examples of 'suicide', as well as highlighting the victims' alleged connections to Andanson, are also intended to show how 'evidence' is so easily trumped up and, when necessary, on occasion, even falsified, in order to make the case hang tight. The scandals surrounding Mitterrand, for example, were not only career-threatening on a personal level, they were dangerously compromising at state level as well. Besides selling arms and defence technologies to Iran *and* Iraq, Mitterrand and his son were involved in all manner of nefarious dealings, particularly regarding arms-for-oil-and-diamond deals in Rwanda, Congo-Brazzaville and Angola. Indeed, with specific regard to Diana's landmines campaign in Angola, and the effect that campaign had on stifling the supply of illegal arms to neighbouring countries such as Rwanda and Congo-Brazzaville, DST and CIA collusion in Diana's assassination should not be underplayed. Likewise, Mitterrand's links to the Bush-Cheney oil syndicate, proactively involved in securing a $1 billion in illicit loans deals in 1998 for Angola's new De Santos government—in return for future oil at a drastically reduced rate—should also be noted. More: they should be investigated. As should the fact that James Andanson's neighbour, notorious arms dealer and agent for Elf Aquitaine and the DST, Jacques Monsieur, was one of *the* primary conduits for illicit arms deals between the West and developing nations in the 1990s, shifting US $60 million worth of materiel to Congo-Brazzaville over a 3-month period in 1997 alone. The helicopters, rockets, missiles and bombs were paid for by the French oil giant, Elf Aquitaine, again, a perverse kind of advance against the promise of future oil. But the Congo-Brazzaville deal was only one of numerous illicit arms deals masterminded in the 1990s by the DST and DGSE, funded by Elf and run by Jacques Monsieur. Two other countries in particular would also receive massive shipments of arms by way of Monsieur and his powerful friends during this period, namely: Angola and Bosnia, the very two countries highlighted by—indeed, visited by—Diana at the height of her landmines campaign. The most important thing to remember is that all of this was happening during those few volatile years leading up to Diana's murder—the French-and-former-Zaire-backed massacre in Rwanda in 1994, 1,000,000 dead; the conflict in Congo-Brazzaville involving CIA-equipped Angolan troops in 1997, 10,000 dead, 800,000 displaced; the civil war in Angola itself, 500,000 dead, 200,000 maimed, widowed or orphaned, an inestimable number unaccounted for and displaced.

Was Diana assassinated? Was James Andanson murdered? Did Bush and Cheney win the White House on the proceeds of this arms-for-oil war?

Answers on a postcard.

A Significant Location
A Badly Charred Corpse
And A Bullet Hole In The Head

We should cast our focus back to the alleged suicide of James Andanson, because there are other anomalies to explore—the so-called 'significance of the location' of Andanson's death, for example.

We are told in the report that the location of the paparazzo's death, near Montpellier in southern France, was not random, as many investigators have claimed, but was significant for the fact that it was near the home of someone Andanson had visited two months prior to his death. For the record, this someone was well-known French activist, José Bové, famous in France as the man who dismantled a branch of McDonald's because he believes the fast food mega-chain, with its imported hormone-injected beef, is a flagship for productivist agriculture and intensive farming, quite evidently something Bové strongly disagrees with. In any event, Andanson had visited the activist on a photographic assignment around two months prior to his death, and Lord Stevens deems this significant in that Andanson was familiar with the area and therefore we should not think it unusual that he chose this particular corner of France, 240 miles from his home and some 400 miles from where he was supposed to be, in which to kill himself. But the fact is, James Andanson was familiar with many parts of France; in the course of his work he visited many hundreds of towns and villages across the country, and even further afield—his photographic assignment with Gilbert Becaud in Corsica on the day Diana died being a primary case in point. Indeed, earlier in the report Elisabeth Andanson assures us that her husband was not a paparazzo, but a photographer who worked mostly by appointment. And what's more, he undertook on average between 75 and 90 assignments a month.

"I should point out that my husband was not a paparazzo, but a photographer, who did between roughly 150-180 assignments in two months, the majority by appointment." [Operation Paget Report, Page 694]

That amounts to around 20 assignments a week. Given this schedule it is hard to imagine any region or town in France that James Andanson would not have visited in the months leading up to his death. Yet the fact that he visited this particular place, not a few days, not even weeks, but two months prior to his death, is to be understood as significant, we are told. Under the heading: *The Significance Of The Location*, Lord Stevens boldly asserts:

"James Andanson had recently visited this secluded and isolated area and was familiar with it." [Operation Paget Report, Page 718]

Reminder: when Lord Stevens says *"recently"*, he actually means two months previously.

Without meaning to be flippant, then, it has to be said this is precisely the kind of statement that reveals Lord Stevens as a man with an agenda, making something of nothing, so desperate to prove Andanson's death a suicide that he endeavours to find significance where there is clearly none at all. As stated, there are some points raised in the report that are difficult to challenge—points that, viewed in isolation, would seem to suggest Andanson committed suicide. The big problem for Stevens, though, is sustaining his case, because there are also points that clearly do not fit the suicide story, while others still blatantly suggest foul play: *murder*. In order to manufacture a case strong enough to challenge these inconvenient points, Stevens is thus seen to brazenly and unashamedly cheat his way to the required outcome, the predetermined verdict of suicide, by trumping up ridiculous points such as this one. The clear fact is that James Andanson must have been familiar with virtually every square mile of the French Republic. He was, as his wife affirmed, constantly travelling from one assignment to the next, which means that, according to Lord Stevens' logic, the location of his death could have been deemed *"significant"* had he died anywhere between Omaha Beach and the French Riviera, or even in the Swiss Alps, where, according to Françoise Dard, he photographed the Dard family *"two or three times a year"*. Indeed, in explicit relation to Andanson's death, it is our contention that this location bears no special significance at all.

For the record, the report states:

"In March 2000 he [Andanson] visited José Bové, a well-known French activist, in relation to a photographic assignment. José Bové's home was situated approximately 500 metres further along the road that runs adjacent to the scene. James Andanson's diary showed meetings with José Bové on 7 and 13 of March 2000. His bank account showed a stay at the Hotel Campanile in Millau on the 7 of March 2000." [Operation Paget Report, Page 718]

James Andanson died on 4th May 2000, 2 months and some 150 photographic assignments later. As stated, the fact that he was murdered *"approximately 500 metres further along the road"* from the home of one of his many hundreds of clients bears no special significance at all. Case closed.

What could bear special significance, though, is not only that Andanson was burnt so badly that his head had detached and fallen into the gap between the two front seats, a mystery we will come to in a moment. But also that he was found with what appeared to be a bullet hole in his left temple. Chief Jean-Michel Lauzun of the local Gendarmerie was the first senior officer to arrive at the scene.

"He described the position of the body and cranium, noting that there was a hole in the left temple." [Operation Paget Report, Page 717]

The French police had their work cut out, then. If it could be proved that Andanson had been shot before he was set on fire, thus implicating a third party in the paparazzo's death, allegations that he had been involved in Diana's murder would surely have assumed new proportions. Explaining away the deaths of 'suicide' victims such as former French Prime Minister, Pierre Bérégovoy, and Mitterrand's right-hand man and former *conseiller du président*, François de Grossouvre, both of whom were discovered with two bullets in their head, is difficult enough. But how on earth do you explain away the fact that the victim first shot themselves in the head, then wandered off to find a suitable location to dispose of the weapon, *then* wandered back, jumped in the car and set fire to themselves? Tricky. Perhaps we should not be too surprised to learn, then, that pathologist, Professor Eric Baccino, announced following the autopsy on Andanson's cindered remains that the hole had not been made by a bullet after all, but by the paparazzo's brain exploding due to *"the intense heat of the fire"*. Evidently the contents of Andanson's cranium had become so hot they had erupted, volcano-like, forming a neat little hole in the side of his head which, though similar in every respect to a bullet hole, was not in fact a bullet hole. As Lord Stevens faithfully reports:

"These observations, while initially sounding suspicious, were explained by the pathologist Professor Eric Baccino as occurring due to the intense heat from the fire." [Operation Paget report, Page 717]

The report goes on to assure us:

"Professor Baccino explained that the hole in the left temple area was solely due to the intense heat of the fire. In any event, examination at the scene and the subsequent examination of the car revealed no missiles or projectiles that could have been used to inflict deliberate harm." [Operation Paget Report, Page 718]

Presumably these *"missiles"* and *"projectiles"* include Andanson's car keys, which were never found, either. This must be considered particularly curious as the car was locked when it was discovered.

In any event, just to seal the lid on this one, make it watertight, the report concludes:

"Dr Richard Shepherd, adviser on pathology issues to Operation Paget, confirmed that this was a rational explanation for the hole observed in James Andanson's head. (Operation Paget Message 972)" [Operation Paget Report, Page 718]

Thank heavens for that. We wouldn't want people to think he was murdered, now would we?

The next few pages of the report enlighten us with more details that—like the *"significance of the location"* detail cited above—show implicitly, of course, that James Andanson committed suicide. *"There were no signs of violence or blunt trauma to the body of James Andanson,"* we are assured. *"He was alive when the car was set on fire as indicated by the high CO levels. There was no evidence to suggest the involvement of any other person in his death."* The significance of the high levels of CO (carbon monoxide) found in his blood is that James Andanson was alive when the fire started, and the absence of any evidence of foul play, we are told, means that *"accidental or technical cause for the fire was ruled out"*. In other words, the fire was started deliberately, by James Andanson, all by himself. No assassins involved.

However, we discovered one or two facts for ourselves—facts that might just cast a new perspective on Lord Stevens' 'suicide' verdict. One point in particular we were keen to explore, something Lord Stevens failed to even consider, is the complete disintegration of James Andanson's body, surely signifying that the fire in which he died must have reached extraordinarily high temperatures. As we know, *"the intense heat of the fire"* was not only to blame for causing Andanson's 'bullet wound', it was also responsible, we are told, for separating his head from the rest of his body, which in turn was so badly incinerated that only a small pile of cinders and fragments of fractured bone remained. As former MI5 officer David Shayler commented when we spoke to him, burning a body at these kind of searing temperatures is "*a classic technique of people trying to hide forensics*". OK, maybe the assassins were unable to hide the bullet wound, but the French police were able to explain it away, while any other evidence of beating or torture was indeed destroyed in the intense temperatures, along with Andanson himself.

In any event, it seemed to us a tad suspicious that there was so little left of James Andanson. As the report grimly describes:

"*As a result of the intense heat there were only burnt remains and multi-fractured bones left. The body had been separated, but in the main was on the driver's side.*" [Operation Paget Report, Page 718]

And further:

"*During the removal process the cranium disintegrated due to the intense heat damage. Identification of the body was made through DNA.*" [Operation Paget Report, Page 718]

According to the local undertaker in Lignières, Christian Bonventi, this total disintegration of Andanson's body is not only highly unusual, it is *suspiciously* unusual. Certainly in his 25 years as an undertaker Monsieur Bonventi claimed he had never seen such a badly carbonized body. "*In my experience there always remains a recognizable body,*" he confirmed. "*More or less carbonized, but complete, or almost complete, and quite recognizable.*" Interestingly, he went on to question whether a "*gasoline fire*" burning inside a modern, 3-door BMW Series 3 Compact, with its fire-resistant interior and paintwork, could burn long enough, or generate temperatures high enough, to completely destroy a human carcass. For the record, the ignition temperature of gasoline or petrol is around 246° Celsius.

Monsieur Bonventi explained: "*For cremations we use a furnace which burns at 1200 degrees Celsius for an hour and a half, and even then it is necessary for us to finish the work with a crusher before we can give the family an urn containing the ashes.*"

And further: "*In the case of Monsieur Andanson, the gendarmerie asked us to recover his remains from the mortuary at Montpellier, a month after the event. All they gave us was an envelope with some ashes and an end bone. Incredible!"*

Monsieur Bonventi joked that there were so few remains he did not believe James Andanson had actually died.

There is another point to consider. The report informs us that the fire was started deliberately, by Andanson, who poured a canister of 4-star petrol over himself and into the driver's foot well, and then ignited that petrol with a burning cigar. We begged to challenge this explanation, and in so doing came across an article in *The Guardian* (February 27th, 2007). Penned by the paper's Science Correspondent, James Randerson, the article in question referred to experiments carried out at the Bureau of Alcohol, Tobacco and Firearms Research Laboratory in Beltsville, Maryland. Of note is that, contrary to popular belief, the experiments proved beyond any doubt whatever that petrol can not be ignited by a burning cigarette or cigar.

Referring to the experiments, the article, entitled *'Petrol Lit With A Cigarette? Only In The Movies'*, states:

"They dropped burning cigarettes into trays of petrol. They sprayed a fine mist of petrol at a lighted cigarette. They even used a vacuum device to produce the higher temperature (900-950C) of a cigarette being sucked. In more than 2,000 attempts the petrol did not ignite."

Well, well. Evidently nobody informed James Andanson—or indeed, Lord Stevens—of this scientific fact.

More Anomalies

From here the report moves on to explain James Andanson's movements and actions on the day he died. Interestingly, we are told that, having spent time at home with his son, chatting about the next race meeting they were planning to attend, and having then informed his wife he was off to Paris to attend two scheduled meetings, James Andanson jumped in his car, drove 240 miles in the opposite direction and set fire to himself. He did this, we are assured, because he was depressed.

As we know, one of his scheduled meetings in Paris that day was with former *Paris Match* Deputy Editor, Christophe Lafaille, who says Andanson phoned him and cancelled the meeting at some stage during the morning. Seeing as he left home, according to the report, at around 11.30 am, and that, evidently, he left his mobile phone at home, we have to conclude that he'd already cancelled his Paris appointment prior to sitting down with his son and chatting about when the two of them might attend the next motor race meeting together. One has to ask: why would he casually sit down and make future plans with his son if he'd already decided to kill himself later that day? Not only strange, but particularly spiteful. Was James Andanson the kind of man to inflict such unnecessary pain on those closest to him, like he was playing some kind of sick, morbid joke? For a man who couldn't bear to be away from his wife and family too long, to the extent that he took them with him each summer to the south of France for the 'celebrity season'; and again, a man who was so close to his son that he'd not only invested in the region of £75,000 (US $150,000) in his ambitions to become a racing driver, but that he was also known to attend his son's race meetings at every opportunity, it seems very unlikely that Andanson would have acted in this way. Surely he would instead have said little, if anything at all, just slunk off, quietly, out the back door, and driven himself unceremoniously to his final destination.

> *"Hey Son, shall we go to the next race meeting together, just like we always do?"*
> *"That would be great, Dad. I'll really look forward to it."*
> *"Ha ha! Only joking. I'm actually just off to kill myself. Have a nice life!"*

Something really does not hang together here. We are told in the report that James Andanson killed himself because he was depressed and because he was worried about how he might be able to continue financing his son's ambition to become a racing driver. Yet in the same breath the report also informs us that:

> *"James Andanson's circumstances seemed very comfortable. He lived in a large house with his wife, son and daughter. The bank accounts checked by police were in credit and it was shown that in 1999 [the year before his death] James Andanson earned a generous income."* [Operation Paget Report, Page 723]

Indeed, let us not forget that James Andanson was already a millionaire, and even Lord Stevens reported that his *"circumstances were very comfortable"* and that *"in 1999 [the year before his death] James Andanson earned a generous income.*" No doubt with the photographs he had taken of Diana and Dodi that summer he was about to increase his wealth ever further, and as the report goes on to reveal, he was about to increase his wealth further still by selling his deceased mother's apartment. Let us get one thing clear: James Andanson did not have to busk for his supper. And other than statements from one or two conspicuous 'friends' and 'associates' that Lord Stevens seems to have plucked from his magic box, there is no real evidence that he was depressed, either. Certainly one could not assume from his vaunted outbursts about blowing himself away if ever his wife was unfaithful, or blowing himself up if ever anything happened to a member of his family, that he was suicidal. This kind of big talk is common among certain types of men, especially after a few drinks in social situation. Besides, so far as we know, Andanson's wife was not unfaithful and nothing untoward *did* happen to a member of his family. So how can these ridiculous boasts be used as evidence that Andanson had shown suicidal tendencies prior to his death? Again, this is nothing but trumped up nonsense.

And here's more nonsense. Following his scheduled meeting with Christophe Lafaille in Paris on the day he died, the meeting he cancelled prior to arranging a day out with his son, Andanson was also scheduled to meet, later that same afternoon, Sophie Deniau of the Sipa photographic agency. We know this because, as stated in the report, the meeting was recorded in James Andanson's diary. It was, moreover, the *final* entry in his diary, a fact by which the ever vigilant Lord Stevens was of course alerted.

"*James Andanson would normally have numerous appointments recorded in his diary for the coming days and weeks. However, Sophie Deniau at 4pm was the last appointment entered in his diary.*" [Operation Paget Report, Page 721]

The insinuation here, of course, is that James Andanson knew he was about to commit suicide, had planned for "*days and weeks*" to commit suicide, which is why there were no further entries in his diary. Seems an open and shut case. But is it? Is it usual for people to plan their suicides this far in advance? "*Days*", and even "*weeks*", in advance? As Lord Stevens informs us, "*James Andanson would normally have numerous appointments recorded in his diary for the coming days and weeks,*" from which we can safely conclude that he had not entered any appointments in his diary for some days, possibly even weeks. Assuming this is correct information, then, we must assume also that, not only had he planned for some time to commit suicide, but that he had actually named the day of his suicide as 4th May, 2000—the day of his last known appointment. But that bothered us. If he'd planned for some weeks to commit suicide on 4th May, 2000, near Montpellier, the 'significant location' identified by Lord Stevens, then why did he bother entering his Paris appointments with Christophe Lafaille and Sophie Deniau in his diary for that day? On the other hand, if he had not planned to commit suicide on 4th May, 2000, why are there no further entries in his diary after that date? We couldn't help feeling at this point that James Andanson's diary might have been 'modified' by an unseen hand. After all, was his 'depression' so manageable that he knew in advance he could hold out until 4th May? What was so special about this day? What if his 'depression' had got the better of him on, say, 1st May, or 2nd, or 3rd, would Lord Stevens have afforded the same significance to Sophie Deniau's entry on 4th May? No, of course not. How could he have? And why, anyway, did Andanson bother to cancel his appointment with Christophe Lafaille yet not bother to cancel with Sophie Deniau?

"*Sophie Deniau also had an appointment with James Andanson at 4pm on 4 May 2000, at the Sipa Press agency in Paris. She stated that when he did not turn up for this appointment, she waited an hour and then left.*" [Operation Paget Report, Page 720]

The words 'smell' and 'rat' spring to mind. Indeed, the fact that Andanson had actually gone to the trouble of arranging an outing with his son at some time after 4th May, 2000, that he'd arranged this outing on the day he planned to commit suicide, and that his alleged suicide had been planned for days, possibly even weeks—together with the many other inconsistencies contained in the report—serve only to make that rat smell all the more pungent.

In short, the section in the report covering James Andanson's death stinks of a cover-up. Their is little more to be said.

Armed Break-In

Another cover-up, this one even more blatantly fabricated than anything thus far presented, although this time it would appear to be more what is implied through things left unsaid than what is insinuated by actually trumping up lies. For the record, and to refresh our memories of this highly significant incident, on June 16th 2000, less than a week after James Andanson's death was first made public, the Sipa press and photographic agency in Paris, which housed much of Andanson's photographic archive was broken into by three masked gunmen. During the raid a security guard was shot in the foot, members of staff were bound and held hostage, while the intruders roamed the premises for a full three hours unchallenged by police, who failed to attend until after the gang had fled. Clearly knowing in advance precisely what they were looking for, and moreover, where to look for it, the gang searched only specific offices on the second floor, leaving the first and third floors untouched. In the end they made off with five desktop computers, five laptop computers, a few scanners, a few screens: and most significantly, *"photographs from a safe in relation to celebrities"*. No details of who the celebrities might have been, or in what situation the photograph might have captured them, has ever been released. Evidently not even Lord Stevens was permitted access to this information. But then, as can be clearly surmised from the heavily weighted tenor of Paget Report, Chapter Fourteen Section 5, entitled: *"Burglary / Robbery at Sipa Press Agency,"* even if it could have been proved that the stolen photographs included Andanson's incriminating crash-scene shots, Stevens would doubtless have found a way to rubbish that evidence anyway.

In the first instance, he tells us:

"James Andanson shared an office at the premises. The photographers using the offices did not tend to leave equipment at the premises and their computers were not provided by Sipa Press. The only property on the premises that could be connected with James Andanson was archived photographs. He kept his laptop computer with him and did not leave it in the office." [Operation Paget Report, Page 723]

The implication here, though not directly stated, is that none of the equipment stored at the Sipa offices, and thus none of the equipment stolen on the night of the raid, belonged to James Andanson. Therefore this perfectly straightforward criminal break-in had nothing whatever to do with Andanson or his alleged presence at the crash scene, where it is further alleged he took photographs of an incriminating nature. Indeed, almost as an afterthought, in what can only be understood as a deliberate and insidious attempt to underplay the point, make it seem insignificant, Stevens informs us that *"The only property on the premises that could be connected with James Andanson was archived photographs."* But surely this is the point. The very fact that James Andanson stored his photographic archive at the Sipa offices is the sole reason suspicions were raised when the offices were raided and *"photographs from a safe in relation to celebrities"* were stolen. Again, it is not so much that he attempts to underplay this point, but that he does it so brazenly, as if he knows beforehand that he will get away with it. As if he's been given the nod.

> *"This investigation is far more complex than I first thought. There are some points I simply cannot explain or conceal."*
> *"Underplay them, make them seem insignificant."*
> *"But surely people will notice, won't they?"*
> *"Just do as you're told. We'll take care of everything."*

The armed gang arrived at the Sipa building at half-past midnight, we are informed, whereupon one of the gang shot the security guard following a struggle. The guard and a computer programmer working the night shift were subsequently tied up and ordered to lay face down on the floor of one of the offices occupying the second floor, at which point:

> *"The first suspect said to another (in French)* "This one plays the hero. If he moves kill him" *and handed over his gun."* [Operation Paget Report, Page 724]

The two other gang members then started to search the building, or at least the offices on the second floor, which they seemed already to know would contain what they were looking for. For the record, the report fails to reveal how many other of Sipa's 200 staff were present during the raid or what happened to them, but it is known that the agency operated, for obvious reasons, on a round-the-clock, 24-hour basis, so we should assume that at least some other employees were also in the building during the three-hour siege. Indeed, initial reports claimed that one of the employees managed to call the police while the raid was in progress, but that the police did not respond. The official line after the event, of course, denied this claim, stating that the police were not called until forty minutes after the gang had fled. Not for the first time the official line and the true version of events seem curiously at odds.

But certainly one of the points that has always intrigued us regarding this armed break-in is that the gang were able to operate freely in the building for such a long time. By any measure, three hours is a considerable amount of time for thieves to be able to go about their business undisturbed by police, particularly in the centre of one of Europe's largest and busiest cities. And even more so inside one of the world's biggest and most prestigious press agencies. For the record, the Sipa offices occupied four floors and covered 3000 square meters of a vast office block, and housed tens of thousands of dollars worth of equipment, not to mention hundreds of thousands—if not millions—of dollars worth of photographs. And yet we are expected to believe there was only one security guard and a computer programmer in the building when the thieves arrived. Someone somewhere is surely having a laugh. We are further told that the armed gang dismantled all the CCTV cameras in the building and disabled the alarm system, although this was after they had already shot the security guard with a *"chrome barrelled Berreta 9mm pistol"* that presumably made no noise when it was fired. Leastwise the report makes no mention of anybody having heard the gunshot or having reported it to the police. Indeed, according to the official version contained in the report, which, as stated, is clearly at odds with other stories that filtered out soon after the raid, the French police claim they were not contacted until after the gang had left the building at 3.30 am, but even then they did not arrive until 4.16 am, some forty-six minutes later and an astonishing three-and-three-quarter hours after the gang had first arrived, in any event easily sufficient time for the gang to have found what they had come for and disappear into the night. Which is precisely what happened. In point of fact, the entire operation would seem to have run oily smooth, suspiciously so—like it might had the French security service orchestrated the raid, and the French police colluded. We are of course not saying that this is what happened. Just that it seems that way.

In any event, as we have by now come to expect, Lord Stevens duly offers the official version of why it took so long for the police to arrive at the crime scene, thus:

"Before leaving the building, the suspects tied up the Security Guard and the computer programmer in the toilets using handcuffs and electrical cables. The victims waited for about 20 minutes, during which time they did not hear any noise. They then managed to untie themselves and called for help. The suspects left the scene at around 3.30 am." [Operation Paget Report, Page 725]

Forgive us for playing the cynicism card here, but even if it is true that nobody alerted the police to the break-in until after the gang had left, a point we are still not convinced of, it still seems mighty odd to us that it was a further forty minutes before the victims *"managed to untie themselves and called for help".* Not that we are questioning the integrity of the victims nor the veracity of their accounts. But it has to be said that the police, certainly in Britain, have been shown in the past to have altered case notes and falsified statements in order to shore up a case that otherwise would have collapsed. Given the sheer magnitude of this particular case, and that everybody other than Lord Stevens seems convinced the break-in was orchestrated by the French security service in order to ensure Andanson's photographs would never see the light of day, we see no reason at all why this same subterfuge might not, on this occasion, have prevailed in France, as well.

A Stranger At The Door
And Conspicuous Time Discrepancies

We also have to scrutinize other claims made by the French police, not least that two paparazzi contracted to Sipa arrived at the building that night to offload some photographs, yet neither contacted the police to inform them that the place was being burgled. Indeed, what we find particularly strange about this official version of events is that, according to the French Judicial Dossier, neither of these paparazzi—both of whom were regular visitors to the Sipa offices—suspected anything amiss when a complete stranger answered the door to them and told them to leave their photographs at reception.

"Nikola Arsov, a photographer, attended the Sipa Press building at 12.30 am, during the course of the burglary, to deliver some photographs. A male, unknown to him, answered the door. He asked where the Security Guard was and was told he was on the first floor where an alarm had been set off. Nikola Arsov placed some photographs in an envelope, which he then left at reception. It was only the following morning that he realised that he may have seen one of the suspects. He gave a description of the man he saw." [Operation Paget Report, Page 725]

And further:

"Alain Benainous, another photographer, attended the Sipa Press building at 1 am to drop off some photographic film. A man opened the door and told him that the Security Guard was on the first floor. He also told him to drop his envelope off at the reception. Alain Benainous then left and it was only later that he discovered that he had seen a suspect. He also gave a description of the suspect." [Operation Paget Report, Page 725]

As well as anything else we have a real problem with times, here. The report tells us that Nikola Arsov arrived at the Sipa offices "*at 12.30 am, during the course of the burglary,*" yet in the same breath we are told:

"*On 16 June 2000 at 12.30 am a suspect went to the building of Sipa Press, 101 Boulevard Murat 75016 Paris and said that he was delivering photographs. When the Security Guard, Youssef Belaid, answered the door, the suspect drew a firearm from a holdall and threatened the guard.*" [Operation Paget Report, Page 724]

Should we deduce from this that Nikola Arsov and the "*suspect*" are one and the same? Certainly the report would seem to imply this.

"*Nikola Arsov, a photographer, attended the Sipa Press building at 12.30 am … to deliver some photographs.*"

And further:

"*On 16 June 2000 at 12.30 am a suspect went to the building of Sipa Press … and said he was delivering photographs …*"

In any event, the report goes on to inform us that the "*suspect*" and the security guard then went up to the second floor, that following a struggle the security guard was shot in the foot, that a second member of staff, a computer programmer, was overpowered by the "*suspect,*" that the "*suspect*" then proceeded to tie both the security guard and the computer programmer up, and that then, and only then, were the second and third members of the gang given the signal by mobile phone to enter the building and make their way up to the second floor. According to the report, they arrived "*about five minutes later*".

Here is the account directly lifted from the Paget report. Apologies that some of the lift is repeated, but we wish to make a valid point here, and we want you to see that we are not making this up!

"*On 16 June 2000 at 12.30 am a suspect went to the building of Sipa Press, 101 Boulevard Murat 75016 Paris and said that he was delivering photographs. When the Security Guard, Youssef Belaid, answered the door, the suspect drew a firearm from a holdall and threatened the guard. Both men went up to the second floor. At one point, the Security Guard tried to disarm the suspect and during the struggle was shot in the left foot. The suspect overpowered both the Security Guard and another person on the premises, Marek Kaserzyk, a Polish computer programmer working on Sipa Press's computers at the time.*

"The two victims were secured, face down on the floor of one of the offices and the suspect telephoned someone and said (in French) "François you can come up". Two further hooded suspects came to the office about five minutes later. The first suspect said to another (in French) "This one plays the hero. If he moves kill him" and handed over his gun." [Operation Paget Report, Page 724]

Somewhat conspicuously we are told that paparazzo, Nikola Arsov, arrived at the Sipa offices at precisely the same time as the first gang member: 12.30 am, which, assuming they are different people, means they would have arrived at the security door guarding the building's entrance together, simultaneously. Interesting. But even if the times are slightly out, and the gang member actually arrived first, say, a minute or two—or even five minutes—before Arsov, we still have to ask ourselves how long it would have taken him to then muscle the security guard up to the second floor, engage him in a tussle, shoot him in the foot, overpower the computer programmer, tie him and the security guard up, call his accomplices—who arrived *"about five minutes later"*—and then for one of the gang to run back down the two flights of stairs to the ground floor and open the door to Nikola Arsov. Including the five minutes it took for the other gang members to arrive, we must surely be talking at least fifteen minutes, possibly longer, which means Nikola Arsov could not possibly have arrived at the offices when the report claims he did, not unless, as stated, he was part of the plot. This really is a serious and massive discrepancy; either someone made a gigantic error in compiling the French police report—in which case a new investigation needs to be opened—or someone is blatantly lying.

But what is even worse is that Lord Stevens does not question this discrepancy nor even acknowledge that it is there. Which probably explains why he does not go on to ask the obvious questions that arise from it. Did Nikola Arsov see any of the armed gang as he approached the entrance to the Sipa offices, in particular the "Ωsuspect" who arrived at precisely the same time as he did? We do not know; unbelievably, the question is not asked. Did Nikola Arsov, a familiar face known to the security guard, either willingly or otherwise aid the gang in gaining entry to the Sipa offices? Again, we do not know. Again, the question is not asked. Did Nikola Arsov hear the gunshot that wounded the security guard? After all, if he arrived at 12.30 am, as the report affirms, then he must have been there, at the door, waiting to get in, or at the very least well within hearing range, when the shot was fired. So did he hear the gunshot? We do not know; once again, staggeringly, the question is not asked. What we do know is that, if he Ωdid hear the gunshot, he did not call the police and tell them about it, not according to the official version of events, anyhow.

But what about when the door was answered? Did he not suspect anything when a complete stranger opened the door to him? Arsov was a Sipa employee. He must have dropped photographs off at the offices on a very regular basis, and must therefore have been familiar with the few staff who worked the night shift. Even if he did not think it odd that the security guard was upstairs because *"an alarm had been set off"*, surely there would have been something about the gang member, this strange new night worker, that would have triggered his early warning system. Surely he would have seemed suspicious in some way, flustered perhaps, guarded, particularly as we are told he was part of a gang of *"ordinary criminals"*, and not a specially trained agent. Apart from in the movies, how many other burglaries can you think of where one of the gang might answer the door to an unexpected visitor, bang in the middle of a job, and appear unflustered, perfectly normal, or at least sufficiently normal that he is able to convince the visitor that all is well and good? Indeed, who was this visitor? Who was Nikola Arsov? Moreover, is there any reason why he might have wished to remain uninvolved when he witnessed what he suspected might have been an aggravated burglary in progress? Again, these are questions the Paget team failed to explore. In consequence, we were left to explore them ourselves.

Nikola Arsov
Farid Ledad
And Goskin Sipahioglu

Described as a working photojournalist of Macedonian origin, Nikola Arsov was one of the first paparazzi to arrive at the scene following Diana's crash. In point of fact, he was *the first* paparazzo to be charged with failing to assist people in danger and involuntary homicide following Diana's death, and for the next two years he lived in the shadow of possible conviction and imprisonment. Even after Judge Stephan finally ruled in September 1999, with the conclusion of the French inquiry, that the charges against him were to be dropped, the pressures of further legal actions pending remained with him. Indeed, further charges of privacy invasion were levelled against Arsov the following year, and as highlighted in an article in Britain's *Independent* in August 2002, which revealed the torture suffered by the nine paparazzi charged in connection with the crash, *"the legacy of Diana's death continues to weigh heavily upon the unhappy paparazzi"*. One can understand, then, why perhaps this particular paparazzo would have wished to avoid any further involvement with, or attention from, the police: why he would not have wanted to call the police and tell them about the stranger who had greeted him at the Sipa offices that night, or about the gunshot he had heard coming from inside the building; or indeed, why he might have agreed to remain tight-lipped when, soon after 12.30 am, police thanked him for his phone call and informed him they would get to the scene 'just as soon as they possibly could'. Whether or not Arsov, or indeed, Benainous actually did call the police and inform them of the stranger who answered the door that night, we will probably never know. But we find it difficult in the extreme to believe that an armed gang was able to break into one of the world's leading press and photographic agencies, in the middle of Paris, shoot a security guard, the Ωonly security guard, ransack the place, for three hours, undisturbed, and then disappear into the night having been given a forty-six minute head start. We contend, in fact, that this armed gang, though doubtless, for the most part, made up of *"ordinary criminals"*, was none the less hired by the French security services to ensure Andanson's photographs would never see the light of day. After all, it wouldn't be the first time a criminal gang has been hired by the intelligence services to carry out their dirty work. We doubt it will be the last.

Lord Stevens, of course, offered an alternative interpretation of events.

"It is not proposed to go into the detail of the investigations undertaken, but as a result of these investigations a number of suspects were identified. They were all French nationals.

"Three men were arrested in connection with this and other similar offences committed in Paris. They were Brice Postal, Fabrice Sauzay and Farid Ledad. Brice Postal and Fabrice Sauzay were arrested together on 13 July 2000 committing another armed robbery. Brice Postal was in possession of a mobile phone used during the Sipa Press robbery and a black balaclava and a chrome barrelled Berreta 9mm pistol together with Remington RP 380

auto ammunition." [Operation Paget Report, Page 726]

Subsequent to these arrests there followed a three-year investigation, during which the French *Judiciaire* endeavoured to establish the alleged link between the Sipa break-in and the *"other similar offences committed in Paris"*. Naturally if the link could be established, the inferred consequence would be that the armed gang was just that: a gang of common criminals acting of their own volition. But notably that link could not be established. As the report goes on to state:

"Although the Sipa Press offence appears to be part of the linked series, the records provided are unclear as to the exact venues of the crimes." [Operation Paget Report, Page 726]

And further:

"Two of the suspects named, Brice Postal and Fabrice Sauzay, were convicted of a number of similar offences of aggravated burglary. It is unclear in the case disposal file if the Sipa Press burglary is one of the charges that formed part of the series." [Operation Paget Report, Page 727]

How? *How* is it unclear. The Sipa break-in either formed part of the series of aggravated burglaries or it didn't. Are Brice Postal and Fabrice Sauzay being fitted up here? And whatever happened to the gang's third member, Farid Ledad? How come he wasn't convicted along with his mates? What relationship does Farid Ledad have with the French intelligence and security services? Did anybody enquire?

And why, anyway, is Lord Stevens having to rely on the word of Sipa owner, Goskin Sipahioglu, to enhance his case. Check this:

"Goskin Sipahioglu and his wife who owned Sipa Press were interviewed by CBS for the programme 'Diana's Secrets' first broadcast on 21 April 2004. In the interview they stated that they did not believe this aggravated burglary to have been carried out by Intelligence and Security Services, claiming it was amateurish to shoot the Security Guard in the foot; that the suspects did not touch any of James Andanson's work, and did not find his computer; and that they were more likely to be looking for some compromising photographs of a particular French celebrity, although he did not name the person." [Operation Paget Report, Page 727]

Goskin Sipahioglu *"did not believe this aggravated burglary to have been carried out by Intelligence and Security Services"*. Is Lord Stevens serious? Did we read that right? The godfather of the Metropolitan Police again having to quote what random citizens *"believe"* in order to make his case sound more appealing, more compelling? Or is Goskin Sipahioglu some kind of special witness, an expert on these matters, particularly qualified in determining which burglaries are carried out by the intelligence services and which ones are not? Indeed, what does this say about Goskin Sipahioglu? Or perhaps more to the point: what does this say about Lord Stevens? The indomitable former police chief scrabbling around for corroborative evidence like some penniless bum looking for cigarette butts. Unbelievable. Embarrassing, even. In any event a very unconvincing attempt to uphold the version of events peddled by the French police.

Andanson's Laptop
And His Photographic Archive

There is a further point of note in Goskin Sipahioglu's interview with CBS. The Paget report explicitly claims that James Andanson's laptop was not at the Sipa offices on the night in question. Rather, the report tells us that Andanson *"kept his laptop computer with him and did not leave it in the office."* Why, then, should Goskin Sipahioglu have told CBS that *"the suspects did not touch any of James Andanson's work, and did not find his computer"*? This statement clearly contradicts Stevens' claim, suggesting instead that Andanson did, on occasion, leave his computer at the Sipa offices, no doubt in the company safe along with his photographic archive. Otherwise, how else would Sipahioglu have known that the thieves *"did not find his computer"*, unless it was still there, in the safe, after the thieves had left? And if Andanson's computer was in the safe during the raid, then there is every reason to suspect that the thieves either took it with them and Sipahioglu was mistaken when he claimed that the thieves *"did not find his computer"*, or more likely, they simply wiped his hard drive, having first made a backup copy of its contents. In any event Sipahioglu's further claim that the thieves *"did not touch any of James Andanson's work"* clearly confirms that Andanson's photographic archive was in the building that night, indeed, that it was locked in the safe with all the other celebrity photographs, a fact that surely indicates, despite Goskin Sipahioglu's contrary claim, that Andanson's photographic archive—film and digital—was the thieves' primary target. Leastwise this remains theory number one.

However, if James Andanson was in possession of such highly incriminating photographs, one might well ask: would he really have left them on his laptop, in the company safe, at the Sipa agency? Would he not have kept the photographs with him, or at least have stashed them in a secure place, somewhere he knew they would be safe? Well, possibly. But what we have to remember is that the Sipa company safe housed any number of highly valuable photographs, worth in total tens, if not hundreds of thousands of dollars. Indeed, the Sipa company safe would surely have been considered by James Andanson perhaps *the most* 'secure place' to have kept his photographic archive, film and digital, including his crash-scene photographs. Where else would he have kept them?

There is one final point we should clear up. The report claims Andanson *"kept his laptop computer with him"*, but we could find no real evidence of this. On the contrary, Lord Stevens made a real point of informing us that, on the day he died, Andanson left all the *"objects that he would normally keep with him"* at home, but no mention is made of his laptop, only his attaché case, mobile phone, Cartier watch and his wallet. Where was his laptop, this other elusive *"object that he would normally keep with him"*? If it seemed odd to us that he left his wallet at home on the day he died, it seemed even more odd that he would have taken his laptop with him, a scenario clearly implied by the conspicuous dearth of information in the report regarding James Andanson's laptop computer. Indeed, what did become of his laptop? No mention of its fate is to be found in the Paget report, nor even, so far as we are aware, in the French police report. If he did not leave it at home on the day he died, as confirmed in the Paget report, then unless for some inexplicable reason he chose to take it with him to his fiery grave, the only place, realistically, it could have been is in the Sipa company safe. And if it was in the Sipa company safe on the day he died, then there is every reason to assume it was still there when the offices were raided. True, following his death his personal effects could have been collected by his family or the police, but there is no mention of this in either the French or the Paget reports. Quite the opposite. Lord Stevens tells us that the reason Andanson's laptop was not at the Sipa offices that night is purely because he *"kept his laptop computer with him"*, not because it had been collected after his death. Sipa owner Goskin Sipahioglu makes no mention of Andanson's laptop being collected from the building, either, stating only that the thieves *"did not find his computer"*. Indeed, all the evidence would seem to suggest that James Andanson's laptop containing a digital archive of his crash-scene photographs was in the company safe at the Sipa offices on the night of the raid, and that it had been there since the day he died. Andanson, remember, was scheduled to meet Sophie Deniau at the Sipa offices on the day he died; indeed, his appointment at the press agency was the last entry in his diary. Did he intend to collect the laptop at that meeting? The photographs? Both? Did he intend to reveal to Sophie Deniau that he had retained some of the crash-scene photographs he had secretly taken, and that he was now prepared to sell them? Sophie Deniau, according to the Paget report, was someone *"who used to buy photographs from James Andanson"*, and was obviously also someone Andanson knew intimately—at least sufficiently well that he felt able to confide his personal feelings in her. It was Sophie Deniau, we recall, who claimed Andanson had told her that if anything happened to a member of his family *"he would commit suicide by sitting in his car with a good cigar and setting fire to himself"*. Not something you might confide in a stranger. One wonders what else James Andanson might have confided in Sophie Deniau—that he planned to publish his crash-scene photographs in a book just as soon as he had found someone to help him produce the text? A writer? Is it purely coincidence, then, that the last two appointments in his diary, in his life, two appointments he was destined not to attend, were with Chrisptophe Lafaille, an experienced editor and writer, and Sophie Deniau, the woman he knew intimately and who used to buy *photographs* from him? Indeed, is it purely coincidence that less than a week after his death was made public the very safe in which his photographic archive was stored was cracked open and emptied of its contents? Again, your shout.

A Common-Or-Garden Burglary

Given the above scenario, then, inclusive of all its varying accounts and other inconsistencies, can we honestly conclude that this was a common-or-garden break-in carried out by *"ordinary criminals"*, as the report claims? Or might we surmise that these *"ordinary criminals"* were in fact hired by the French security service to make sure Andanson's photographs were never published? Certainly we can conclude that the raiders were not themselves intelligence agents; that would surely be preposterous. No intelligence agency would send in its own men when *"ordinary criminals"* could do the job just as well, better even: their bungling, amateurish 'burglary' would seem far more authentic than the slick operation we might expect from trained agents, and the paper trail, of course, would lead back to the city crime web rather than DST HQ. Mission accomplished.

As for identifying what the thieves were actually after, we could perhaps find clues in analyzing what, apart from the photographs, they eventually made away with: a few computers, scanners, screens, plus one or two other bits of saleable gadgetry, all tolled around £54,000, not an insignificant sum, true. But does it really take three hours to nick a few computers and scanners, chuck them in the back of the van and vamoose? It would certainly seem to us that an ulterior scenario was happening here, and that the computers were taken purely to make the raid look like an average, common-or-garden burglary. Which, in effect, it was.

"The suspects made an untidy search, cabinets were opened, and damage caused. Doors to some offices appeared to have been forced but none of the filing cabinets appeared to have been searched." [Operation Paget Report, Page 727]

At the same time, of course, the deal could easily have been that the thieves were permitted to keep the stolen equipment as reward for their night's work—in return for handing over the photographs to their secret employers: the French security service. Certainly it would seem the photographs were priority, a fact acknowledged even by the French police, as well as by Lord Stevens, even though they deny the photographs had anything to do with James Andanson or Princess Diana. None the less it is acknowledged that Sipa's photographic archive occupied top spot on the gang's priority list, a fact that would also explain why they spent so long in the building. As we know, the archive was locked in the company safe, and that safe had first to be located and then broken into—a task that would have taken even the most experienced safe cracker some time to achieve. In any event there is no other reason why the gang should have remained in the building for such a long time if all they had come for were a few computers and scanners. The photographs, on the other hand, even if the thieves knew beforehand precisely where the safe was located—which, by every account, they did—would have taken longer to remove. Thus we contend the photographs, and not the computers and scanners, comprised the thieves holy grail. Once again, the evidence speaks for itself.

Indeed, the only question remaining is: were these the photographs Andanson had taken in the crash tunnel, the ones he had subsequently bragged about to his friend Françoise Dard, the ones for which, five weeks earlier, he had been murdered? Or were they, as claimed by Sipa owner,

Goskin Sipahioglu, nothing more than *"some compromising photographs of a particular French celebrity"*?

We'll leave you to decided for yourselves.

24

The Central Intelligence Agency
and
The National Security Agency

Standard Denials

This otherwise pointless chapter in the Paget report sets out solely to prove that America's CIA and NSA played no role whatever in the alleged conspiracy to assassinate Princess Diana. It fails miserably. In fact it offers no evidence at all that these highly secretive agencies are innocent of the charges levelled at them. Rather, in response to *"the claims made by Mohamed Al Fayed"*, it merely proceeds to trot out the standard claims and denials we would envisage being dealt by the two agencies in question. For example:

"The Director of Central Intelligence personally requested records searches when the allegations were first raised. An independent review of CIA files was conducted by the CIA Inspector General, who stated that the files:

"...yielded no information shedding any light on the automobile accident or deaths of Lady Diana and Dodi Fayed .../... (MORI DocId 869046)." [Operation Paget Report, Page 734]

Did you see that? "An *independent* review of CIA files was conducted by the *CIA Inspector General* [our italics]. Not even subtle about it, are they? The report further states:

"... The CIA Directorate of Operations (DO) had informed the Inspector General that DO records searches did not locate or identify:

"... any cables containing information about an alleged involvement of the British Royal family, government or intelligence services in the deaths of Princess Diana or Dodi Fayed" or *" that CIA in any way might have been supportive in such a conspiracy. (See MORI DocID 869055, dated 27 April 1998)."* [Operation Paget Report, Page 734]

The CIA Office Of Public Affairs was even more insistent, thus:

"Any allegations of CIA involvement in the death of the Princess were ludicrous and absurd. (See MORI Do c ID 869029, dated 27 July 1998)." [Operation Paget Report, Page 735]

Nothing less than we would expect, then. Indeed, it should come as little surprise to learn that the NSA was equally trite in its seemingly scripted denials. As the report tells us:

"The Director of Policy, NSA, Central Security Service, Louis Giles stated:

"I have personally reviewed the 39 NSA-originated and NSA-controlled documents referenced by Ms JoAnn Grube, NSA Deputy Director of Policy, in her 5 November 1998 response to a Freedom of Information Act request referencing Princess Diana. I can state that these documents contain no information shedding any light on the circumstances surrounding the death of Princess Diana and Dodi Fayed in the 1997 Paris car accident." [Operation Paget Report, Page 735]

And again:

"Furthermore I can categorically confirm that NSA did not target Princess Diana nor collect any of her communications. The NSA documents, acquired from intelligence gathering of international communications, contain only short references to Princess Diana in contexts unrelated to the allegations being made by Mr Mohamed Al Fayed." [Operation Paget Report, Page 735]

Of course, the NSA's claim that it *"did not target Princess Diana nor collect any of her communications"* is a ludicrous one, though hardly one worth contending here. Like the CIA, the NSA has shut up shop on the matter, citing National Security as its justification, thus:

"The documents ... must remain classified as their disclosure could reasonably be expected to cause exceptionally grave damage to the national security of the United States by revealing intelligence sources and methods." [Operation Paget Report, Page 735]

The NSA concluded that the *"grave damage to the national security of the United States"* would be caused, not by revelation of the files or their contents, but by exposure of the agency's intelligence-gathering *"sources and methods"*. Quite why the agency would necessarily expose its *"sources and methods"* in disclosing the contents of its files on Princess Diana is a mystery in itself, one, presumably, the NSA is not prepared to discuss for fear of exposing its 'sources and methods'. Nice one, chaps.

In any event, there is little we can say here to challenge the stance assumed by either the NSA or the CIA. We know both agencies possess files on Diana, but we of course are utterly powerless to force their release. In all fairness, so is Lord Stevens, which is why this chapter in the report is a fairly pointless inclusion. Even America's much-vaunted Freedom of Information Act (FOIA) is powerless against such mute beasts, as the following CIA document shows. Evidently, every ten years the Director of Central Intelligence (DCI) reviews which CIA operational files will be subject to the FOIA, and perhaps more pertinently, which ones will not, thus:

"On 13 April 2005, based on the decennial review required by and conducted in accordance with the CIA Information Act of 1984, and taking into account the review criteria set forth in the Act, the then-DCI designated the following categories of CIA operational files as exempt from the search, review, publication, and disclosure provisions of the FOIA:

Files within the Directorate of Operations:

$\sum$ • *Personality Files*

$\sum$ • *External Organizations Files*

$\sum$ • *Operational Interest Files*

$\sum$ • *Operational Activity Files*

$\sum$ • *Policy and Management Files (including Clandestine Service History Program Files)*

$\sum$ • *Cover Arrangements Files*

Files within the Directorate of Science & Technology

$\sum$ • *Signal Intelligence Activities Files*

$\sum$ • *Operational and Technical Support Files*

$\sum$ • *Intelligence Collections Systems Files*

$\sum$ • *Imagery Analysis and Exploitation Files*

Files within the Security Center

$\sum$ • *Covert Security Approval/SECRET Files*

$\sum$ • *Provisional Covert Security Approval/SECRET Files*

$\sum$ • *Operational Approval Files*

$\sum$ • *Provisional Operational Approval Files*

$\sum$ • *Anonymous Personnel Actions Files*

$\sum$ • *Approval to Polygraph for Operational Purposes Files*

$\sum$ • *Diversified Cover Officer Files*

$\sum$ • *Contract/External Files*

$\sum$ • *Covert Security Approval/SECRET Files*

$\sum$ • *National Resources Division and Name Check/ Operational Program Files*

$\sum$ • *Industrial Special Security Approval/Covert, Industrial Security Approval/Covert, and Industrial Special Security Approval/Covert Reinvestigation Files*

$\sum$ • *Internal/Covert Files*

$\sum$ • *Consultant External/Operations and Consultant Internal/Operations Files"*

The CIA Information Act of 1984, then, prevents the FOIA from searching, reviewing, publishing or otherwise disclosing the contents of any of the above-listed file categories. One wonders, are there any categories left?

It has to be said, though, that the biggest disappointment is not so much the trite denials trotted out by the two agencies; rather, the gleeful way in which Lord Stevens appears to receive them. And the sly, insidious way he then proceeds to use them to bolster his case. In his defence, he does at least admit that:

"The NSA, having provided attributed responses, either does not have information relevant to the crash or is concealing it." [Operation Paget Report, Page 739]

But in the same breath he concludes:

"Operation Paget was satisfied that there was no evidence that communications relating to the events in Paris had been received from any American agency. There is no evidence to support the claim of concealment of relevant material." [Operation Paget Report, Page 739]

Not that we should be in the least surprised that the former top cop reached this conclusion, foregone as it always was. But having admitted that the NSA might well be lying about the information it has on Diana, and in particular on whether or not she was about to become engaged, or married, or indeed, that she might already have been pregnant; and having further admitted that, in consequence, *"it is not possible for Operation Paget to be categorical in its conclusions"*, how then can he categorically state: *"There is no evidence to support the claim of concealment of relevant material"*? Why does the report not instead say: *"While there is no evidence to support the claim of concealment of relevant material, neither is there evidence to the contrary"*, thus presenting the true picture, the *whole* picture, including the fact that the NSA might well be concealing relevant information, or lying, rather than a picture that wrongly infers that the NSA is guiltless? The answer is of course that, by carefully wording his conclusions in this way, they appear to support his case more so than if he'd been straight and honest. This is deceit; it is wrong. If a suspect in a murder case were so ambiguous in their denial of guilt, do you think the Crown Prosecution Service—or its US equivalent—would conclude: *"We know this person might be lying, but there is no evidence to support the claim of their guilt,"* and leave it at that? Of course it wouldn't. On the contrary, it would order that the suspect be brought to trial where their denial would be challenged by proper counsel and their ambiguity judged by a democratically elected jury. True, as previously acknowledged, Lord Stevens has little power over the mighty NSA, and we do not, therefore, seek to criticize him for failing to establish the truth regarding its 'Diana files'. But we must call him to account for the way he tends to use the situation to reinforce his own case. In short, no reprimand for the failure, my Lord. But shame on you for the insidious manner in which you seek to twist that failure to your own advantage.

Before we move on, we should just remind ourselves here of one or two other points regarding the involvement of American intelligence agencies in Diana's death. Of course the two major players, the CIA and NSA, are bound to deny involvement, in any form, even that the files they admit to possessing reveal information relevant to the investigation into the princess's death. Indeed, both agencies are bound by their official allegiance to the President to deny any illegal activity, and whichever way you look at it, eavesdropping phone calls between Diana and Dodi and passing the content of those phone calls back to MI-6 is illegal. True, that the NSA and CIA might conduct such an operation would come as little surprise to most of us. But that the President might in any way have been involved, or even that he might have known about the operation, well that's another matter entirely. And make no mistake, the President is indeed implicated in all CIA activities. According to the CIA mission statement, in fact, the agency's main function is to conduct *"covert action at the direction of the President"*, thus implicating the President in any actions carried out by the CIA and its operatives. For the CIA to admit, therefore, that it passed information on Diana or Dodi back to MI-6 prior to their deaths, fully implies that this *"covert action"* was carried out, officially at least, *"at the direction of the President"*, in effect announcing that then President Bill Clinton directed the CIA to keep MI-6 informed on Diana's relationship with Dodi and thus implicating Clinton in the plot to assassinate the couple. Thus the CIA owning up to possessing files revealing Diana's marriage plans, or indeed, her pregnancy, like the NSA owning up to targeting Diana and collecting her personal communications, is unthinkable. It just ain't gonna happen. Hence why both agencies were policy-bound to deny their involvement in Diana's death, and thus why Lord Stevens' investigation into their involvement was pointless from the outset.

Stealth
And National Security

We should also briefly mention Stealth, the CIA contract agent who first informed us regarding Diana's death (see *Introduction* and *Chapter 7*). According to Stealth, who was still working for the CIA when we spoke to him in 1997, the CIA and MI-6 have always worked very closely together, particularly at the highest, most covert level. In point of fact, Stealth informed us that he was at that time assigned to a joint CIA/SIS cell operating out of Britain (SIS: *Secret Intelligence Service*, or MI-6), and that the cell had been formed to carry out covert operations for a joint British-US military-industrial cabal. In other words, as though to evidence his claim, he implied to us that he was involved in military-industrial espionage on behalf of some British-US defence interest rather than the British and US governments.

"SIS and CIA do the bidding of these people," he revealed. *"We always do the bidding of these people."*

Stealth went on to reveal that the higher echelons of MI-6 and the CIA *"work hand-in-glove"*, and that they always have done, further affirming that, at the highest, most covert level, cooperation between the two spy agencies with regard to Diana's assassination would have been seen as normal rather than abnormal practice. He further explained that, again, at the highest level, decisions were taken that did not always involve, or originate from, the President or Prime Minister, but rather from a group of extremely powerful industrialists and military/intelligence chiefs who Stealth described as *"democratically unaccountable"*. He further described this powerful cabal as being made up of *"financial, industrial and political godfathers... [who] operate quite independently of the law"*.

He also said that *"many of the highly covert, highly illegal operations carried out at the behest of these people are done so behind the smokescreen of National Security"*. This is of particular note when we remind ourselves of the reasons given by the NSA for refusing to release the documents held on Diana and Dodi.

"The documents ... must remain classified as their disclosure could reasonably be expected to cause exceptionally grave damage to the national security of the United States by revealing intelligence sources and methods." [Operation Paget Report, Page 735]

In other words, as Stealth affirmed, the NSA is here seen to be hiding behind *"the smokescreen of National Security"* in its efforts to outmanoeuvre the law. The request for these documents to be released was carried out under America's Freedom Of Information Act, and by law should, therefore, have been granted. But as Stealth also affirmed, the cabal of *"financial, industrial and political godfathers"* who really call the shots *"operate quite independently of the law"*, and thus the NSA documents will remain under lock and key indefinitely. Indeed, even if Stealth did not mean to be taken literally when he inferred that these guys disregard the law with impunity, we can none the less see from the above-cited CIA Information Act that, when necessary, the law is manipulated in their favour anyway. They do not need to break the law. They make it.

"It's the kind of behaviour that flies in the face of democracy and the democratic freedoms on which our world is allegedly run," Stealth affirmed. *"And it is wholly unacceptable. These people are getting away with murder, sometimes literally."*

We still do not know, of course, whether Stealth himself was a double-agent of sorts (see *Chapter 16—Set Up*); whether or not the information he provided a week before Diana's death was part of the plot, or a genuine attempt by him to 'surface' that plot. But then, as another intelligence operative we interviewed, David Shayler, wryly stated: *"The problem with this game, Jon, is that you find yourself in a world of smoke and mirrors"*, a sentiment with which Stealth, in his own unambiguous way, concurred: *"If I were to tell you all I know about the military-industrial complex, Jon—about the quasi-security and intelligence agencies and their underhand operations; about the modus operandi of some of the complex's most powerful chiefs—you would quickly become as old and embittered as I am."*

He concluded: *"They are using the laws of National Security to further their own secret political ends. It riles me. It is fundamentally wrong."*

As is the assassination of a princess.

The Sources

One final point before we move on. As alluded to in the Introduction, as well as other chapters throughout this book, a few short weeks after speaking to Stealth we contacted another source, someone we knew to be very well-connected within British military intelligence. Via this source we were introduced to a second source who told us he had learned of the plot to assassinate Diana some three or four months prior to the Paris crash, who indeed claimed to have been present at a meeting held at MI5 HQ in which Diana's assassination had been discussed, and who also confirmed to us that Camilla Parker Bowles' near-fatal car crash a few weeks prior to Diana's death had been plotted and carried out by the Security Service (see *Chapter 10*). This is something we will elaborate on a little later in view of new evidence presented in the Paget report.

(For the record, we have deliberately disguised these two sources by blending them into one composite character, as well as amalgamating the information received from them for security reasons. They agreed to talk to us on the understanding that we protect their anonymity at all times. Thus the two sources are often referred to in the singular.)

In any event, this source confirmed much of what Stealth had revealed—not only that Diana's assassination had been planned for *"several months"*, but that the CIA had indeed assisted MI-6 operationally, as well as informing them that Diana and Dodi were expecting a child. This same source also explained the reasons for CIA involvement in the plot. Without wishing to repeat ourselves (as these reasons are presented at various points throughout the book), briefly, this source informed us that during the year or so leading up to her death, Diana had started to make something of a real nuisance of herself within US defence industry circles. Her landmines campaign had started to forge a momentum all its own, he said, quite unexpectedly so, to the point even that not only had she thrown the spotlight of world attention on, among other things, the CIA-brokered arms-for-oil-and-diamonds deals shaping the future of Angola and other oil-rich African countries. But she had also, he assured us, single-handedly, and virtually overnight, persuaded the President of the United States to overturn American defence policy, thus pulling the rug on untold billions of dollars in defence revenue—profits that would otherwise have been won by US-based defence corporations. Indeed, the day she convinced then President Bill Clinton to support her campaign by agreeing to sign up to an accord banning the manufacture, sale and deployment of antipersonnel landmines worldwide— with the added threat of anti-tank mines and airborne mines (cluster bombs) being absorbed in to the equation—the CIA was finally encouraged to whisper severe warnings in Bill Clinton's ear (see *Chapter 13*). At the same time the agency finally agreed to throw its weight behind the MI-6 plot to assassinate Diana, we were assured, and so began feeding the information it had collected from its telephone intercepts back to London. As our source revealed: *"This was the reason the CIA got involved with MI-6 to take care of the princess. MI-6 had their own reasons for wanting rid of Diana. But from this point on it became a joint operation ... Diana's fate was effectively sealed then."*

And further: *"The CIA assured Clinton that Diana would be out of the way by the time the deal was to be signed ... [by the time of] the conference in Oslo. With Diana gone, they knew that public focus on the [landmines] issue would diminish quickly—and that would leave the way clear for Clinton to opt out of the agreement without too much fuss."*

And so it came to pass. As we now know, less than three weeks after Diana's death Clinton duly opted out of the treaty, something Lord Stevens failed to take into account when glibly assuring us that he could find *"no evidence to support the claim"* that the CIA was involved in Diana's death. Perhaps it would have helped if he'd looked in the right places ...

Oswald LeWinter And The CIA Documents

... Here, for example, at claims that the CIA documents 'surfaced' by former high-ranking CIA disinformation officer, Oswald LeWinter, in 1998, were actually copies of genuine documents. Indeed, though immediately branded forgeries by the CIA, the documents in question, together with the subsequent suppression of evidence and the refusal to prosecute law proceedings against the CIA by the US government, clearly raise further suspicions regarding CIA involvement in Diana's death.

For the record, early in 1998, Oswald LeWinter, together with several other very serious players—including CIA agents, a high-flying Beverly Hills lawyer and a deep-throat investigative journalist—hatched a plan to extort US $20,000,000 from Mohamed Al Fayed by selling him CIA documents and telexes proving that Diana and Dodi had been assassinated by MI-6; and indeed, that Diana had been pregnant at the time of her death. In the event, the sting went amateurishly wrong, suspiciously so, given the calibre of the conspirators. Mohamed Al Fayed informed the US authorities of LeWinter's approach and, in consequence, a joint FBI/CIA counter-operation was launched. While LeWinter, the apparent fall guy, was arrested and spent several years in jail, all others involved, including the lawyer hired to broker the deal, Keith Fleer; the journalist, George Williamson; former CIA officer, Pat McMillan; plus notorious cold-war Czech double agent, Karl Koecher, (the only mole ever known to have penetrated the CIA), escaped justice. The perfect CIA disinformation sting. Indeed, if the CIA did possess files documenting its involvement in Diana's death, what better way to repudiate the fact than 'surfacing' those documents as 'forgeries'? And this, it would seem, is precisely what happened. Following the bungled sting operation, the documents were indeed branded forgeries, in the best way possible—in a court of law, thus exonerating the CIA, officially and legally, from any involvement whatever in Diana's death. It really was the perfect operation, and Oswald LeWinter, of course, like another 'Oswald' who notably springs to mind, was the perfect CIA fall guy. Indeed, LeWinter was caught red-handed with documents he maintains to this day were authentic—or at least that they were copies of authentic documents rather than straight forgeries. Given that he was tracked all the way to Austria—where the sting took place—by a posse of FBI and CIA operatives, one has to concede, at least, that the documents must have been deemed pretty damn precious by the US authorities, and that, therefore, the chances of them being straight forgeries are low. After all, why would the FBI and the CIA send a team of agents to Austria to apprehend someone selling false documents? Surely the only reason they would go to such lengths would be to prevent *genuine* documents from being surfaced in the public domain. Selling *false* documents in Austria, on the other hand, would be a matter purely for the Austrian authorities; indeed, LeWinter was tried, convicted and sentenced in Austria, by an Austrian judge and an Austrian jury in an Austrian court of law. No yanks in sight. And the only reason the documents were in the end branded forgeries was because LeWinter was forced to confess they were forgeries in order to save his own butt. He'd been well and truly stung. Confess that the documents are forgeries, he was told, and you will be charged with fraud. He did. He was. He spent two and a half years in jail. Admit that the documents are genuine, on the other hand, and you will be charged with treason for attempting to sell classified documents and spend the rest of your life behind bars. Notably, no one else involved in the operation was or ever has been prosecuted, either in Austria or the United States. In point of fact the US government assigned the case 'low priority' and then promptly closed the case entirely, one can only assume to protect the CIA from being found out, a fact that, to us anyway, indicates that the entire episode was a carefully planned sting operation orchestrated by the CIA to surface and discredit the documents for the very fact that they prove the agency's involvement in Diana's death. The added fact that LeWinter, both during his incarceration and since his release in December 2000, has maintained that the documents were indeed genuine, or at least genuine copies, serves only to bolster this probability. As the US District Court for the District of Columbia itself asked in September 2000, when Mohamed Al Fayed attempted to force the CIA to release these and other documents relating to the princess's murder:

"Was the criminal investigation into LeWinter and others for the attempt to defraud Al Fayed over the alleged CIA documents deliberately assigned low priority and then closed by the United States government in an effort to shield the actions of current or former CIA employees from scrutiny or avoid adverse publicity?"

In true tradition, the CIA simply refused to answer this question and the US government shut up shop. As the US District Court of the District of Columbia also revealed:

"The Austrian justice ministry sent a request concerning the documents taken from LeWinter's hotel room to the CIA to ascertain their authenticity, and also requested that a United States government expert be sent to testify under oath at LeWinter's trial concerning the documents. The United States government delayed its response for three months, and finally simply replied that the documents were "not authentic" and refused to send any expert to testify under oath."

Not that this in itself proves a thing, of course. But there certainly are details in the documents that give rise to suspicions that Oswald LeWinter, like his namesake, was indeed an operational patsy, and thus that he might actually have been telling the truth—i.e. that the documents were copies of authentic originals rather than straight forgeries. For the record, the US District Court of the District of Columbia also revealed the nature of the documents recovered in the joint FBI/CIA operation:

"Among the papers found in LeWinter's hotel room were an airmail

*pouch addressed "U.S. Government Property, Return to Commander USA
FAC, Indianapolis IN 46249", and a multiple-use U.S. government
messenger envelope with the last noted addressee "U.K. liaison." Inside this
envelope were two telexes and a Domestic Intelligence Information Report
that appeared on their face to originate within the CIA."*

Below is a reproduction of, strangely, the only document ever
released to the press. You will note that the telex is dated 17th June, 1997—
some ten weeks before Diana's death.

Domestic Collection Division

Foreign Intelligence Information Report
Directorate of Intelligence

WARNING NOTICE - INTELLIGENCE SOURCES AND
METHODS INVOLVED

FURTHER DISSEMINATION AND USE OF THE INFORMATION
SUBJECT TO CONTROLS STATED AT BEGINNING AND
END OF REPORT

REPORT CLASS: TOP SECRET REPORT NO: 00.D 831/173466-97

COUNTRY: France

DATE DISTR: 17 June 1997

SUBJECT: File overview: Diana Princess Of Wales-Dodi

REFERENCES DCI Case 64376

SOURCE: CAS Paris/ CAS London/ COS Geneva/ CAS Kingston/ UK
citizen Ken Etheridge

1. Relationship initiated between Diana POW and Dodi aF according
to reliable intel sources in November 1996. Intimacy begins shortly
after they meet. (Report filed)

2. Reliable source reports Palace seriously disturbed by liaison. PM

considers any Al Fayed relationship politically disastrous. Edinburgh (Prince Philip -ed) sees serious threat to dynasty should relationship endure. Quote reported: "Such an affair is racially and morally repugnant and no son of a bedouin camel trader is fit for the mother of a future king," Edinburgh. (Report filed)

3. Request from highest circles to DEA attachÈ UK for 6 on Dodi re: Cocaine. See File forwarded to UK embassy DC. (Copy filed)

4. US liaison to MI-6 requested by David Spedding for assistance in providing permanent solution to Dodi problem. Blessing of Palace secured (Twiz filed)

5. WHuse (White House -ed) denies Spedding request. Harrison authorized only to arrange meeting for MI-6 representative with K-Team Geneva. (Twiz on file)

6. Meeting in Geneva reportedly successful (Report filed)

7. Al Fayed Mercedes Limo stolen and returned with electronics missing. Reliable intel source confirms K-team involved. Source reports car rebuilt to respond to external radio controls. (Report filed)

8. COB Geneva reports that on May 28, 1997 heavily weighted Fiat Turbo...(end of page text)

TOP SECRET

We are not familiar with all the spy lingo employed in the telex, but we can clarify one or two terms and abbreviations which tend to show that whoever 'forged' the document certainly seemed to know their art. For example, the telex purports to originate from the Domestic Collection Division, a department within the CIA tasked with collecting overseas information, largely from American citizens either travelling or otherwise situated abroad. These days this department would appear to be known as the National Resources Division, but as the telex states, in 1997 it was still known as the Domestic Collection Division (DCD). True, it does seem a little odd that the DCD would have been tasked with collecting information on Diana and Dodi, as its main area of operation is more commercial, financial and industrial espionage. The citing of American nationals in the document as source(s) of the information, however, would certainly be consistent with DCD procedure. We are told, for example, that the source in Paris, as in London and Kingston, was designated 'CAS', or 'Controlled American Source', signifying that these sources, whether officially attached to the CIA or not, were none the less American citizens either travelling or living abroad. We have to say, however, that we find it difficult in the extreme to believe the CIA would have used regular American citizens to inform them regarding Diana and Dodi; far more likely that these designations refer to 'Covert Action Staff' stationed abroad. 'CAS' is a known CIA acronym for either or both.

A further source cited in the document and situated in Geneva is designated 'COS', the CIA acronym for 'Chief Of Station'. As the COS, certainly in Switzerland, would have worked on a 'declared' rather than a covert basis, this designation is significant, as the CIA's COS in Geneva in June 1997 would be easily identifiable and therefore should be questioned in connection with the LeWinter documents.

As should 'Ken Etheridge', also identified in the document as a source, though unlike the 'CAS' sources, Mr Etheridge is identified as a *"UK citizen"*. This is a very intriguing inclusion. Though we are not claiming that this Kenneth Etheridge is the one cited in the LeWinter document, we *are* saying that a man bearing this very name shares a very well-publicized and somewhat acrimonious history with Mohamed Al Fayed, and should therefore have been questioned when the document was surfaced. Indeed, was Mr Etheridge ever questioned, we wondered? Was Kenneth Etheridge, the former City of London police chief who in 1989 let Fayed's most hated adversary, Tiny Rowland, off the hook regarding his company's dodgy deals in Rhodesia and off-shore tax-avoiding schemes, questioned when the document was surfaced? Was former Detective Chief Superintendent Kenneth Etheridge, who retired following his investigation of Tiny Rowland's Lonrho company, only to be made the company's head of security, ever questioned over his alleged status as a CIA informer? Moreover, was *"UK citizen Ken Etheridge"*, who helped Tiny Rowland gain compromising information on Mohamed Al Fayed via his old, high-ranking contacts at the City of London Police, ever asked why his name should have appeared on a CIA telex in connection with Mr Al Fayed's son? Just a thought.

It is also of note, to us at least, that the telex states: *"Relationship initiated between Diana POW and Dodi aF according to reliable intel sources in November 1996. Intimacy begins shortly after they meet."* As stated in the opening chapter of this book, our sources have always maintained that Diana and Dodi had been friends, if not lovers, since November 1996. And as Mohamed Al Fayed himself has always maintained: *"Diana and Dodi met long before the summer of 1997 and during their romance had more time together than people knew."* One can understand why Dodi's father might wish people to know this critical detail, but there is no reason we could think of why a 'forged' document should contain such information. In any case, who would have known it? Other than Mohamed Al Fayed and perhaps one or two well-informed intelligence agents, who would have known that Diana and Dodi had been seeing each other since November 1996? LeWinter? Possibly. But how? How would LeWinter have known unless the CIA had told him? The CIA would of course have known because they had been listening in on Diana's telephone calls and passing the transcripts back to MI-6. Which means, presumably, that MI-6 would have known, as well. But LeWinter? How would he have known unless his former employers had been in on the plot from the outset? The charge was, remember, that LeWinter and his buddies had acted alone in forging these documents in order to extort money from Mohamed Al Fayed. Had the CIA tripped up by including this nugget of truth in what was purported to be a forged document, we wondered? We made a note.

We also noted that documents containing disinformation are invariably based on genuine documents; certainly that a 'surfaced' document would typically take the form of a genuine document containing genuine information artfully laced with a few untruths. The LeWinter document was beginning to appear this way to us. Reference to the couple's relationship having started sooner than publicly known, allusions to Dodi's alleged cocaine abuse and mention of a *"heavily weighted Fiat Turbo"* being procured by the CIA Chief of Station in Geneva seemed authentic enough, as did the reference to *"US liaison to MI-6"* requesting CIA assistance. Mention of Prince Philip being *"seriously disturbed by liaison"*, and inclusions such as *"Blessing of Palace secured"*, on the other hand, seemed a little scripted, as did the CIA's unlikely referral of Spedding's request for assistance to the White House and the White House's subsequent denial of that request. But genuine or false, one has to agree that surfacing the document via a 'patsy' such as LeWinter was the perfect way to 'prove' it was false, and thus exonerate the CIA from any involvement whatever in Diana's death. Job done.

As for us, we simply have to believe the CIA played at least some part in the operation that killed Diana; we do have, after all, Stealth's words indelibly etched on the pages of our personal history. We have the testimonies of our other sources to consider, as well, in particular the two sources who were to play such an important role at the very beginning of our investigation. Indeed, while we have to acknowledge that, aside from the LeWinter documents, our only real evidence of CIA involvement in Diana's death is motive based, and that we have no smoking-gun evidence to offer (indeed, we doubt such evidence will ever surface), we do none the less stand by the information we gleaned from our two original sources—not only because the information they gave us makes sense, but also because it fits so perfectly well with all the other information we have uncovered and gathered over the years. The more time moves on, in fact, the more sense that information seems to make; the more perfectly it seems to fit with the rest of the picture, which is of course still evolving, revealing new evidence that serves even further to corroborate the information we received from these two sources so early on in our investigation. And so the wheel turns. It is a real acid test that, when new information emerges, it validates rather than invalidates information already in the frame, corroborates rather than undermines the evidence already presented. This has certainly been shown time and again with the information received from these two sources, a fact surely deserving of special recognition when we realize also that the information they offered was both original and seminal: it did not stem from the rumour mill; rather it stemmed from the very smoke-filled dens in which the plot was first hatched, and thus provided a unique and comprehensive background to the unfolding conspiracy. Indeed, we should make a point of acknowledging, not only their courage in stepping forward, but also their contribution in terms of revealing the plot from the inside—what that plot was really all about, why it was really formulated, what was really going on behind the scenes, the scheming and manoeuvring that finally led to the operation being given the green light. This inside information, for the most part, is contained in *Chapters 8* and *9*, which were written fully nine years before the release of Lord Stevens' Paget report. But it is only now, with the release of that report, that the information we received from these two original sources—in particular the information pertaining to Camilla Parker Bowles' near-fatal car crash some two months prior to Diana's death— has not only been corroborated. It has also been added to. The result: an even greater insight into why Prince Charles would have wanted both Diana *and* Camilla assassinated, as we shall see.

25

THE SECURITY SERVICE
AND THE
SECRET INTELLIGENCE SERVICE

A Battle Royal
And The Royal Nanny

T he amount of time, effort and money it must have taken to investigate and eventually trash all the allegations surrounding Britain's two intelligence services is quite simply phenomenal. Over 50 separate allegations regarding MI-6 alone are listed, explored, and finally dismantled by the Paget team, expertly, with a subtle twist of arrogance. At the end of it all they must have felt so good, thinking they had finally put this whole conspiracy craze to bed. Well bad news, guys. Welcome to the twenty-first century—where people have minds of their own.

The vast majority of the claims regarding British intelligence involvement in Diana's death refer to MI-6. According to the Paget report, at any rate, MI5 would seem to be off the hook, a fact supported by former MI5 counter-terrorism officers, David Shayler and Annie Machon, both of whom, when interviewed, were keen to assure us that MI5 was more lawfully accountable than MI-6 and thus less likely to get involved in operations such as eavesdropping telephone calls, wiretapping, or indeed, political assassination. Our other sources did not fully agree with David and Annie, stating contrarily that factions within MI5 had clearly been involved in the plot to assassinate Diana—and indeed, Camilla Parker Bowles—pretty much from the beginning. Certainly from as long ago as November 1995, they assured us, a battle royal had ensued between the two agencies over which of the two rivals to kill off in order to *"clean up the constitutional mess"* caused by Prince Charles's philandering (see *Chapter 9*). Clearly our original sources were in little doubt that the Security Service had played a role in determining Diana's fate, even if only that it had bungled its attempted assassination of Camilla Parker Bowles in June 1997, and that this failure had resulted in MI-6 finally being given the green light to proceed with its plan to assassinate Diana. Indeed, David Shayler did confess to suspicions that MI5 had been penetrated by agents from other agencies, including MI-6, and that these renegade factions within MI5 could well have been involved in the plot. Certainly new evidence presented in the Paget report tends to corroborate this claim, showing that, once again, our two original sources were probably right. See what you make of this.

In October 2003, Diana's former butler Paul Burrell shocked the world by publishing a note that he claimed Diana had written some seven years earlier, in October 1996. It turns out, however, according to evidence presented in the report, that the note had been written a year earlier than Burrell claimed—in October 1995, just a few short weeks before Diana's now famous *Panorama* interview. But in any event, as the report also acknowledges, the real significance of the note is in what it contains rather than when it was written.

The note, perhaps the most chilling handwritten message in modern times, reads:

"This particular phase in my life is the most dangerous. My husband is planning an accident in my car, brake failure and serious head injury, in order to make the path clear for him to marry."

The assumption at the time, by us as well as most everybody else, was that the name 'Camilla' should be tagged on the end of this note, so that it might read *"in order to make the path clear for him to marry [Camilla]"*, as this was obviously the woman Diana was referring to. Thanks to Lord Stevens, however, we now know that Mrs Parker Bowles was not the woman Diana was referring to, thus:

"There is a generally held perception that this reference is to Camilla Parker Bowles, now the Duchess of Cornwall. This is not so. The Princess of Wales did name a woman in her note. It was not Camilla. Operation Paget knows the identity of the woman named." [Operation Paget Report, Page

103]

So do we. Indeed, at about the same time Diana wrote her now famous note, it is alleged the philandering Prince Charles was not only romping with his long-term mistress, Camilla Parker Bowles, but with someone else from the royal harem, as well: former royal nanny, Alexandra 'Tiggy' Legge-Bourke, the woman he had been caught kissing while on a skiing holiday in Klosters earlier in the year. Ironically, the man who captured the tell-tale photograph was none other than James Andanson, and it reportedly netted him a tidy £100,000. Not bad for a morning's sight-seeing. In any event, as our sources rightly maintained so many years before, as a result of Charles's affection for Tiggy Legge-Bourke, Diana feared both she *and* Camilla had been placed on the Establishment hit list.

"The Princess of Wales ... believed that there was a conspiracy and that both she and Camilla were to be 'put aside'." [Operation Paget Report, Page 97]

While everybody suspected that Charles wanted rid of Diana, nobody really thought he might have wanted rid of Camilla, as well. We were all wrong. No wonder Establishment czars were frantic in their efforts to *"clean up the constitutional mess"* caused by Charles's philandering. The man was rabid. And as a result, the looming constitutional crisis would have been seen as an even bigger challenge than it already was. The problems that already existed, as outlined in Chapter 9, would surely have been compounded by the addition of yet another prospective royal spouse, in particular with regard to Charles's position as future Supreme Governor of the Church of England. True, time has moved on; over the years a lot has been achieved to relax the rules and soften opinion regarding the remarriage of divorcees in church, even to the extent that when Charles eventually did marry Camilla Parker Bowles—albeit in the local town hall rather than in church—the marriage duly received its appropriate blessing from the Archbishop of Canterbury, something that could simply never have happened in the 1990s. Back then things were different. Very different. Indeed, we should perhaps remind ourselves just how different they were: just how seriously the Church and the Establishment viewed the problem and just how frantic Church hierarchs had become at the prospect of having an openly adulterous King as their Supreme Governor. As Tony Wright, then Parliamentary Aide to the Lord Chancellor, publicly stated in July 1997, *"a constitutional crisis"* resulting from the marriage of Prince Charles and Mrs Parker Bowles would *"end in disestablishment"*. In layman's terms that means that the Church and the State, unlike Charles and his copious harem, would no longer be sleeping together, and in consequence, Britain would become a secular state for the first time in its history. Words scarcely suffice to describe just how far-reaching a problem this had become. Indeed, by comparison, bumping off a princess would have been considered child's play.

"Either you have a Supreme Governor who can manage his life in the way other people manage it, and when they encounter difficulties, have to solve them," Tony Wright told the BBC's *Today* programme, *"or be told by this established Church that they can't do it. In which case we shall have a constitutional crisis and it will end in disestablishment."*

Evidently Charles's local vicar, Rev John Hawthorne, agreed, stating on the same programme that the naughty prince should not become Supreme Governor of the Church *"unless he repented of his adultery and gave up Mrs Parker Bowles"*, a sentiment that gained the backing of other, more senior clerics, including the Archbishop of Canterbury, as well as Prime Minister Tony Blair. In point of fact, the day before Tony Wright made his comments, on Thursday 17th July, 1997, Tony Blair held a special meeting at Number Ten in which he was briefed by representatives of the Lord Chancellor's Department (now the Department for Constitutional Affairs) regarding *"the legal and constitutional implications of the divorced prince marrying a divorcee and then ascending to the throne."* Indeed, as stated in *Chapter 9*, the main obstacle back then was always that, if Charles were to marry Camilla and then ascend to the Throne, Camilla would automatically become the Princess of Wales and subsequently the Queen Consort. All well and good, so long as Diana, Princess of Wales, was no longer alive, if you get our drift …

In any event, the reason we know Tiggy Legge-Bourke was prime suspect at this time is that Diana named her in a note, written not by herself, as Lord Stevens wrongly asserts, but by her lawyer, Lord Mishcon. At a meeting between Lord Mishcon and the princess on 30th October, 1995, at which her Private Secretary, Patrick Jephson, was also present, Diana told Lord Mishcon about Charles and Tiggy and cited the situation as a cause for her current anxieties. But more significantly still, Diana also told Lord Mishcon precisely what those anxieties were: that *"reliable sources"* had warned her she was in danger of being killed off in *"car accident"* due to *"brake failure"*. True, she cited Charles's affection for Tiggy Legge-Bourke as the reason for her concern, but there were other reasons, too, good reasons, frightening reasons, that she should fear for her life, as we will see in a moment. Indeed, having spoken in private about the matter with Patrick Jephson, who *"to Lord Mishcon's surprise, said that he 'half believed' the accuracy of her remarks regarding her safety"*, Lord Mishcon recorded what Diana had told him in a note which he kept under lock and key until the princess's death some two years later. And here is where it all gets sticky. Alerted by the fact that Diana's *"reliable sources"* appeared to have been right— that she did indeed die in a *"car accident"* that might well have been due to *"brake failure"*, in any event that she died in a *"car accident"* that *crashed* in *suspicious circumstances*—on 18th September, 1997, a little under three weeks after Diana's death, Lord Mishcon met with then Metropolitan Police Commissioner Sir Paul (now Lord) Condon and Assistant Commissioner (now Sir) David Veness at New Scotland Yard, and brought the note to their attention. But to no avail. Britain's two most senior police officers simply tucked the note neatly away in a secure place and kept all knowledge of its existence a closely-held secret. In other words, they buried it, justifying their actions by stating there was no *"relevant suspicion concerning the death"*, and therefore the note was immaterial. No mention of the note or its contents was ever made again—not, at least, until Paul Burrell decided to publish the contents of a similar note in 2003 (Diana's own chilling note), at which point the Metropolitan Police were forced to admit the existence of the original note submitted by Lord Mishcon. From where we stand, this can only be deemed a deliberate and calculated suppression of vital evidence on the part of Condon and Veness, and we believe they should be brought to account for their actions in this regard. As stated, at the time they were Britain's two most senior police officers, and as such they were— together with former Detective Superintendent Jeffrey Rees, the British/French Liaison Officer for the French inquiry—responsible for ensuring that all relevant documents were made available to Judge Stephan, the inquiry's presiding magistrate. A note lodged by Diana with her lawyer stating that *"reliable sources"* had warned her that she might be killed off in a *"car accident"* due to *"brake failure"* would, one might reasonably assume, have been classed as *highly* relevant by Judge Stephan, especially as the note in question provided information, not only chillingly accurate with regard to the *manner* of her death, but with regard to *motive*, as well. But Judge Stephan was never made aware of the note, of course. The Metropolitan Police made sure of that.

Prince Philip
Nicholas Soames
And The Honourable Rosa Monckton

There were other reasons why Diana so feared for her safety at this time. The looming constitutional crisis had in itself galvanized the full force of the entire Westminster Establishment against her, and according to our sources, Westminster's secret intelligence arm, MI-6, was at the forefront of that attack, already plotting away behind the scenes while its propaganda machine set about destroying the princess's character—and her mind—via the media. With or without Tiggy Legge-Bourke, it seemed, the situation had by now become critical. Indeed, whether or not the royal nanny posed a real threat to Diana's marriage is here only minimally relevant, if at all; by this time it was public knowledge that her marriage was a sham anyway. The real threat felt by Diana at this time, in fact, came not from within the royal harem, but from within Charles's close circle of upper-class cronies and psycho-spooks—friends, courtiers, servants, and other highly paid protectors—many of whom made no secret of their intense dislike for the nonconformist princess. Prince Charles's close friend, former Minister of State for the Armed Forces, Nicholas Soames, for example, who the Establishment trotted out every time it wanted to publicly slate Diana or defend Prince Charles, was perhaps Diana's foremost nemesis. He had already stated that the princess appeared to be suffering from *"mental illness"* and that she was *"in the advanced stages of paranoia"*, a public insult for which he was firmly rebuked by his boss at the time, former Prime Minister John Major. But it was what Soames and his accomplices were thinking and plotting behind the scenes that really worried Diana. As the Paget report tells us, Soames was one of three people Diana feared above anybody else, the others being Lord Fellowes (accused of being in the British Embassy in Paris on the night of the crash—see *Footnote II*), and the royal godfather himself, Prince Philip. Speaking of Fellowes in the report, Diana said:

"'He hates me. He will do anything to get me out of the Royals. He cost me the friendship with my sister' and added 'Prince Philip wants to see me dead.'"

Indeed, there are several instances in the report where Diana makes her fears regarding Prince Philip known, loud and clear. Following her *Panorama* interview in November 1995, for example, she told her close friend, Roberto Devorik:

"After this they are going to kill me ... I am sure Prince Philip is involved with the security services. After this they are going to get rid of me." [Operation Paget Report, Page 108]

And again, speaking to Devorik, this time in August 1996:

"I am a threat in their eyes. They only use me when they need me for official functions and then they drop me again in the darkness... they are not going to kill me by poisoning me or in a big plane where others will get hurt. They will either do it when I am on a small plane, in a car when I am driving or in a helicopter." [Operation Paget Report, Page 109]

It would seem beyond question, then, that Diana not only knew her life was in danger, but that she also knew the people most likely to have been plotting her death. Moreover, it would seem she had also been told by her *"reliable sources"* the method most likely to have been used to murder her, which in itself is significant. Surely most people fearing they might become a victim of political assassination, in particular those suffering *"the advanced stages of paranoia"*, would fear they might be shot, like JFK, or poisoned, like former KGB spy, Alexander Litvinenko. Diana, on the other hand, was quite specific. Though she did mention the possibility of crashing in a small plane or helicopter, she stated quite confidently that she would not be the victim of poisoning, and indeed, most frequently spoke of dying in a pre-planned car crash due to *"brake failure"*. She could not have been more explicit. And yet Establishment stalwart Lord Stevens simply ignores this evidence and instead focuses his entire effort behind the opinions of fellow Establishment spooks like Nicholas Soames, who insisted the princess was simply 'paranoid'.

"Dear Simone, as you know, the brakes of my car have been tampered with. If something does happen to me it will be MI5 or MI-6 who will have done it. Lots of love, Diana." [Operation Paget Report, Page 105]

Of course, these kind of remarks, expressing these kind of fears, were perfect ammunition for sharks like Soames; though expressed privately following an incident in which Diana's brakes had failed, they would none the less create a feeding frenzy for the MI-6-controlled media outlets to which they were mysteriously 'leaked' at the time. For the record, the comments were expressed in a note Diana wrote shortly after her *Panorama* interview, a note she subsequently sent to her close friend, Simone Simmons—who, incidentally, has something to say herself about the razor-toothed Mr

Soames. Check this.

In the report, Simone Simmons reveals details of a telephone conversation between Diana and Nicholas Soames in February 1997. Nicholas Soames, remember, was and still is a personal friend of Prince Charles and was Diana's most viciously outspoken critic. In any event, during the telephone call, Diana beckoned her friend, Simone Simmons, over to where she was standing and indicated that she should listen in on the call. She held the telephone so that they both could hear what Soames was saying. In the Paget report, Simone Simmons says that she heard Soames say in a menacing and *"threatening"* voice:

"Don't meddle in things that you know nothing about because you know accidents can happen." [Operation Paget Report, Page 110]

This blatant and undisguised threat was allegedly made by the man who was at the time Britain's Armed Forces Minister. The phone call took place on Diana's return from Angola, where she had been campaigning to have landmines banned. Two plus two equals four. Yet the only attention Lord Stevens gives to this threat is to be found in the following statement:

"Nicholas Soames provided a statement to Operation Paget (Statement 187) in which he categorically denied ever having such a conversation with the Princess of Wales." [Operation Paget Report, Page 110]

End of story. Top-end aristocrat, grandson of Winston Churchill, son of Baron and Baroness Soames and personal friend of Prince Charles, Arthur Nicholas Winston Soames, is let off the hook by Knight of the Realm and recently elevated Life Peer of the United Kingdom, John Arthur Stevens, Baron Stevens of Kirkwhelpington. Talk about the old school tie. True, evidence of Soames' alleged telephone threat will also be presented to the inquest, but that too will of course be presided over by a woman who was recently elevated to the peerage, Baroness Elizabeth Butler-Sloss, Deputy Coroner of the Queen's Household, Dame Grand Cross of the Order of the British Empire, sister of the late Lord High Chancellor and Chairman of Britain's Security Commission, a somewhat anonymous organisation tasked with protecting the security of the Crown and its secret intelligence arm, MI-6. Do you honestly suppose we could expect the Baroness to pay any more attention to the threat made to Diana by Nicholas Soames than Lord Stevens?

Doubtful, isn't it. Indeed, it makes interesting reading, scrolling down the list of gilt-edged names Stevens turned to for help in building his case against Diana's assertion that Prince Charles and MI-6 were out to get her. Lady Sarah McCorquodale, Diana's estranged sister; Lucia Flecha de Lima, wife of the Brazilian Ambassador to Britain and supposed 'friend' of Diana; the Honourable Rosa Monckton, another supposed 'friend' of Diana; Lady Annabel Goldsmith, etc, etc. All these flowers of the nobility, of course, stated precisely what Lord Stevens wanted them to state—that Diana's fears were unfounded, that MI-6 wouldn't do such a thing and we all think Prince Charles is lovely. *Rule Britannia*. What else could they have said? Even if they thought differently, how could they possibly have said so? How could they possibly have admitted that Diana might have been murdered by the very Establishment that lines their breeches with diamonds? Lucia Flecha de Lima, for example. Who is this woman? What gave her the right to order Paul Burrell to burn Diana's *"blood-stained clothes"* following the crash? Why did Lord Stevens defend this action?

"Paul Burrell has openly stated that he burned the clothing on his return to Kensington Palace following a discussion with a friend of the Princess of Wales, Lucia Flecha de Lima. Having been given the clothing by the authorities in the first place there is no indication that this was anything other than an innocent act to deal with what could have been a health hazard." [Operation Paget Report, Page 560]

A health hazard? Could it not also have been vital forensic evidence going up in smoke? Sweep the tunnel clean, embalm the princess, burn her clothes. Not that there was a cover-up in progress, of course, and not that these women, these so-called 'friends' of Diana, were forced by their status to participate in that cover-up. But why, when Simone Simmons tells us that the letters Diana received from Prince Philip were *"nasty"*, does Lucia Flecha de Lima state:

"'Prince Philip tried to help her during the difficult period of her marriage, in his own way. He was sometimes a bit brutal. I have read the letters. They were not unkind. He is a clever man. He would not hurt her. The divorce was over and the finances were settled. There was no reason for anyone to kill her." [Operation Paget Report, Page 125]

Oh really? Then why do you suppose Diana said *"Prince Philip wants to see me dead"*? Not *"Prince Philip isn't all that keen on me"*, or *"I know he's only trying to help me, but don't you think he's being a bit brutal?"*. No. Having stated her fear that her father-in-law was *"involved with the security services"*, she explicitly said: *"Prince Philip wants to see me dead."* One can only wonder why she should have made such a dramatic assertion as this if in truth it contained no substance.

And speaking of the security services …

What about the Honourable Rosa Monckton, publicly the princess's closest friend? It was Lucia Flecha de Lima who introduced Diana to this society sophisticate, who over the years certainly became one of Diana's closest confidantes. It was Rosa Monckton with whom Diana went on an Aegean cruise prior to her Mediterranean holiday with Dodi, and it was at the end of this cruise, according to the Honourable Mrs Monckton, that Diana came into her menstrual cycle, thus proving—somewhat conveniently—that the princess could not possibly have been pregnant when she died. Needless to say, Rosa Monckton does not believe Diana was about to get engaged to Dodi, nor even form a long-term relationship with him. And neither does she believe Diana was murdered. But then, like her good friend, Lucia Flecha de Lima, how could she? How could she possibly accept that the very agency her younger brother Anthony has allegedly worked for since 1987, MI-6, might have assassinated her close friend, Princess Diana? Simple. She could not. Especially as her husband, Dominic Lawson, Editor of *The Sunday Telegraph*, has also been accused, in the press *and* in Parliament, of being an MI-6 agent. Indeed, accusations that Rosa Monckton is herself an MI-6 asset, and that she befriended Diana purely to keep an eye on her, just as her grandfather, Sir Walter Monckton, is said to have 'kept an eye' on the errant King Edward VIII on behalf of the same agency, can only call her 'friendship' with Diana even further into question. Problem is, nobody seems able to ask this question, leastwise not with any authority or meaning. Nobody seems able to call Rosa Monckton to the witness stand and impel her to answer this question, under oath: What is your relationship with the Secret Intelligence Service? Do you, or any of your family, have a relationship with MI-6? Certainly Mohamed Al Fayed seems to think that maybe this is the case. As he stated in court, under oath, during his libel case against Neil Hamilton in 1999:

"The Editor of The Sunday Telegraph definitely works for MI-6 … his brother-in-law works for MI-6 … these are the people who control democracy in this country. Let MI5 and MI-6 sue me. Let Prince Philip sue me, then I

will go through everything. They killed my son."

Did Rosa Monckton pass information about Diana to MI-6? One must presume Lord Stevens interrogated her in this regard, as the following statement is included in the report:

"Rosa Monckton stated that the claim that she was 'recruited' by MI-6 to befriend the Princess of Wales was totally wrong." [Operation Paget Report, Page 808]

And again:

"There was no evidence to show that Rosa Monckton passed any information about the Princess of Wales to the SIS [MI-6] during their seven year friendship." [Operation Paget Report, Page 808]

One wonders: precisely what might constitute *"evidence"* that Rosa Monckton had passed information about Diana to MI-6? A double-page advertisement in the New York Times, perhaps? An announcement on CNN?

Good evening. In London today, the Honourable Rosa Monckton finally broke her silence and confessed to passing information about the late Princess of Wales to Britain's MI-6. She went on to confirm her belief that Diana was murdered by agents of the notorious spy agency because of her plans to marry Dodi Fayed, the father of her unborn child. Here's Dan with the weather.

Or maybe Lord Stevens simply popped round to MI-6 HQ and asked if they had received any information about Diana from the Honourable Mrs Monckton, and was satisfied when MI-6 assured him they hadn't. In any event, here's what he had to say about Rosa Monckton's husband, Dominic Lawson, accused by Mohamed Al Fayed of being an MI-6 agent and helping to write Trevor Rees-Jones' book, *The Bodyguard's Story,* together with Martyn Gregory.

"There is no evidence that Dominic Lawson was involved in the writing of that book. Trevor Rees-Jones has denied this claim.

"There is no evidence that Dominic Lawson was involved in any action linked to any of these claims."

Dominic Lawson's brother-in-law, then, Rosa Monckton's brother?

"The only reference to Rosa Monckton's brother allegedly being linked to the SIS comes from articles in the media and postings on web sites." [Operation Paget Report, Page 824]

Notice how Lord Stevens cunningly presents his conclusions, with an air of dismissiveness, as though *"articles in the media and postings on web sites"* of course bear no credibility at all, and thus could not possibility hold any truth whatever. But what he fails to mention is which newspapers carried the stories revealing Anthony Monckton as the most senior MI-6 officer in Serbia before being exposed and sent back to Britain, as well as the credibility of the sources who exposed him. Indeed, not only was he exposed by name; his photograph, email and credit card details were also published in the Belgrade newspaper that broke the story, which also appeared in the *London Times* and subsequently in the *Guardian*. Given Anthony Monckton's family and background, of course, we shouldn't be too surprised to discover that he is an MI-6 career officer. As previously inferred, and as stated in an article by Jane Tawbase in the now defunct *EuroBusiness Magazine*, the Monckton's are *"a British spy family"*, the claim stemming back to Rosa Monckton's grandfather, Walter Turner Monckton, 1st Viscount Monckton of Brenchley, who was Britain's Attorney General during the 1930s and who served also as King Edward VIII's confidant and 'advisor' during the abdication crisis, in much the same way as Rosa played confidante and 'advisor' to Diana during the constitutional crisis surrounding her divorce. In fact it would appear that Walter was keeping a watchful eye on the errant Edward—and of course, his sexually deviant wife, Wallis Simpson—on behalf of the very same agency for which his descendants work today. According to Mohamed Al Fayed, in fact, another of Rosa's brothers, Christopher, 3rd Viscount Monckton of Brenchley—famous for inventing the Eternal Puzzle—is also an MI-6 agent, though we could find no evidence to substantiate this claim. But claims that Rosa Monckton herself has a relationship with MI-6, even if only as the wife of Dominic Lawson and sister of Anthony Monckton, should not be ignored. Indeed, they should be properly investigated by the Metropolitan Police with regard to claims that MI-6 was involved in the unlawful death of Princess Diana. Did Rosa Monckton pass information about Diana to MI-6? We await a full and proper investigation in this regard.

THE SECURITY SERVICE
AND THE SECRET INTELLIGENCE SERVICE

Another One Bites The Dust

One snippet of news just in. Unbelievably, Baroness Elizabeth Butler-Sloss has this morning announced that she is quitting her post as presiding judge at Diana's inquest, thus becoming the third coroner in nine months to do so. Evidently she is unaccustomed to working with democratically elected juries, and claims on this basis that she does not have the experience necessary to see the case through. In a statement to the press, she said:

"I do not have the degree of experience of jury cases that I feel is appropriate for presiding over inquests of this level of public interest." In other words, as a result of Mohamed Al Fayed winning his appeal, just last month, to overturn Butler-Sloss's ruling so that a jury will now sit at the inquest; and further, that Butler-Sloss is not deemed to *"have the degree of experience"* necessary to intimidate and manipulate that jury into submission, the Establishment has replaced her. As Mohamed Al Fayed said on hearing the news this morning (quote, *Daily Mirror*, 25.04.07):

"Why wasn't this lack of experience made public months ago, before time and effort were wasted? This is a further indication of the Establishment's intention to cover up the murders of two innocent people. If the first coroner doesn't do what the Royal Family want, they change for another coroner."

He added: *"Clearly, Butler-Sloss was pushed. They just want to put someone in who'll say it was an accident and not murder."*

Indeed, and they haven't wasted any time finding that someone. The buck has already been passed to former High Court Judge Lord Justice Scott Baker, Assistant Deputy Coroner of the Queen's Household, Knight Grand Cross of the Order of the British Empire and member of the Queen's Bench since 1993. Baroness Butler-Sloss? Lord Justice Scott Baker? Aside from gender, sounds like the same person.

Richard Tomlinson
and The Boston Brakes

In an attempt to put paid to any lingering doubts that Diana might have been assassinated, the final chapter of the Paget report sees Lord Stevens grabbing Richard Tomlinson firmly by the throat and squeezing, relentlessly, unforgivingly, until every last breath has been wrung from the former MI-6 man, like life from a chicken. Not that these actions so much as dent the body of still-solid evidence implicating MI-6 in Diana's death. But by utterly discrediting Tomlinson, Lord Stevens is able also to discredit *"the allegation made by Mohamed Al Fayed"*, and in the process dupe the rest of us into believing MI-6 was innocent all along. We have to remind ourselves that Stevens sets out not to investigate whether MI-6 played a part in Diana's death, but whether *"the allegation made by Mohamed Al Fayed"* regarding MI-6 involvement in her death should be recommended to the coroner as credible, or not. As Al Fayed's allegation regarding MI-6 is based almost entirely on disclosures made by Tomlinson, it falls at the first hurdle. Stevens wins the day. But not the war. The real allegations, independent of Tomlinson's whistle-blowing claims, remain. There can be little question of that.

Because of the extraordinary nature of the information received from Stealth a week before Diana's death, of course, John and I were on the trail of MI-6 from the outset. Indeed, we were the first to name MI-6 and the CIA as having colluded in her death, purely because we had been given the information so early on. We did not need to rely on Tomlinson's disclosures, which in any case did not appear in the public domain for at least a year or so after the crash. True, when the Tomlinson affidavit started to do the rounds, it seemed to support what we had been saying and so naturally we were happy to associate ourselves with its contents. When you're taking on MI-6 you need all the help you can get. But it has to be said we were never entirely comfortable with all of Tomlinson's claims, not least that he cited the now famous 'Milosevic Plot' as bearing startling similarities to the operation that killed Diana. That he claimed he had learned of this plot in 1992, and that it involved staging a car crash in a tunnel so as to minimize the presence of witnesses, seemed intriguing enough. But his further claim that it involved the use of an antipersonnel flash gun, or strobe gun, something, he claimed, MI-6 officers are taught to use during their training, simply did not fit with the picture that seemed to be emerging. We could never quite understand why an antipersonnel flash gun should have been used if the operation was, as seemed evident to us, a 'Boston brakes' operation. A simple microchip transceiver fitted to the car's EMS was all that was needed for the car to be remotely controlled. No flash gun required. Indeed, we always felt that the use of a flash gun would have been too risky, too arbitrary. Blind the driver and the car might crash. But it might not. As we know, the 'Boston brakes' method involves the car's steering and brakes being completely taken over: the brakes fail and the car is remotely driven into its target, in this instance a concrete pillar. No doubts. No variables. A simple, straightforward and devastating accident causing death or serious injury, every time. This is the 'Boston brakes', and according to world famous explorer and former SAS officer, Sir Ranulph Feinnes, it has been used by known 'hit squads' around the world since at least 1986, not only for its reliability, but for its deniability, as well. Perhaps this is why Lord Stevens chose to exclude the 'Boston brakes' from his investigation, and instead focus his entire effort on discrediting Tomlinson's 'Milosevic Plot'. Which he did, ruthlessly.

But the 'Boston brakes' was not the only method sidestepped by the Paget team. Lord Stevens also failed to investigate the use of the 'Blockbuster bomb', a very small explosive used to blow out a tyre or the brakes. In Chapter 2, former SAS Sergeant Dave Cornish revealed that this device is sometimes used in conjunction with the 'Boston brakes'. Indeed, in support of this claim, we cited the assassination of Major Michael Marman in 1986, killed in a staged road traffic accident by a known professional hit squad, internationally known as 'The Clinic'. As explained, eyewitness Aubrey Allen testified to the inquest into Major Marman's death that he saw a small explosion moments before the car lost control. *"The BMW was travelling normally down the centre of the road in front of me when a large puff of smoke came out of the left rear side of the car."* As a result of the explosion, Mr Allen said, the BMW spun out of control. But it did not spin in a random manner. Rather, there appeared to be a pattern, as the car's driver, Sir Peter Horsley, explained: *"...With alarming suddenness my BMW spun sharply to the left, and then, with tyres now screeching, equally sharply to the right and then back again."* Why did Lord Stevens not take note of this characteristic and check it against the manner in which Diana's Mercedes behaved when Henri Paul lost control? According to computer-simulated reconstructions of the crash, Diana's Mercedes swung *"sharply to the left"* then *"equally sharply to the right and then back again"* into the concrete pillar, behaving in a remarkably similar fashion to Sir Peter Horsley's BMW. Is this a characteristic of the 'Boston brakes'? Is this what happens when the driver loses control and the remote kicks in? We do not know. Lord Stevens did not investigate it.

Indeed, it has to be said that we found this investigation wanting on many fronts, not least that any ambition for uncovering the truth was easily outdone by an unashamedly ruthless desire for covering it up. Whether this was a symptom of some hidden agenda, some or other hidden directive, and that Lord Stevens himself was forced to work hands-tied, who knows. But that Operation Paget was designed purely to arrive at a predetermined outcome seemed to us evident from the outset. No doubt about that.

It is today May 7th, 2007, almost ten years since Diana's death, and one wonders what further revelations might come to light in the course of the Royal Inquest, due to reopen in October 2007. One wonders if John and I will be called to give evidence, or whether the coroner will take into account the evidence presented in this book. We doubt it. But then, quite frankly, neither must we care. Our book is there to be read. The evidence is there to be seen. Both John and I feel we have given enough of our lives to the cause and we must now move on. Should either of us be called to give evidence, of course, we will do so without hesitation. But in the end what we really care about is not who presents the evidence, but who receives it and how it is judged. In the end what we care about is not that the evidence be attributed to any particular person, but that it be properly investigated by people of integrity and conscience. In this regard we should at least be grateful that, thanks to the persuasive powers of Mohamed Al Fayed's legal team, the inquest will now be held in public and heard by a democratically elected jury. Still a far cry from the fully independent public inquiry called for by the majority of British people, true. A start, none the less. Indeed, let us hope that coroner Lord Justice Scott Baker and his democratically elected jury are indeed people of integrity and conscience, and that they, unlike Lord Stevens, are courageous enough to face the evidence head-on. Because in the end what we care about is not what form the inquiry might take, but that justice might prevail.

BIBLIOGRAPHY

The Feather Men, Sir Ranulph Fiennes, 1991 (ISBN0747510490), Bloomsbury, London.

Sounds From Another Room, Sir Peter Horsley, 1997 (ISBN085052810) Leo Cooper, London.

INDEX